# The Indian Diaspora

## *Historical and Contemporary Context*

Essays in Honour of Professor Chandrashekhar Bhat

*Edited by*
**Laxmi Narayan Kadekar**
**Ajaya Kumar Sahoo**
**Gauri Bhattacharya**



**RAWAT PUBLICATIONS**
Jaipur • New Delhi • Bangalore • Mumbai • Hyderabad • Guwahati

ISBN 81-316-0210-9




*Published by*
Prem Rawat for **Rawat Publications**
Satyam Apts, Sector 3, Jawahar Nagar, Jaipur 302 004 (India)
Phone: 0141 265 1748 / 7006 Fax: 0141 265 1748
E-mail: info@rawatbooks.com
Website: www.rawatbooks.com

*New Delhi Office*
4858/24, Ansari Road, Daryaganj, New Delhi 110 002
Phone: 011 2326 3290

*Also at Bangalore, Mumbai, Hyderabad and Guwahati*

Typeset by Rawat Computers, Jaipur
Printed at Chaman Enterprises, New Delhi

# The Indian Diaspora

☙ Professor Chandrashekhar Bhat ❧

# Contents

# Preface

The present volume was planned in 2006 when the faculty associated with the Centre for the Study of Indian Diaspora, University of Hyderabad thought of celebrating the decade of existence of the Centre, established in 1996, by the University Grants Commission (UGC) under its Area Studies Programme. The Centre is the only one of its kind in India. Since its inception it has been involved in teaching and research and helped the Government of India in its efforts to understand various issues of the Indian diaspora. Prof Chandrashekhar Bhat, the founder Director of the Centre, alone managed the Centre, with all odds, till his retirement in 2006 and brought it to the notice of the outside world. So this volume is a humble attempt to recognize and honour his contribution to the field of Indian diaspora. For this volume we have invited those scholars who have been associated with the Centre to contribute a paper on 'Indian diaspora'. We are grateful to all the authors for their contribution to this volume and to Prof E. Haribabu, Director, Centre for the Study of Indian Diaspora, University of Hyderabad, and Dr Gangu Bhat for their cooperation in preparing the volume. We sincerely thank Mr. Pranit Rawat of the Rawat Publications for his kind support in bringing out the volume in time.

# Introduction

## I

The last two decades have witnessed a sudden rise in publications related to diaspora and its politics, international migration, and transnational community formation. Journals such as *Diaspora: A Journal of Transnational Studies, Global Governance: A Review of Multilateralism and International Organization, Public Culture, Global Networks, Demography, Population and Development Review, International Migration Review, South Asian Diaspora* and *Transitions* have been publishing studies related to these areas. The folk term 'diaspora' which was till recently used to connote the plight of Jewish people dispersed in various nations, became fashionable and acquired a wide usage during the recent years. Since the 1970s, the term 'diaspora' is increasingly used to denote almost every group living far away from its ancestral or former homeland. John Armstrong applied the term "... to any ethnic collectivity which lacks a territorial base within a given polity" (1976: 393). The broad usage of 'diaspora' became common later. In 1991, when the journal *Diaspora* was launched, its editor Khachig Tölölyan wrote: "We use 'diaspora' provisionally to indicate our belief that the term that once described Jewish, Greek, and Armenian dispersion now shares meanings with a larger semantic domain that includes words like immigrant, expatriate, refugee, guest worker, exile community, overseas community, ethnic community" (Tölölyan, 1991: 4).

There has been an appreciable increase in international migration since the mid-1960s. The number of international migrants rose from 75 million in 1965 to 120 million in 1990. International migration contributed close to half of the population growth in the developed countries and about 90 per cent in Europe (United Nations, 1998: 166). The intensity of international migration further increased with the second wave of globalization (Helleiner, 2001: 243–264). Globalization of production and decline in birth rates led to the immigration of substantial workers from Asia, Africa and the Caribbean to the developed countries of Europe, North America, Australasia, and Japan.

International migration became a major problem facing the industrialized countries during the post-1960s. Prior to the 1960s, only 13 per cent of the nations had enacted legislations pertaining to immigration. But by the mid-1990s, 40 countries had immigration policies (United Nations, 1998: 166). International migration was one of the important issues on the agenda of the Cairo International Conference on Population and Development in 1994.

William Safran has listed six basic characteristics of contemporary diasporas. They are: (1) dispersal from an original centre to at least two peripheral places; (2) maintenance of a memory, vision, or myth about their original homeland; (3) belief that they cannot be fully accepted by their host country; (4) longing to return to the ancestral home when the time is right; (5) commitment to the maintenance and/or restoration of the homeland; and (6) development/construction of a consciousness and solidarity as a group defined largely around the continued relationship with the homeland (Safran, 1991: 83–84).

International migration is different from transnational migration. Glick Schiller (1999: 96) has defined transnational migration as:

> a pattern of migration in which persons, although they move across international borders and settle and establish social relations in a new state, maintain social connections within the polity from which they originated. In transnational migration, persons literally live their lives across international borders. That is to say, they establish transnational social fields .... Transmigrants are people who claim and are claimed by two or more nation-states, into which they are incorporated as social actors, one of which is widely acknowledged to be their state of origin.

The transnational perspective on migration became popular among migration researchers in the 1990s (e.g., Waldinger, 1998). They studied not merely the adaptation of the migrants to the new societies, but also their ties, real or imagined, to their homelands and lands outside where the diaspora has settled.

The present-day global migration has produced transnational diasporic groups related by culture, ethnicity, language and religion. There is intense and constant interaction between these groups. Developments in the field of information and communication technology have brought the diasporic groups closer and the movement of people involves the circulation of money, technology, goods, information, ideas, lifestyles, etc., what Appadurai describes as ethnoscapes, mediascapes, technoscapes, financescapes, and ideascapes (1993). Tölölyan (1991) defines diasporas as exemplary communities of transnationalism and therefore of complex processes of exchanges, material, cultural and mental.

The Indian diaspora is the third largest diaspora next only to the British and the Chinese. Recent population estimates suggest that the Indian diaspora has crossed the mark of 20 million, dispersed around the globe in more than 70 countries. Its population is above 10,000 in 48 countries and more than half-a-million in 11 countries. The people of Indian origin in Guyana (51.93%), Fiji (41.34%), Trinidad and Tobago (38.63%), Surinam (36.04%), The United Arab Emirates (32%), Reunion (30.51%) and Nepal (27.12%) form a substantial proportion the country's population. They have a large presence in Qatar (24%), Bahrain (20%), Oman (15%), Kuwait (13%), Malaysia (7.20%), Saudi Arabia (7%), Sri Lanka (6.28%), Singapore (5.40%), and Myanmar (5.26%) (Ministry of External Affairs, 2001: xvii–xx). Several other countries have significant presence of expatriate Indians/people of Indian origin/non-resident Indians.

The 19th and early part of the 20th centuries witnessed unprecedented emigration of indenture and contract labourers, traders, professionals, and employees of the British government, to the British, French, Dutch and Portuguese colonies in Asia, Africa, Latin America and the Caribbean. During the post-World War II period, there was far-reaching emigration of Indians (mainly professionals) mainly to the developed countries namely, the United Kingdom, the United States of America, Australia and New Zealand. During the oil boom in the 1970s and the 1980s, millions of Indians emigrated to the Gulf and West Asian countries. Large-scale emigration of software engineers and other professionals took place since the 1980s to the developed countries.

The first wave of Indian emigration comprised mostly indentured labour to the European colonies to fill in the vacuum created by the emancipation of African slaves on the plantations following the ban on the practice of slavery. The indenture labour was a new concept of plantation work on contract for a period of five years. The system kept the plantation economy thriving on labour under captivity. Hugh Tinker has rightly described it as the new name for slavery.

Indian labour emigration under the indenture system first started in 1834 to Mauritius, Uganda, Ceylon and Nigeria. Later the labourers emigrated to Guyana (1838), New Zealand (1840), Hong Kong (1841), Trinidad and Tobago (1845), Martinique and Guadeloupe (1854), Grenada, St. Lucia and St. Vincent (1856), Natal (1860), Malaya (1860), St. Kitts (1861), Japan (1872), Surinam (1873), Jamaica (1873), Fiji (1879), Burma (1885), Canada (1904), and Thailand (1910). On the arrival in the colony, the immigrants were assigned to the plantations to which they were 'bound' for five years. At the end of the five years, they were free to reindenture or to work elsewhere in the colony, and at the end of ten years, depending on the contract, they were entitled to a free or partly paid return passage to India or a piece of crown land in lieu of the fare (Jain, 1993: 6; Clarke et al., 1990: 8). Under the indenture system, some 1.5 million persons migrated. Today, they constitute more than ten million dispersed across the above mentioned parts of the world, including 'twice migrants' in the developed countries (Bhachu, 1985). The indenture system was terminated in 1917 due to the anti-indentureship campaign led by Indian nationalists.

Another system prevalent to get the contract labour mainly to the tea plantations of Ceylon and the rubber plantations of Malaya was the *kangani* system. The word *kangani* is an anglicized form of the Tamil word *kankani* meaning overseer or foreman. The *kanganis* were Indians who were employed by the plantation owners to recruit labourers in India. *Kanganis* were men with some capital who advanced money to the prospective coolies for travelling and settling down on a plantation (Jain, 1970: 199). The *maistry* system used to acquire labourers for plantations in Burma was more or less similar to the *kangani* system except that the former was characterized by a gradation of middlemen-employers and the innumerable deductions. In contradiction to indenture labourers, coolies under these systems were largely free. There was no contract and no fixed period of service (Jain, Prakash, 1989: 162). During the period 1852 and 1937, 1.5 million Indians went to Ceylon, 2 million to Malaya and 2.5 million to Burma (Davis, 1951: 104). The Sastri Report of 1936 brought about the formal abolition of *kangani* plantation recruiting (Thompson, 1943: 122).

The second wave of emigration from India took place mainly to the developed countries in North America, Europe, Oceania and West Asia during the post-World War II period. Phenomenal changes in the political and economic scenario of the receiving and sending countries led to their new wave of international migration. There was a shift during this period in the direction and magnitude of international migration and composition of the migrants. The history of emigration from India and other Asian countries to the four English-speaking developed countries, namely, the United States of America, Canada, Australia and New Zealand, has been similar. In the 1960s, in these countries the immigration restrictions were removed and Asians (mostly professionally trained and skilled) were allowed to immigrate.

The third wave emigration of Indians on a large-scale to the West Asian countries is a post-World War II phenomenon. There were only 14,000 Indians in the Gulf in 1948 (Kondapi, 1951: 528). By 1971, their population had risen to 40,000 (Tinker, 1977: 12). During the 1970s and 1980s, there was large-scale immigration to the Gulf due to the oil boom. The population of Indian workers which was 1,51,418 in 1975 rose to 5,99,500 in 1981, and to 11,50,000 in 1992. In 1990, there were about 1.4 million Indians in the West Asian countries (Jain, Prakash, 1994). In 2001, according to the Ministry of External Affairs Report (2001: xvii–xx) there were 32,82,600 Indians in the Gulf countries, namely, Saudi Arabia, The United Arab Emirates, Oman, Kuwait, Bahrain and Qatar. Most of the Indians working in the Gulf are unskilled and semi-skilled labourers.

The fourth wave of Indian emigration was of software engineers to the western countries, USA in particular, since the 1980s. They are considered to be the cream of India, trained in her premiere educational institutions such as IITs, IIMs and universities. They are highly mobile and keep very close contact with India in terms of socio-economic interests (Bhat et al., 2002).

## II

The present volume consists of twelve chapters besides a profile of Professor Chandrashekhar Bhat by K. Laxmi Narayan. The twelve chapters are arranged thematically into two broad sections on the basis of historical/colonial or 'old Indian diaspora' and contemporary/postcolonial or 'new Indian diaspora'. The chapters offer rich insights into the historical processes, dynamics of contemporary global forces and influences on identity issues, generational differences, and issues arising in the Indian diaspora. The chapters in the first section address the issues of struggle for retention of cultural identities of Indians in countries like Mauritius (Vinesh Hookoomsing), South Africa (P. Pratap Kumar, Brij Maharaj), the Caribbean (Kumar Mahabir), and other old Indian diasporic countries (Mohan Gautam). The last chapter (Karthiyaini Devarajoo) in the section focuses on the diasporic writings of Malaysians of Indian origin and their depiction of culture and society of Malaysia where large number of Indians have migrated and settled.

The migration of professionals to the developed countries especially after the 1960s was designated by scholars as the period of 'brain drain' which had many negative impacts on India (see Khadria, 1999; Desai et al., 2002). However, the last two decades have witnessed what the scholars have designated as 'reverse migration', 'brain circulation' or 'brain gain', which has several positive impacts on India (see Hunger, 2002; Kale et al., 2006; Biao, 2006; Saxenian, 2005). Although there are multiple factors for this sudden change in the migration trend, important among them are the liberalization policy of India since 1991 and the growth of software industry. These changes have transformed the economy of India.

The chapters in the second section focus on the contemporary context of migration of professionals to the developed countries and their contribution to the economy of host societies as well as to the country of origin (Binod Khadria, Eric Leclerc and Margaret Walton-Roberts). The section also focuses on other important issues in the contemporary context like the linkages between India and the Indian diaspora (Basil Hans), and the comparative perspective on the first and the second generation Hyderabadi Muslim identities in the diaspora (Karen Isaksen Leonard). Like the first section, the second section also concludes with a chapter (Dolores Herrero) on the writings of the Indian diasporic scholars focusing on gender issues in the post-colonial India.

The major issue of any diaspora is the retention of cultural identities of the homeland. While in many diasporas this feature is either lost or mixed with the dominant host culture, Indian diaspora still has retained in several countries its cultural heritage of homeland intact. Diasporic Indians have been able to construct their identities since their physical displacement from the homeland. They share among themselves and with the next generations not only the history of their dispersion but also the culture of Indians in general, including their myths, legends, and traditions that constitute an integral part of their contemporary identity.

The first section starts with a paper by Vinesh Hookoomsing titled "Language Loss, Language Maintenance: The Case of Bhojpuri and Hindi in Mauritius". It focuses on the social construction of languages of Indians in Mauritius and how these languages have played an important role in shaping the identity of Indians over the years. During the course of the indentured migration, Indians took their cultural baggage which consisted of among other things, (a) a predefined social identity, (b) a set of religious beliefs and practices, (c) a framework of norms and values governing family and kinship organization, and food habits, and (d) language (Jayaram, 1998). One of the many manifestations of Indian culture in Mauritius today is the retention of Indian languages. Different Indian languages have been transplanted in Mauritius over the years. Important among them are the three languages namely Bhojpuri, Hindi and Urdu which have survived with varying ups and downs under the combined influence of internal and external forces.

P. Pratap Kumar, in his paper "Urbanism and Death of Religion: Strategies of Religious Manifestation in Modern Society", has analyzed the various strategies that the Indians (especially Hindus) in South Africa have adopted over the years to perpetuate their religious traditions alive through the historical evidences of invention of homogeneity to that of contemporary context of public performances of religions. The reconstruction of religion in the diasporic context occurs in two ways. First, religion attaches itself to culture, and second, it becomes identified with ethnicity, which the author has demonstrated in his paper by giving examples of three Hindu religious festivals such as (1) the festival of Chariots of the ISKCON, (2) the Mariamman festival, and (3) the fire walking festival.

Brij Maharaj's paper "Ethnicity, Class, State and Conflict: The 'Indian Question' in Natal, South Africa", examines various contesting issues that the ethnic minority communities in South Africa face and how Indians [as an ethnic minority community] have resisted the racism over the years. He argues that formation of ethnic identity is influenced by struggles within groups, between groups, and between the state and its various ethnic populations. Indians in South Africa have struggled against discrimination, poverty, and lack of political and civil representation. Today they have achieved South African Citizenship as 'temporary sojourners', although this status is still the 'second grade'.

Mohan Gautam, in his paper "The Autobiography of Munshi Rahman Khan in Understanding the Indian Diaspora", says that life histories constitute an important methodological tool in understanding the historical processes and the structure of the Indian diaspora. The paper examines the following questions: What is the need to study the autobiography of diasporics? What is its importance in the context of Indian diaspora research? In what way can we place the autobiography of Munshi Rahman Khan in the methodology of social sciences?

The paper titled "The Indian Diaspora in the West Indies/Caribbean: A Cultural History of Triumphs and Tribulations" by Kumar Mahabir, examines the history of migration of Indians and their retention of cultural identities in the smaller Caribbean islands. The author contends that although the Indians have lost many of their valuable traditions as a result of the dominant Afro-European culture, they have still retained several aspects of Indian cultural heritage. Their growing presence has contributed to the creation of a cosmopolitan Caribbean society at the beginning of the twenty first century. Notwithstanding their impoverished means and limited opportunities, they have advanced in every field of endeavour, including literature, law, medicine, science, business and politics.

Karthiyaini Devrajoo, in her paper "Transforming Diaspora: Familiarity with Alien Terrains", depicts the socio-cultural, economic and political life of the Malaysian society through the literary works of diasporic Malaysian Indian writers. She demonstrates that, although these writers have evolved over time and transformed their writing, some common themes could be discerned in their writings, viz., themes covering diasporic issues, national issues and finally global issues. She has also examined the factors contributing to the success of the writings of the Malaysian Indians at the international level.

Section II is devoted to the papers on the new Indian diaspora. Binod Khadria's paper titled "Migration of Highly Skilled Indians: Case Studies of IT and Health Professionals", presents a contrasting picture of the return migration of IT professionals in Bangalore and out-migration of health professionals in New Delhi. He has examined several reasons for such out-migration of health professionals and reasons for return migration. The study finds that young IT professionals' migration to the developed countries generally has occurred as a result of pull factors like gaining professional international experience, higher earnings, perks and high quality of life, whereas migration of health professionals, especially the nurses, occurred as a result of push factors like lack of job opportunities and better environment for career advancement at home.

A similar kind of study of returnee migrants is presented by Eric Leclerc in his paper "Circulation of Indian IT Professionals to Hyderabad and Beyond: Integrating India in a Global Workforce". He has analyzed how the Indian diaspora has made significant impact on the growth of IT sector in India, focusing on the new city of Cyberabad (as a part of the Greater Hyderabad) in Andhra Pradesh. The last decade has witnessed significant transformation in Hyderabad, especially in the field of Information and Technology (IT). The creation of the IT city called Cyberabad shows how IT has transformed the geo-economic position of Hyderabad in the international arena. Drawing from the fieldwork data collected from Hyderabad and Kuala Lumpur, the author asserts that it is the 'brain circulation' that serves as an imperative factor for the growth of IT sector in India.

Margaret Walton-Roberts's paper "Globalization, National Autonomy and Non-Resident Indians", probes the important contribution of Indian diaspora (includes both NRIs and PIOs) for the overall development of India. The growth of Indian diaspora, its transnational nature and its diverse roles in the economic growth and poverty reduction in the homeland suggest a case for the mainstream international development sector to embrace these communities as full partners in the development cooperation. The author has supported her discussion with the example of Punjabi diaspora's contribution to the homeland—the Doab region in Punjab.

V. Basil Hans, in his paper "Indian Diaspora: Emerging Issues in the Context of Greater India", deliberates some of the emerging issues between India and Indian diaspora and the role of Indian diaspora in the construction of 'greater India'. He thinks that although the contribution of Indian diaspora is visible in the economic field, there are several other areas which need to be addressed. He calls for a new approach to forge the linkage between India and Indian diaspora.

Karen Isaksen Leonard's paper titled "Is there a Second Diasporic Generation? The Case of India's Hyderabadis" offers a contrasting picture of the identities of first and second generation Hyderabadis living abroad. Drawing from the long-term multi-sited fieldwork data, she shows that the first generation Hyderabadis, who left the country after independence, is more cosmopolitan and transnational in their character than the second generation Hyderabadis, who is born and brought up abroad. While the first generations, in many cases, still identify themselves as Hyderabadis and claim certain collective memories of the old Hyderabad state and its urban Indo-Muslim culture, the second generation is not bothered about their Hyderabadi identity. She has examined how the Hyderabadis have retained their cultural memories of the homeland in the diaspora and what are the effective means through which they maintain their linkages and networks with the homeland.

The last paper in this section, as in the first section, focuses on the literary works of diasporic scholars. Dolores Herrero in her paper titled "Meena Alexander's *Nampally Road*: Female Subjectivity and the Ethics of Care and Commitment at the Shock of Return", explores how the diasporic Indian writers have managed to depict in their writings the gender inequalities experienced by women in the post-colonial India in comparison to the women in the diaspora where they manage to bind themselves together cutting across social, educational and cultural boundaries.

Together, these papers provide a glimpse of the demographic, socio-cultural, economic and political changes that have taken place in the Indian diaspora and the contribution of Indian diaspora for the overall development of India.

## References

Appadurai, A. 1993. "Disjuncture and Difference in the Global Cultural Economy", in P. Williams and L. Crisman (eds.), *Colonial Discourse and Post-Colonial Theory*. London: Harvester Wheatsheaf.

Armstrong, John. 1976. "Mobilized and Proletarian Diasporas", *American Political Science Review*, 70(2): 393–408.

Bhat, C.S., K. Laxmi Narayan and Sadananda Sahoo. 2002. "Indian Diaspora: A Brief Overview", *Employment News*, Vol. XXVII, No. 38: 21–27.

Biao, Xiang. 2006. *Global "Body Shopping": An Indian International Labour System in the Information Technology Industry*. New Jersey: Princeton University Press.

Clarke, Colin, Ceri Peach and Steven Vertovec (eds.). 1990. *South Asians Overseas: Migration and Ethnicity*. Cambridge: Cambridge University Press.

Davis, Kingsley. 1951. *The Population of India and Pakistan*. Princeton: Princeton University Press.

Desai, Mihir A., Devesh Kapur and John McHale. 2002. "The Fiscal Impact of High Skilled Emigration: Flows of Indians to the US". http://www.people.hbs.edu/mdesai/fiscalimpact.pdf (visited on 15th May 2007).

Glick Schiller, Nina. 1999. "Transmigrants and Nation-States: Something Old and Something New in the US Immigrant Experience", in C. Hirschmann, P. Kasinitz and J. De Wind (eds.), *The Handbook of International Migration*. New York: The Russell Sage Foundation. pp. 94–119.

Helleiner, Gerald K. 2001. "Markets, Politics, and Globalization: Can the Global Economy be Civilized?", *Global Governance*, 7(3): 243–64.

Hunger, Uwe. 2002. "The 'Brain Gain' Hypothesis: Third-World Elites in Industrialized Countries and Socio-Economic Development in their Home Country". Working Paper 47, Centre for Comparative Immigration Studies, University of California, San Diego.

Jain, Prakash C. 1989. "Emigration and Settlement of Indians Abroad", *Sociological Bulletin*, 38(1): 155–168.

—— 1994. "Gulf Migration and Its Impact on India". A Paper Presented in the International Conference on the Indian Diaspora at the University of Hyderabad in 1994.

Jain, Ravindra K. 1970. *South Indians on the Plantation Frontier in Malaya*. New Heaven: Yale University Press.

Jain, Ravindra K. 1993. *Indian Communities Abroad: Themes and Literature.* New Delhi: Manohar.

Jayaram, N. 1998. *The Study of Indian Diaspora: A Multidisciplinary Agenda.* Hyderabad: Centre for the Study of Indian Diaspora, University of Hyderabad. http://csidss.googlepages.com/oc1.pdf

Kale, Dinar, David Wield and Joanna Chataway. 2006. "Diffusion of Knowledge through Migration of Scientific Labour in India", IKD Working Paper, No.17. http://www.open.ac.uk/ikd/workingpapers/workingpaper_17.pdf

Khadria, Binod. 1999. *The Migration of Knowledge Workers: Second Generation Effects of India's Brain Drain.* New Delhi: Sage Publications.

Kondapi, C. 1951. *Indians Overseas, 1838–1949.* Madras: Oxford University Press.

Ministry of External Affairs, Government of India. 2001. *Report of the High-Level Committee on the Indian Diaspora.* New Delhi: Indian Council of World Affairs.

Safran, William. 1991. "Diaspora in Modern Societies: Myths of Homeland and Return", *Diaspora,* 1(1): 83–99.

Saxenian, AnnaLee. 2005. "From Brain Drain to Brain Circulation: Transnational Communities and Regional Upgrading in India and China", *Studies in Comparative International Development,* 40(2): 35–61.

Thompson, Virginia. 1943. *Postmortem on Malaya.* New York: Macmillan.

Tinker, Hugh. 1977. *The Banyan Tree: Overseas Emigrants from India, Pakistan and Bangladesh.* London: Oxford University Press.

Tölölyan, Khachig. 1991. "The Nation-State and its Other: In Lieu of a Preface", *Diaspora: A Journal of Transnational Studies,* 1(1): 3–7.

United Nations, Department of Economic and Social Affairs, Population Division. 1998. *World Population Monitoring, 1997: International Migration and Development.* New York: United Nations.

Waldinger, Roger. 1998. "Commentary". International Conference on Nationalism, Transnationalism and the Crisis of Citizenship. Davis: University of California.

# Chandrashekhar Bhat and His Works

LAXMI NARAYAN KADEKAR

Chandrashekhar Bhat is a familiar name in India as a Professor of Sociology, Convenor of the UGC Special Assistance Programme in Sociology, and Convenor of the Centre for the Study of Indian Diaspora (CSID), in the prestigious University of Hyderabad. He is known for his active association with the academic bodies of various universities, University Grants Commission's Committees, the Indian Sociological Society's and its journal *Sociological Bulletin*'s activities. As the Convenor of the Centre for the Study of Indian Diaspora, he has provided a platform for researchers working on the Indian diaspora to participate in the seminars, workshops and conferences organized by the Centre, the only centre of its kind in India funded by the University Grants Commission.

## The Beginning

Chandrashekhar was born in Bayar, a village in Manjeshwara taluk of Kasargod district in Kerala, on 23rd November 1944. His forefathers had migrated from Karad in Maharashtra. He had schooling in Dharmathadka Primary School, Sajankila Durga Parameshwari Middle School and Vittal High School. During 1961–64, he studied in St. Philomena's College, Puttur (Karnataka) and graduated from the University of Mysore.

He joined the Master's degree programme in Social Anthropology at the Department of Social Anthropology and Social Welfare, Karnatak University in 1965. At that time, it was one of the two best departments of Anthropology in India (the other was

Lucknow University's), having eminent Anthropologists like K. Ishwaran, T.N. Madan, M.C. Pradhan, Gopala Sarana and B.G. Halabar. The credit of recruiting some of the best minds in the field should go to Prof D.C. Pavate, the founder Vice-Chancellor of Karnatak University. The department was well-known for its village, community and tribal studies. He secured first rank in M.A. (Social Anthropology) in 1967 and was offered a Junior Research Fellowship by the Anthropological Survey of India. He worked for some time in the Anthropological Survey of India at its South India station in Mysore. Pramod Kumar Misra was its regional director and on his initiative the Survey at that time was involved in the ethnographic studies of nomadic communities throughout the country. He did an ethnographic study of the Waddars of Mysore with special reference to their nomadism. The findings of this study were published in the *Bulletin of the Anthropological Survey of India* in 1968 and 1969.

Chandrashekhar's paper 'Marriage Among the Waddars' (1968) deals with the role of endogamy, incest, types of marriage, selection of mate, preferential marriage, age at marriage, dowry, bride price, marriage, adultery, secondary marriage, widow marriage, and residence of the married couple. The study was conducted in Vinoba Colony of Siddapur in Mysore district. Vinoba Colony is at a distance of three miles to the south of Hunsur town. It is a settlement built by the Waddars of Nellore district of Andhra Pradesh. In March 1968, it had 484 persons. The residents are Telugu speaking people.

The Waddar community consists of three endogamous groups namely Kallu Waddars, Mannu Waddars and Uppu Waddars. Among the Mannu Waddars, there are two exogamous groups namely Raju and Pathani. Wadders considered sexual union with a person with whom it is prohibited is an incestuous union. If an incestuous union leads to pregnancy, the only solution sought is abortion. Monogamy is the socially accepted norm. Though not popular, polygamy is not prohibited. Marriages are arranged by the parents. The cross-cousin marriage is the preferred type of marriage. Both the types of cross-cousin marriages, i.e., the one in which a man marries the daughter of his mother's brother and the other in which he marries the daughter of his father's sister, are prevalent. A girl is married usually after she attains puberty. The age at marriage for a boy is above twenty years, when he is able to support his family. The practice of dowry exists in marriage along with the custom of bride-price known as *oli*. Marriage consists of two stages—betrothal ceremony (*tambulam bettedi*) and the marriage (*pendli*). Marriage is celebrated at the bride's residence and the presence of the elder members of the community and a person maintaining the hereditary office of the minister of functions (*samayagadu*) is very essential.

Adultery on the part of a woman is considered as a serious offence. When such a case comes into light, it is taken to the caste *panchayat*, and they may sanction a divorce. She may be remarried to the person with whom she commits adultery after paying the penalty fee to the caste *panchayat*. If a man commits adultery, it is not treated with the same seriousness. A second marriage is normally permitted on account of either divorce or widowhood or childlessness. If a man is to take a second wife, either during the life time of his first wife or after her death, he prefers his first wife's sister. Only in the absence of a marriageable sister-in-law, does he look for some other bride. Widow marriage is allowed with the consent of the caste *panchayat*. Usually a bride follows the bridegroom to his parents' house after her marriage.

His other paper 'Ethnographic Study of the Waddar of Mysore with Special Reference to Their Nomadism' (1969) is a detailed study covering social structure, nomadism, internal structure of the community, material culture, economic activities, and social life. In many places in Mysore and Andhra, the Waddars are seen leading a nomadic life. Wherever they find work (within a certain region) they go and stay there as long as the work lasts. There are others who now live permanently at one place and have stabilized their sedentary life by obtaining landholdings and cultivating the land. As per the 1961 Census, their population was 1,82,000 in Mysore State and were listed under Scheduled Castes. The Waddars migrated to Mysore to work as labourers during the construction of the Krishna Raja Sagar Dam across Kaveri river. After the completion of the project they took up petty contract works under the Public Works Department of the state. It was only after 1960 that they started acquiring land and taking more interest in agricultural work than in the earth-work. A large number of them are owner-cultivators owning two to four acres of land. The Mannu Waddars continue to maintain their old social ties with their relatives and friends of Nellore district. But they prefer to give their children in marriage to the local Waddars. They have built permanent houses that give them the status of a villager. Though it cannot be said that they have carved out a position for themselves in the local caste system, they are given a status which is higher than that of the untouchable castes.

Among the Kallu Waddars there are three endogamous subdivisions. Mannu Waddars form a single endogamous group. A household consists of closely related agnatic kinsmen of one to three generations. The most common form of households consist of husband, wife and children. The parent-children and the husband-wife relationships form the core of Waddars' family life. The duties and obligations on the part of parents and children can be viewed through different angles—genetic, moral, religious and economic. Agricultural activities among the Waddars are aimed at the production of goods for their direct consumption. Paddy is the only crop they raise on wet land and ragi, jawar and cereals and vegetables are dry crops. They are classified under three categories on the basis of their role in contract work. They are contractors, *maistries* (supervisors) and labourers. They undertake work both from private and governmental agencies. As a result of diversification of their economic activities, there are sure signs of increase of wealth and quality of life among them.

They continue to have their own caste *panchayat* formed by their traditional leaders. In them they deal all the cases concerning property disputes, disputes arising during marriages and sex offences. Though it continues to function, its influence on its members is declining. Even now all the cases are first referred to the caste *panchayat*, and it is only when it fails to deliver an agreeable judgement, the case is taken to the law court. *Panchayat* still continues to play its role in the organization of communal celebrations such as 'Sri Rama Navami' and 'Peddamma Pandu' (Festival of Peddamma, the goddess of smallpox).

Their religious life has been least affected by their taking to settled life. They worship their traditional family deities as in the past, and in addition they offer *puja* to the local deities Shani, Hanuman and Parvathi. The rituals involved in birth, first tonsure, puberty, and death are said to continue in their traditional way. But as regards marriage celebrations, they have deviated from the traditional practice. Marriages nowadays are celebrated during day time which was till recently prohibited.

**D'school Influence**

In 1969, Chandrashekhar was awarded a research fellowship to pursue doctoral studies at the Department of Sociology, University of Delhi and worked on 'Social Mobility among the Waddars of Karnataka' with the renowned sociologist M.S.A. Rao. The

Department of Sociology was established in 1959 as a constituent of the Delhi School of Economics. In 1968, the Department was recognized as a Centre of Advanced Study in Sociology by the University Grants Commission. The Department had reputed sociologists and anthropologists like M.N. Srinivas, M.S.A. Rao, A.M. Shah, Andre Beteille, J.P.S. Oberoi, Baburao Bhaviskar, Anand Chakravarti and Anita Minocha. As an active member of the Faculty and Research Scholar's Tea Club, which encouraged informal interactions between the research scholars and the faculty every afternoon around 3 p.m., he developed a close rapport with the entire faculty. Some of the younger faculty members of the department and the neighbouring Hindu College, namely, Anita Minocha, Veena Dua, Anand Chakravarti, S.D. Badgayan and P.D. Khera became his personal friends and included him in their 'lunch group'. It was a rewarding experience to be part of this department. Students from all parts of India and abroad were part of the department. He was awarded the Ph.D. degree in 1978.

His doctoral work was later published under the title *Ethnicity and Mobility: Emerging Ethnic Identity and Social Mobility among the Waddars of South India* (1984). This work analyzes the process of spatial and social transformation of the Waddars of Mysore through the phenomenon of ethnicity. The author illustrates the *modus operandi* of ethnic formation and examines the role of ethnicity in social mobility with the help of the case study of Waddars of Karnataka who have transformed from a semi-nomadic to a settled mode of life during the mid-1940s. He has studied in detail three Waddar settlements at Siddapur in Mysore district, Bhakshi Colony in Bangalore city and Waddar Bande of Bellary city during 1968–1971. He provides a rich ethnographic material concerning the Waddars of Karnataka.

The study examines two important dimensions of the changing life of the Waddars: firstly the process of transformation from a nomadic to a settled way of life in so far as it provides a territorial base for social mobility in a local system; secondly, the process of social mobility following their sedentary life. The Mannu (earth workers) and Kallu (stone workers) Waddars of Siddapur and Bellary have taken to agriculture and stone work respectively, whereas the Uppu Waddars of Bangalore (once salt traders) have taken to securing municipal employment. Persons belonging to all these three castes have migrated from different parts of former Madras Presidency and settled in the princely state of Mysore. The sedentarization of the Mannu Waddars of Siddapur has been dealt within the earlier paper covering their ethnography. The Kallu Waddars migrated from the Telugu speaking areas due to frequent droughts and lack of sufficient work. Certain parts of the princely state of Mysore and Madras Presidency provided them ample opportunities for work and also higher wages. They obtained, over a period of time, either free land from the government or vacant land to be cleared for cultivation. The nomadic life of the Uppu Waddars who were also migrants from Telugu areas was different in certain respects. They were traders in salt, jaggery, tamarind, curry leaves and a few urban products and maintained regular routes. During the early part of the 20th century, their trade and agriculture suffered due to frequent droughts. Under these conditions they migrated to the neighbouring states. They took to sweeping in the towns and cities of the Mysore state. It provided them a regular income and also a settled way of life. Sedentarization has given the Waddars various benefits of settled life. Besides facilitating a place in the local caste hierarchy, it has also provided them opportunities for participation in the local economic, political and religious life. Once they are incorporated in the life of the community, it allows them scope for social mobility in the context of the existing social system of castes.

Social mobility among the Waddars may be analyzed along two axes: ritual and secular. The ritual and the secular spheres of life are closely linked to each other. The reformatory movement among the Waddars was led by a school teacher Yellamma of Kolar in 1939. She propagated the lifestyle of the twice-born castes in terms of dietary habits, rituals and modes of worship in an effort to claim equality with them. With the help of others she started educational institutions and hostels for boys and girls. Since then several caste associations have sprung up throughout, which have fostered the growth of ethnic identity and collective mobilization for improving their ritual and educational status. They adopt different reference groups under different situational contexts. For instance, they emulate Brahmins and Vokkaligas in the religious sphere of life, to raise their status in the ritual hierarchy, whereas they compare themselves to the Scheduled Castes in the political context to facilitate mobility along the secular axis. They claim superior status to the barbers and watermen. Thus these two castes provide the Waddars the reference groups for comparison and negation. The secular avenues of mobility—spatial, occupational, educational and political—have provided them with greater opportunities to acquire a better status than the one attributed to them by society.

As a result of their spatial mobility from Andhra Pradesh to Mysore, the Waddars acquired a higher position in Mysore, in terms of their caste rank, than what they enjoyed in their home state. Agriculture has enhanced their status in a society which is predominantly agricultural. Political participation has provided the Waddars greater access not only to political but also to greater educational and employment opportunities. The political activities initiated by them helped in getting Scheduled Caste status in the erstwhile state of Mysore. This has provided vast scope for improving their status through exploiting the secular avenues of mobility. While the Waddars are in a position to obtain all the secular benefits, they are also in an advantageous position to utilize these benefits to improve their ritual status. Unlike the untouchables, the Waddars are above the line of untouchability (except Mannu Waddars) and their attempt to elevate their ritual status has succeeded to a certain extent. Politicization of the Waddars has also fostered an ethnic identity. "Dr Bhat's contribution to the study of social mobility in situational context of ethnicity is refreshing and path breaking, as it goes beyond the routine category of caste. It serves as a pointer to future sociological studies in India" (Rao, M.S.A., 1984: viii).

**Career Courting**

At the end of his senior research fellowship at Delhi in 1973, Chandrashekhar joined the Department of Anthropology, University of Mysore as a lecturer. I had by then joined the department to pursue my doctoral research. Soon this debonair, handsome young man became popular as a teacher. In 1974, he married Gangu, his former colleague from the Anthropological Survey of India. His stay at Mysore helped him to complete his doctoral dissertation. He did help me in finalizing my thesis too. In 1977, M.S.A. Rao organized a National Seminar on Social Movements in India in which he presented a paper. 'The Reform Movement among the Waddars of Karnataka' which was later published in M.S.A. Rao (ed.), *Social Movements in India: Studies in Peasant, Backward Classes, Sectarian, Tribal and Women's Movements (1979).*

In 1979, he joined the newly launched Department of Sociology and Anthropology in the Central University of Hyderabad. He was one of the founder members of the department. Other faculty members were Ratna Naidu, Vijay Kumar Kochar, Kodanda Rao and Mithilesh Pande. G.S. Aurora joined the department soon after. During the initial years, the intake of the department was small which gave an opportunity for the teachers and students to interact closely. Some of the students of this period became his lifelong friends.

Chandrashekhar received a Commonwealth Academic Staff Fellowship to pursue post-doctoral research at the School of Oriental and African Studies, London University during 1983–1984. It was here that he was introduced to the newly emerging field of overseas Indian studies by the well-known Indologist Professor Adrian C. Mayer, who had the distinction of carrying out the first ethnographic study of Indians in Fiji. The interest that Chandrashekhar evinced in the study of Indians in London was instrumental in the establishment of the Centre for the Study of Indian Diaspora at the University of Hyderabad a decade later. In 1985, I joined the department along with Uma Ramaswamy, P. Venkata Rao, Vidyasagar Reddy and K. Vijayatilakam. In 1986, A.K. Imadi and M.V.T. Raju joined the department.

The premature and sudden demise of M.S.A. Rao in 1985 was a shock to us. His close association with M.S.A. Rao's family continues even to this day. He is the affectionate 'Chandrashekhar Bhayya' to Vasudev and Venkatesh, the sons of M.S.A. Rao. M.S.A. Rao left behind many things unfinished. One such undertaking was the manuscript of the complimentary edition of *Urban Sociology in India*. Published in 1974 by Orient Longman, it was the first Reader which brought together a number of significant sociological studies on urban India. This soon became a source book in many universities in India and abroad. The book reflected the state of the art in the later 1960s. Chandrashekhar and I undertook the task of completing this volume with the title *A Reader in Urban Sociology* which was published by Orient Longman in 1991. It was also simultaneously published in London. Within a year its paperback edition was also brought out. The present Reader has readings based on two criteria. Firstly, most of the latest research covering various aspects of urbanization and urbanism were included. Secondly, sections on two new fields were incorporated: 'Caste, Class and Ethnicity' forming one section, 'Urban Poverty and Slums' the other. The Reader has elaborate chapter introductions.

Chandrashekhar, Ranga Rao (former Professor of Sociology, Andhra University) and I have also edited *Sociology of Development and Change: Essays in Memory of Prof M.S.A. Rao* which was published by Orient Longman in 1993. Its paperback was also brought out in 1994. It analyzes the issue of development and change in relation to various aspects of Indian society. The essays span four broad areas—rural and urban development, migration, food and nutrition, and education. The volume has two papers by Chandrashekhar. The first is titled 'Prof M.S.A. Rao and His Works'.

The second is titled 'Indian Ethnic Associations in London: Search for Unity in Diversity'. This paper is based on a three-month field study in the Croydon Council Area of Greater London during 1983–1984 as a Commonwealth Academic Staff Fellow. The paper discusses the working of Indian ethnic associations in London focussing on their unity in diversity. It examines the extent of diversity in the composition and activities of these associations and analyses their attempt towards unification under a different definition of the situation. Indians constitute 1.4 per cent of the country's total population. Most of the minority associations fall under one of the two broad categories: 1) those offering cultural services specific to the immigrant group, and 2) those promoting the adjustment and adaptation of the immigrant group to the socio-economic and political environment of the host society.

Ethnic associations of both types have been increasing since the early 1970s. Most of the associations in London and in the United Kingdom are based on diverse factors like religion, region, language and caste which are major cohesive forces. These diversities have made it difficult, if not impossible, for the emergence of national identity in a significant way. There have been attempts made to establish associations based on a pan-Indian identity, overriding the parochial and dogmatic ones. But these pan-Indian associations are extremely ephemeral due to meagre support and participation. The *Section 11* Funding is a grant offered by the Home Office, Government of United Kingdom to initiate new programmes for the promotion of education and cultural activities among the minority groups to enable them to participate in wider society beyond their own ethnic boundaries. This scheme has initiated the process of bringing various associations closer in order to coordinate, if not merge, their politico-economic and cultural interests. The birth of the South London Indian Council is a response to this scheme as well as the long felt need for unity among the Indians. The Council has already been recognized by the Croydon Borough Council as the representative of the Asian Indians. This has set in motion the organization of Indian associations with a pan-Indian identity at the local, regional and national levels (e.g., United Kingdom Indian Council).

Chandrashekhar along with G.S. Aurora compiled a trend report on the State of Research in the Fields of Science, Technology and Development in India covering the period 1977–1987 for the *Third Survey of Research in Sociology and Social Anthropology* brought out by the Indian Council of Social Science Research (2000). This report examines the linkages between 'science and technology' on the one hand and the process of development on the other. The introductory part of the report covers the concepts of science, technology and development. It is followed by socio-historical trends in science and technology policy and institutional aspects of science and technology as related to development.

In 1988, a separate Department of Anthropology was created out of the combined Department of Sociology and Anthropology. In 1991, E. Haribabu, Satish Deshpande and Surinder Jodhka, in 1998, Sasheej Hegde and Vinod K. Jayarath joined the department. In 1996, the Department of Sociology received the U.G.C. Special Assistance Programme in Sociology. Chandrashekhar was made its coordinator. As the coordinator of SAP he was instrumental in allotting minor research projects to the faculty, organizing annual national seminars, organizing lectures by the visiting scholars, and bringing out occasional papers. His democratic functioning as the Head of the Department and Coordinator of Special Assistance Programme was appreciated by the faculty. The progress achieved by the Special Assistance Programme was phenomenal and the Department got the second and third phases of S.A.P also under his leadership. He continued as the coordinator till his superannuation in November 2006.

### Launching Diaspora Studies

Chandrashekhar organized an 'International Conference on the Indian Diaspora', jointly sponsored by the University Grants Commission and the Rajiv Gandhi Foundation during November 1–2, 1994. The Conference emphasized the long felt need for a Centre for Study of Indian Diaspora, as a coordinating body in India, and recommended to the UGC to set up the Centre. The Commission in its meeting on 23rd March, 1995, approved the establishment of a Centre for the Study of Indian Diaspora at the University of Hyderabad under the UGC Area Studies Programme. Chandrashekhar was appointed as the coordinator of this Centre. The Centre for the Study of Indian Diaspora (CSID) envisages research on the historical context of the Indian diaspora during the colonial and post-colonial phases, civilizational heritage of diaspora communities, continuities and transformation in culture, economy and political life—besides the communications and linkages between India and the Indian diaspora.

The Centre has done praiseworthy work during the last ten years under the leadership of Chandrashekhar Bhat. Very good collection of books on diaspora has been added to the library. The centre also has built up its own library which possesses valuable set of Xerox collection, newspaper cuttings, albums, and bibliography on diaspora theme. It has provided visiting fellowships, research projects, organized national and international seminars, published occasional papers and organized lectures of the visiting scholars.

The Centre organized a Symposium on 'Indian Diaspora in Asia and the Pacific' in the 'International Conference of Asian and Pacific Studies' held in January 1996. A National Workshop on 'The Study of Indian Diaspora: Conceptual and Methodological Issues' was held in September 1997. In September 2001, a National Workshop on 'India and Indian Diaspora: Linkages and Expectations' sponsored by the Ministry of External Affairs was organized. An International Conference on 'Indian Diaspora: Trends, Issues, and Challenges' was held in February 2005. Another International Conference on 'Globalisation and Diaspora: Changing Contours of Locality and Identity in the 21st Century' was organized in February 2007.

During his tenure as the Convenor of CSID, he published papers mainly in the field of Indian diaspora. His paper with Ajaya Kumar Sahoo, 'Diaspora to Transnational Networks: The Case of Indians in Canada' (2003), examines the nature of Indian diaspora communities in the contemporary context of globalization, especially with the advent of new technologies in transport, information and communication. After a brief note on the Indian diaspora in Canada, the paper discusses the emergence of transnational networks among the two of the most prominent communities, viz., Punjabis and Gujaratis. Canada offers its immigrants a favourable environment to integrate with the socio-economic and political life through its policy of multiculturalism. Recent developments in travel, transport and communication have not only brought the diaspora communities and their motherland close but also the dispersed communities around the world. The social networks are transnational in nature. Punjabis and Gujaratis in Canada have maintained strong socio-cultural, economic and political ties with their relatives, friends and others around the world including the motherland. These networks are manifested through sending remittances to the families left behind in India, investment in industries, business and property, involvement in various national and international associations, and visiting homeland for manifold reasons including marriage, visiting relatives and attending festivals. The Punjab, Gujarat and Indian governments are also maintaining close contacts with the respective diaspora for socio-cultural and economic reasons. They have floated various schemes to attract NRI investments and savings in their home states. These networks between the diaspora communities are mutually beneficial to the communities and the country of their origin.

The paper titled 'A General Note on the Telugu Diaspora in the United States', co-authored with T.L.S. Bhaskar provides a brief history of the Telugu diaspora in the US, associations to maintain its identity, and economic linkages with the homeland. Migration of the Telugus to the US began in the early 1950s but gained momentum only during the late 1960s after the 'quota system' was abolished with the Hart Celler Act in 1965. A large number of doctors emigrated to the US during the early 1960s followed by the engineers, teachers and students. The Telugu diaspora is mainly a result of the people who migrated from the homeland 'in search of work'. The migration of Telugus took a new turn in late 1980s with the software industry expanding in India. Two prominent associations have emerged to preserve and promote the culture and identity of the people of Telugu origin. These associations and other consequent ones have become effective platforms for the Telugu cultural, literary and social activities in the US. They raised funds for various cultural, developmental, and philanthropic activities in the United States and Andhra Pradesh. Andhra Pradesh has become a lucrative destination for the investors, with proper infrastructure and conducive atmosphere to do business. The Government of Andhra Pradesh is showing increasing interest in building strong bonds with the non-resident Telugus by its friendly policy to promote investments and philanthropic contribution. The software industry was exporting not products but people, a process Indians call body shopping. The Telugus formed the major proportion of Indian software professionals in the US from the early 1990s with the enactment of The Immigration Act of 1990. There are about three lakh Telugus in the US. Majority of the Telugus in the US are from the coastal districts of Andhra Pradesh. In order to promote their community living and culture, they have formed associations wherever they are in substantial numbers. Telugu Association of North America (TANA) and American Telugu Association (ATA) are the two prominent ones.

His paper with Ajaya Kumar Sahoo, 'Transnational Networks among the Punjabi and Gujarati Diasporas in the USA' (2003), examines the extensive socio-cultural, economic and political networks among the Punjabis and Gujaratis throughout the world. The Punjabis were the first South Asians to migrate to North America in 1803. In 1990, the USA had about 1,25,000 Sikhs. The Punjabi diaspora maintains strong socio-cultural, economic and political networks with the kith and kin and other members of the community around the world. These are manifested through sending remittances, involvement in various national and international associations, and visiting homeland for manifold reasons. The Punjabi cultural troupes stage *bhangra* and other theatre forms throughout the diaspora. *Kabaddi* tournaments are held in various countries. Punjabi media consisting of newspapers, magazines play an important role in informing overseas Punjabis about their homeland. *Des Pardesh,* a monthly magazine has largest circulation among the Punjabi diaspora. Similarly, the *Gadar* launched from San Francisco is also very popular. There are several transnational TV and radio channels which provide information and entertainment besides the innumerable websites connecting Punjabis around the globe.

There are about 1,50,000 Gujaratis in the USA. They are mainly involved in motel, and diamond industries and retail business. They maintain extensive ties with relatives and friends in Gujarat and elsewhere. These ties are manifested in the form of marriage arrangements, kinship networks, remittances and religious affiliations, etc. The new migrants have invested in India and possess PIO cards. The Government of Gujarat in 1998 established the Non-Resident Gujarati Foundation mainly to attract investments and establish better communication with them. The Gujaratis have established Gujarat Samajs in various states of the USA. They have provided financial help, mobilized men and materials during times of crises in Gujarat and India like the earthquake in Kutch in January 2001. The American India Foundation persuaded Bill Clinton to visit Gujarat and raise funds for relief and rehabilitation programme.

His paper 'India and the Indian Diaspora: Linkages and Expectations' (2003), examines the nature of policy pursued by India towards her diaspora and offers suggestions towards a new approach in the contemporary context. The paper begins with a brief introduction underlining the diversity among the Indian diaspora communities and analyzes India's relationship and policy towards the Indian diaspora during the colonial and post-colonial period. Though the colonial government enacted a few legislative directives for the protection and well-being of the indenture labour in plantation barracks, they were more violated than followed. The only policy that the government followed was to export sufficient low paid workforce to run the plantations. The British encouraged the indentured labour to settle down in their island colonies following the ban on slavery. Independent India preferred to forget her unfortunate children abroad under Nehru's policies of respect to national sovereignties, amicable international relations, non-interference in the affairs of other nations and the pursuit of non-alignment. The Government of India was lukewarm to the issues of overseas Indians until she realized the potential of the New Diaspora, or NRIs who emigrated after independence to the developed world. Liberalization and the new industrial policy sought involvement of overseas Indians in investing both in terms of capital and technology. The non-resident Indians were encouraged to invest in India through certain attractive schemes as much as they were welcomed to launch industrial enterprises along with transfer of technology. The People of Indian Origin Card was launched by the Ministry of Home Affairs in March 1999 to reinforce the emotional bonds of Indians who have made other countries their homes. The Persons of Indian Origin (PIOs) up to the fourth generation are eligible to avail this facility. This scheme will entail a host of facilities to the PIOs which were earlier open to the non-resident Indians. The author says that the new global order has seen that the protection of the interests of its population beyond its national boundaries is justified even if it means undermining the sovereignty of another country. There is an urgent need to review the policy towards the countries with PIOs.

The paper 'Transnational Networks of Indian Diaspora Communities: The Case of Telugu Diaspora' (2005) jointly written with Ajaya Kumar Sahoo, examines the multiple networks of Indian diaspora communities in the contemporary context of globalization with special reference to the Telugu diaspora. The Telugu diaspora is the largest south-Indian diaspora which has its presence in various countries. There were two major waves of overseas migration of the Telugus. The first was the migration as indentured and *kangani* labourers to the British colonies during the 19th and 20th centuries. The second was the migration of professionals such as engineers, doctors, scientists and students to the developed countries such as the USA, the UK, Canada, Australia and New Zealand. The New Diaspora continues to have close contacts with the families and relatives back home and around the globe. Their networks are channelized through various mechanisms such as regular communications over telephone, visits and correspondence, remittance, internet, sending and receiving videos on family events and other celebrations.

The paper 'Continuity and Change in the Perception of "Indianness": Issues of Identity among the Indians and the Indian Diaspora', explores Indianness in the complex socio-cultural milieu of India and the people of Indian origin outside, distinctively diversified into innumerable castes and subcastes, languages and dialects, regions and localities, and religions, sects and sub sects. Any definition of 'Indianness' needs to underline attributes that encompass all diversities that are present among the Indians in India and also elsewhere beyond the national boundaries. The paper initially examines the nature of 'Indianness' in India evolved as a product of political history and civilizational culture. Perception of 'Indianness' among the diaspora communities is analyzed in the later part of paper. Historically, India is a colonial creation in the sense that the map of India was drawn by the British during their rule and redrawn significantly on August 14th in 1947, on leaving the subcontinent. At that very moment, a section of the population became 'Pakistanis' and later in 1972 some of them became 'Bangladeshis'. Implied here is that 'Indianness' is a social/psychological product of colonialism as much as post-colonialism, articulated through the political notion of a 'nation' that bound the population despite the diversities. There was emergence of the very notion of 'nation' and nationalism during the freedom movement and the very process generated cohesion among the diverse sections of the Indian society.

Indianness in India is taken for granted, never questioned, for it is innate and inseparable from every Indian. Like any identity, Indianness comes more often to the fore when encountered with/challenged by non-Indians. Indians among themselves employ any of the multiple identities that the situation demands although the significant ones are mediated by religion, language and caste. These very identities are in extensive operation among the diaspora communities, especially in the New Diaspora or Anglophone Indian diaspora. Perception of 'Indianness' among the Indian diaspora differs on how they are situated in their country of immigration. In a country like Mauritius where people of Indian origin form a majority, Indianness is perceived through its constituents of Hindus, Telugus and Tamils while in Trinidad they are primarily categorized as people of Indian origin, with a distinction based on religion such as Hindus, Muslims and Christians.

Indianness among the old diaspora today is a synthesis of the 'images' of India, passed on by the early settlers to their descendants through oral and institutional modes, and the concrete interaction obtained through the visiting 'culture specialists' such as performing artists, film stars, founders of new religious/spiritual movements, etc. TV, video and audio cassettes, newspapers and internet portals today provide images for 'virtual' interaction that facilitate to reinforce 'Indianness' among the diaspora communities.

In the new diaspora we find that religious, regional, linguistic and caste factors still play an important role. Regional associations have emerged to serve the purpose of both maintaining a separate identity as much as providing a setting for meeting people coming from the same region who also speak the language. While the identity of 'Indianness' becomes significant in India only in situations when the national interests are at stake, it is almost a part of daily interaction with 'others' in so far as the Indian diaspora is concerned. Indian diaspora communities make continuous effort to maintain 'Indianness' as a marker of distinctive identity, transcending the diversities that they uniquely practice, in their interaction with host societies.

Chandrashekhar's interest in Indian diaspora led to presentation of papers/keynote addresses in several Indian and foreign seminars/conferences. Space does not permit to give all the details. He participated in conferences on diaspora in Trinidad and Tobago, the United States of America, Mauritius, Germany, France, Spain, the Netherlands and Armenia.

He presented a paper on 'Indian Diaspora in Transnational Perspective: The Emergence of Global Networking and Community Formation', and chaired Panel 9 on 'International Indian Diaspora' at the 17th European Conference on Modern South Asian Studies, University of Heidelberg, Germany, between September 9–14, 2002. He presented a paper on 'Continuity and Change in the Perception of "Indianness": Issues of Identity among the Indians and the Indian Diaspora", at the International Conference on 'Peripheral Centres, Central Peripheries: Anglophone India and its Diaspora', at the Centre for Transcultural Anglophone Studies (TAS), University of Saarland, Saarbrucken, Germany, during September 29–31, 2002. He chaired a session on 'Countrywise Status Report' at the Global Organisation of People of Indian Origin Convention at New Delhi on 8th January 2003. He presented a paper on 'Spatial Dimensions of Indian Diaspora: A Contemporary Appraisal', at the International Conference on 'Transnational Territories: Myths and Realities', at the Department of Geography, University of Rouen, France, during November 19–21, 2003. He presented a paper on 'India and PIO Diaspora: Networking for Educational Advancement' at the GOPIO International Convention on 'PIO Diaspora Networking with Partners for Global Peace' at Indira Gandhi Cultural Centre, Mauritius, during December 5–7, 2003. He chaired a session on 'Indian Diaspora: Countrywise Report', at the 'GOPIO International Convention' at New Delhi on January 12th 2004.

He delivered a key note address on 'Contextualising Diasporic Identity: Implications of Time and Space on Telugu Immigrants', at the International Conference on 'The South Asian Diasporas: The Creation of Unfinished Identities in the Modern World', held at Erasmus University, Rotterdam, The Netherlands on 23rd June 2005. He was invited to give a keynote address on 'Indian Diaspora: From Indenture to Transnational Networks', at the Seminar on 'Indian Diaspora: Past and Present' at Maulana Abul Kalam Azad Institute of Asian Studies, Kolkata, during March 28–29, 2006. He was invited by the Ministry of Foreign Affairs, Armenia to give a keynote address on 'Challenges of Diaspora in the Globalizing World', at the 'Armenian Diaspora Conference', Armenia during September 18–20, 2006.

He was a Visiting Professor at the University of Rouen, France during May-July 2005. During this period he also visited the MSH, Paris on invitation for a week.

The Department of Sociology expanded during his headship. In 2000, Aparna Rayaprol, N. Purendra Prasad, V. Janardhan, M.V.S. Apparna, and Ajailu Nuimai, in 2004 G. Nagaraju, and in 2006 Satyapriya Rout and C. Raghava Reddy joined the department. The SAP was very vibrant under his coordinatorship. Sociology was the first department to equip itself with computers, printers, Xerox machines, etc. A seminar room with fairly good infrastructural facility was established due to his initiative. Further many seminars, workshops, lectures were organized due to his special drive.

During his tenure in the university, he has mainly taught the courses and guided students in the following areas: social movements, social change and development, urbanization, industrial sociology, ethnic studies and Indian diaspora. Three of his Ph.D. students have worked in industrial sociology, one in organizational sociology and three in Indian diaspora. Eight M.Phil students have worked in different areas under his supervision. He maintains a special bond with his research students. They are all members of his extended family.

**Academics and Beyond**

He shouldered different administrative responsibilities during his service. He was Head of the Department of Sociology during 1992–1993, 1996–1999 and 2003–2005; Dean, Students Welfare including Foreign Students' Advisor; Ex-Officio Chairman, Sports Board, University of Hyderabad during 1992–1996; Convenor, Centre for the Study of Indian Diaspora during 1996–2006; Coordinator UGC-Special Assistance Programme, Department of Sociology during 1995–2006; International Students' Advisor, University of Hyderabad between 2003 and 2005; Chairman, Road Safety and Hygiene Committee; and Secretary, Faculty Club. His services were sought after by the successive vice-chancellors due to his pleasant manners, commitment, and management skills.

He served the subject 'Sociology' at the national level in different capacities. He was a Member of the Subject Panel on

Sociology, University Grants Commission (1994–1996). He was a Member of Academic Council, Madras Institute of Development Studies, Madras. He was an elected member of the Managing Committee, Indian Sociological Society and also a member of the Editorial Board, *Sociological Bulletin*.

Throughout his service his wife's support has been praiseworthy. She throughout encouraged and helped him in achieving his goals sacrificing her own professional career. On several occasions she took long leaves to support him in organizing seminars or conferences. I am one of the fortunate ones who have enjoyed throughout the warmth, generosity and hospitality of the couple.

He superannuated in November 2006. We wish him a long, healthy and active academic life. His friends and admirers have many expectations from him.

## References

1968. "Marriage among the Waddars", *Bulletin of the Anthropological Survey of India*, 17(3): 257–72.

1969. "Ethnographic Study of the Waddars with Special Reference to Their Nomadism", *Bulletin of the Anthropological Survey of India*, 18(4); 255–310.

1979. "The Reform Movement among the Waddars of Karnataka", in M.S.A. Rao (ed.): *Social Movements in India: Studies in Peasant, Backward Classes, Sectarian, Tribal and Women's Movements* (169–189). New Delhi: Manohar.

1983. "Ethnicity and Development: The Case of Waddars of South India", *Ethnic Studies Report*, 1(2). Colombo: Institute of Ethnic Studies.

1984. *Ethnicity and Mobility: Emerging Ethnic Identity and Spatial Mobility among the Waddars of South India*. New Delhi: Concept Publishing Co.

1984. Rao, M.S.A., 'Foreword' in Chandrashekhar Bhat, *Ethnicity and Mobility among the Waddars of South India*. New Delhi: Concept Publishing Co.

1991. With M.S.A. Rao and Laxmi Narayan Kadekar (eds.): *A Reader in Urban Sociology*. New Delhi: Orient Longman.

1993. With Laxmi Narayan Kadekar and K. Rangarao (eds.): *Sociology of Development and Change*. New Delhi: Orient Longman.

1993. "Indian Ethnic Associations in London: Search for Unity in Diversity", in Chandrashekhar Bhat, Laxmi Narayan Kadekar and K. Ranga Rao (eds.): *Sociology of Development and Change* (15–27). New Delhi: Orient Longman.

2000. With G.S. Aurora. "Science, Technology and Development", in M.S. Gore (ed.): *Third Survey of Research in Sociology and Social Anthropology*, Vol. I. (1–28). New Delhi: Manak.

2002. With Sadananda Sahoo and Laxmi Narayan Kadekar. "Indian Diaspora: A Brief Overview", *Employment News*, 27(38): 21–27.

2003. With Ajaya Sahoo, "From Diaspora to Transnational Networks: The Case of Indians in Canada", in Sushma J. Varma and Radhika Sheshan (eds.): *Fractured Identity: Indian Diaspora in Canada*, pp. 141–167. New Delhi: Rawat Publications.

2003. With Ajaya Sahoo, "Transnational Network among Punjabi and Gujarati Diasporas in the USA", in R. Goopa Kumar (ed.): *Indian Diaspora and Giving Patterns of Indian Americans in USA*, pp. 69–94. New Delhi: CAF India.

2003. With T.L.S. Bhaskar, "A General Note on the Telugu Diaspora in the United States", in R. Gopakumar (ed.): *Indian Diaspora and Giving Patterns of Indian Americans in USA*, pp. 69–94. New Delhi: CAF India.

2003. "India and the Indian Diaspora: Linkages and Expectations", in Ajay Dubey (ed.): *Indian Diaspora: Global Identity*, pp. 11–22. New Delhi: Kalinga Publications.

2005. With Ajaya Sahoo, "Transnational Networks of Indian Diasporic Communities: The Case of Telugu Diaspora", *Man in India*, 85 (1 and 2): 61–80.

2006. "Continuity and Change in the Perception of 'Indianness': Issues of Identity among Indians at Home and in the Diaspora", in Martina Ghosh-Schellhorn (ed.): *Peripheral Centres, Central Peripheries: India and its Diaspora(s)*, pp. 243–250. Berlin: LIT Verlag.

# I

# Old Indian Diaspora

# 1

# Language Loss, Language Maintenance

## The Case of Bhojpuri and Hindi in Mauritius

VINESH HOOKOOMSING

In its coverage of the 2007 edition of Pravasi Bharatiya Divas, Webindia123's news site[1] came up with a rhetorical questioning: "Can Bihar, one of the most backward states in India, be transformed into Mauritius, a fascinating island nation in the Indian Ocean?", before adding: "This is precisely the task Prime Minister Manmohan Singh has in mind for the large number of Biharis settled in Mauritius." The Press Trust of India[2] put it more forcefully: "'Go to Bihar and inspire people there to make a Mauritius out of Bihar.' This is the message of Prime Minister Manmohan Singh to Persons of Indian Origin (PIOs) in Mauritius having roots in Bihar."

The Delhi Divas was followed by the Bihar Global Meet (19–21 January, 2007), during which the High Commissioner of Mauritius, "speaking in excellent Bhojpuri", recalled how his ancestors came to Mauritius from Ara. He also met with Bihar's Chief Minister and "discussed ways to develop Bihar on Mauritius model with sugarcane industry as its backbone", while assuring his host that "the Mauritius government was keen on setting up a sugarcane research institute in the state".[3]

This was confirmed by a Cabinet decision of the Government of Mauritius taken on 9 February 2007 and which reads as follows:

> Concerning the possibility of Mauritius investing in Bihar in areas of interest namely, in power and sugar production, the Prime Minister proposed the creation of a business forum to facilitate its process. It was, also, proposed that the Mauritius Sugar Industry

Research Institute could be called upon to provide technical assistance to sugar cane growers in Bihar.

The Prime Minister, Navinchandra Ramgoolam, "also conveyed his appreciation and gratitude to the chief minister for his endeavour to erect a statue of Sir Seewoosagur Ramgoolam in the native village of his forefathers."

This almost umbilical link with India, celebrated at the global Indian diaspora meeting, sets Mauritius apart for a number of reasons, the most significant being the achievement and status of the Mauritians of Indian origin, who comprise more than two-thirds of the Island's population, in terms of:

- Political power and state control which has shaped and oriented the process of nation-building since independence obtained in 1968;
- Educational, social and economic progress resulting in the creation of a large, increasingly urbanized middle-class;
- Maintenance of a cultural and religious framework of symbols and references for collective identity.

Last but no less important, modern India's presence, proximity and policy of privileged "PIO" nation in favour of Mauritius has triggered a new sense of pride in being part of the global cosmopolitan Indian family. A special feeling indeed, heightened by the fact that FDI to India flows abundantly from offshore Mauritius, thus making the tiny island its main, though artificial, FDI provider.

The present focus on India, and Bihar in particular, may be seen as a logical outcome of Indo-Mauritian history. The indentured labourers who migrated to Mauritius in the 19th century originated massively though not exclusively from the central province of India. Similarly, even though labour constituted the bulk of Indian migration to Mauritius, trade was also part of it. While the coolie was mostly from Bihar, the trader came from Gujarat and, in some cases, from the South.

Thus, Indian languages in Mauritius meant not only Bhojpuri and Khari Boli Hindi, but also Gujarati, Bengali, Tamil and other provincial languages. When Gandhi stopped in Mauritius in 1901 on his way to India from South Africa, he addressed the local Indian business community in Gujarati. The first Indian newspaper to be published in Mauritius, *The Hindusthani,* was a bilingual English-Gujarati paper. It was launched in March 1909 by one of

Gandhi's collaborators, Manilall Doctor, with the financial support of the local Indian traders. In the 2 March 1913 issue of his short-lived newspaper, the language spoken by the Mauritian Indians is referred to as a "pedgin-Hindustani, interlarded with Franco-Mauritian or French-Creole words".

While keeping in view the broader multilingual context of Mauritius, the present study will focus on Bhojpuri and Hindi, with due attention to Urdu, all three being languages inherited from Bihar.

**Mauritian Bhojpuri and Hindi**

The linguistic diversity brought by the Indians into the 19th century Mauritius and their recourse to Bhojpuri as a lingua franca are well-known features of Indian settlement in Mauritius. The fact that the bulk of Indian labour was imported from the Bihar region is an obvious explanation of the role played by Bhojpuri as a link language among the different sections of the Indian community during the indenture days.

The importance of Bhojpuri as a factor of cohesion and solidarity has nevertheless not been given due recognition, nor has its presence been adequately assessed as an element of protection from the acculturation process. The pioneering work that Ramessur Ory[4] reports to have conducted on the Mauritian Bhojpuri language and culture in the 1960s has yet to be unearthed. Until then, the credit for being one of the first to acknowledge the contribution of Bhojpuri goes to Jaynarain Roy (1970)[5] when he writes: "It is due to this language that we have been able to survive culturally during the past 150 years or so amidst immense sufferings and hardships."

The same feeling is expressed in more personal terms by P. Mewasingh (1984)[6] when he writes:

> Today, a vast majority of people do not know either Hindi or Sanskrit yet they know the wonderful stories of the *Ramayana, Mahabharata* and the *Bhagavad Gita,* thanks to Bhojpuri as these stories were told to them in that language. I am one of them. It was much later in life that I realized the treasure which I had inherited from my parents. Thanks to that language I imbibed the culture of that great country from where it had come—India.

The need for a re-appraisal of the role and importance of Bhojpuri is a fairly recent development. Indeed the word 'Bhojpuri' itself has only very recently become part of the average Mauritian's vocabulary. The explanation lies to some extent in the low status of the language but especially in the fact that Bhojpuri has never really been considered as a linguistic entity in its own right.

The social and historical context of its transplantation and, subsequently, of its emergence as a lingua franca has been briefly outlined by S. Gambhir (1986)[7] who describes the formation of Mauritian Bhojpuri in a three stage process:

- *First stage:* Bihari and Hindi based multi-dialectalism;
- *Second stage:* Linguistic adjustment and dialect levelling; and
- *Third stage:* Emergence of a common linguistic system—Mauritian Bhojpuri.

Gambhir suggests that the speakers' own perception of their linguistic systems as forms of "Hindi" or "Hindustani" helped to "boost the dialect levelling processes". That the observable structural links between their linguistic systems and Hindi/Hindustani had some degree of psychological reality, is exemplified by the fact that speakers of Bhojpuri often referred to the language they spoke as a form of "broken Hindi or *motya bhasa, "bhasha"* being refined Hindi.

Such value-loaded characterizations indicate at the same time that the perceived links between Bhojpuri and Hindi also have a social reality, which is fundamentally of a diglossic nature. D. Bahadoor (1984),[8] for instance, considers Hindi as "the standard form of Bhojpuri, with a grammar and a literature, a script and a perfect phonology". The first scholarly attempt to reconstruct the social history of Hindi-Bhojpuri in Mauritius goes to the credit of L.P. Ramyead. While discussing the problems of Indian languages and schooling in the 19th century, Ramyead (1985: 32) writes:

> In fact, literacy and vernacular education presented a problem to Bhojpuri speakers because Bhojpuri was not a written language nor was it regarded as being suitable to be so and formal education thus, of necessity, had to be in KHB (Khari Boli Hindi), the language perceived to have both literary and cultural prestige, whether as Hindi or Urdu. It was towards KHB, therefore, that they looked for their educated and cultured modes of expression; there was no hope of Bhojpuri ever achieving this for them.

Already in the early *baithkas,* the language used as medium of instruction was, according to Sarita Boodhoo (2000: 26), "Bhojpuri mixed with some Hindi, developing at that time in India as *Khadi Boli* (language spoken while standing)". With the establishment of

Khari Boli/Hindi as the prestigious variety of *bhasha,* literally meaning refined speech or language, Bhojpuri was progressively confined to the limited sphere of folk language and pejoratively referred to as *motya bhasa.* At that level, Creole was already well established as the main link language within the broader Mauritian context, as a result of which the gradual decline of Bhojpuri as an inter-group lingua franca was inevitable. More seriously, its primary function as mother tongue and home language was at stake. The situation of Bhojpuri at the turn of the last century is aptly summarized by P. Sooriah (1977)[9]:

> At one point Bhojpuri was the dominant single language throughout the island in opposition to Creole. But then the tragedy of Bhojpuri is that it was made an orphan by its own living parents. The decline of Bhojpuri as a rival to Creole began early in the 20th century with the arrival on the scene of Arya Samaj. Firstly they advocated the use of Khari Boli Hindi as the prestigious language as opposed to the "Motiya" Bhojpuri that led many Bhojpuri Hindus to disown Bhojpuri in favour of Hindi. Secondly, the emphasis on a not too familiar Hindi had driven the minority Indian communities away from the main pan-Indian solidarity. Thirdly, a pro Hindu attitude of Arya Samaj coupled with the political developments on the mainland, particularly the Hindu-Muslim divide cast their evil shadows on Mauritius Indian community driving the Muslims away from the mainstream. As a result Bhojpuri Muslims disowned Bhojpuri in favour of Urdu.

The growing shift to Creole resulted in a Creole-Bhojpuri diglossia which was thus superposed to the Hindi-Bhojpuri diglossic couple. According to S. Bhuckory (1967: 108), "in society people knowing Hindi have started making use of it in their conversation in preference to Bhojpuri". In the case of Bhojpuri and Creole, he writes: "In urban areas there is a tendency to use more and more Creole at home with the result that Bhojpuri is very often not known by the younger generation." To counter this, Bhuckory suggests that "social workers and priests, teachers and parents have all to strive to make Bhojpuri, if not Hindi, the language of the home".

**Hindi with, or without, Bhojpuri?**

The Hindi-Bhojpuri-Creole issue gave rise to heated debates in the late 1970s and early 1980s on the options and strategies to be adopted in favour of Hindi and/or Bhojpuri. These can be summarized as follows:

- Bhojpuri being condemned to an irreversible decline in the long term, all the efforts should be concentrated on Hindi;
- Bhojpuri should be promoted for its own sake;
- Bhojpuri should be encouraged for the sake of Hindi.

The first option gives the impression of being realistic: resources are limited, therefore instead of wasting them on Bhojpuri which stands no chance of improving its situation, it would be wiser to focus on the prestige variety, that is, Hindi. Realism however shows that Hindi as well as the other standard Indian languages present in Mauritius mostly occupy the specific culture and identity niche in the general sociolinguistic landscape dominated by their European counterparts, English and French, and by Mauritian Creole, the nationwide language of communication.

The second option does not seem to stand on solid ground because of the status of Bhojpuri and is considered with suspicion. Bhojpuri, as already mentioned, has been constantly losing ground to Creole; it has little prestige and is looked down upon by its users. It is not considered as a language by itself and is perceived or presented as being inseparable from the prestigious Hindi. Any proposal to promote Bhojpuri for its own sake tends therefore to be seen as a calculated move to dissociate it from Hindi in order to do away with it more easily for the benefit of Creole. The short-lived Mauritius Bhojpuri Institute set up in 1982 with the expressed goal of promoting Bhojpuri had some difficulty to drive home the point that the development of Bhojpuri does not go against the interest of Hindi. This point was re-emphasized by its promoter, Sarita Boodhoo (1999: 141), when she writes 'Bhojpuri has no quarrel with Hindi which language it precedes in linguistic history and which it nurtures culturally and emotionally". The Bhojpuri-Hindi issue is actually nothing new in the multilingual context of Mauritius. During the 1970's, the rise of Creole and its possible adverse impact on French were debated along very much similar lines, by those who were opposed to the establishment of Creole as an independent linguistic entity and preferred its limited use as a stepping stone to French.

The most explicit and coherent proposal for Bhojpuri as an indispensable support for Hindi—the third option—is to be found in Barz (1980: 25). Barz starts by making an important and necessary distinction between 'Hindi' as a collective label for an extensive family of related languages and 'Hindi' as a particular member of that family, that is, standard Hindi defined as "the common literary and spoken language for all speakers of dialects belonging to that family". The relationship between Hindi and Bhojpuri is then defined in the following terms:

> The relationship between standard Hindi and Mauritian Bhojpuri in Mauritius is a symbiotic one. Neither standard Hindi nor Urdu will ever become household or native languages in Mauritius. On the one hand it is unlikely that Mauritian Bhojpuri will develop a written literature since, as matters now stand Mauritian Bhojpuri speakers who write in an Indian language write in standard Hindi and almost nothing has been published in Mauritian Bhojpuri (…). However, if there were to be a drastic reduction in the number of people using Mauritian Bhojpuri in daily life it is unlikely that enough cultural impetus would remain for the survival of standard Hindi in the island. The two languages must move along together and the fate of one will determine that of the other.

The crucial role of Bhojpuri as the "necessary living roots" needed for the survival of Hindi depends on the fulfilment of two important conditions:

- The maintenance of a large and "linguistically healthy" body of speakers of Mauritian Bhojpuri.
- The recognition and promotion of Bhojpuri (linguistic description, study in schools, role in nation-building, literary publications, etc.).

What Barz understands by a "linguistically healthy" body of speakers is not clear. It could be interpreted to mean that norms and standards should be prescribed for a healthy "non-contaminated" use of Bhojpuri. Engineering the social use of a language is a fairly complex issue, especially in a contact situation like Mauritius, where the "Bhojpuri-Hindi symbiosis" at the cultural and symbolic level is matched by a close and constant interaction between Bhojpuri and Creole in everyday communication at societal level.

Actions which could lead to the fulfilment of the second condition mentioned by Barz were initiated. Agencies were set up, projects were elaborated and some concrete results were obtained. The Department of Bhojpuri at the Mahatma Gandhi Institute produced cassettes and L–P records of Bhojpuri folksongs; it also started work on a Bhojpuri dictionary project. As mentioned earlier, a Mauritius Bhojpuri Institute was created in 1982, and its main objective was to revive Bhojpuri language and traditions. It had an impressive start with the organization of a spectacular Bhojpuri festival—the first of its kind—and the publication of the first issue of a Bhojpuri newsletter, "Bhojpuri Patrika". But there was no real follow-up and its ambitious action-programme, as announced initially, remained largely symbolical. At the more scholarly level, a number of linguistic studies were undertaken, such as Domingue, N. (1971), Neerputh, N. (1986), Baker and Ramnah, P. (1985) and Ramdin, S. (2006).

But the vital recognition given to the language was its inclusion in the 1983 population census. The limited and derogatory acceptance of Creole in the 1972 census ("For the purposes of the census only 'creole patois' should be considered as a language") was replaced in 1983 by a formal recognition of its status as a language. This recognition was also extended to Bhojpuri and it read as follows: "For the purposes of the census also, Creole and Bhojpuri should be considered as languages".

## Hindi-Bhojpuri and the Gradual Shift to Creole: What the Census Shows

Statistical language data on Mauritius were obtained through the census for the first time in 1931, but at that time they concerned only the European languages, that is, English and French. In 1944, Hindi (as a generic category for Indian languages), Creole and Chinese were added. From 1952 to 1972, specific Indian languages present in Mauritius were added, namely, Urdu, Tamil, Telugu, Marathi and Gujarati. Hindi should therefore be understood to stand for Hindi-Bhojpuri in the absence of explicit reference to the latter. With the inclusion of the various provincial Indian languages, the census authorities felt the need to distinguish between current or usual language, defined as the language usually or most often spoken in the home, and language of forefathers, or ancestral language. The latter category appears under the heading "linguistic group" and serves to differentiate between the Indo-Mauritian sub-groups.

Census language data are not always reliable because of the numerous extra-linguistic considerations which influence language choice. Their value therefore resides not so much in their statistical accuracy as in the relevance of the tendencies they exhibit. Table 1 presents the post-independence census data for the single languages that are relevant to the present study, namely Hindi, Bhojpuri and

**Table 1**

*1972–2000: Evolution of Ancestral (AL) and Current Language (CL)*

| | | *1972* | *1983* | *1990* | *2000* |
|---|---|---|---|---|---|
| *Total pop* | | *826,199* | *966,863* | *10,22,456* | *11,78,848* |
| Creole | AL | 2,72,076 (32.9%) | 2,80,377 (29.0%) | 3,45,802 (33.8%) | 4,54,763 (38.6%) |
| | CL | 4,28,434 (51.9%) | 5,21,950 (54.0%) | 6,18,226 (60.5%) | 8,26,152 (70.1%) |
| Hindi | AL | 3,20,889 (38.9%) | 2,08,450 (21.6%) | 38,142 (3.7%) | 35,782 (3%) |
| | CL | 2,62,128 (31.7%) | 1,11,134 (11.5%) | 12,845 (1.2%) | 7,250 (0.6%) |
| Bhojpuri | AL | 1,80,983 (18.7%) | 3,43,798 (33.6%) | 3,61,250 (30.6%) | |
| | CL | 1,47,050 (15.2%) | 2,01,616 (19.7%) | 1,42,387 (12.1%) | |
| Urdu | AL | 71,669 (8.7%) | 55,347 (5.7%) | 45,274 (4.4%) | 34,120 (2.9%) |
| | CL | 23,470 (2.9%) | 23,572 (2.4%) | 6,809 (0.7%) | 1,789 (0.15%) |
| Arabic | AL | 66,033 (6.8%) | 1,686 (0.2%) | 806 | |
| | CL | 1,813 (0.2%) | 280 | 82 | |
| Tamil | AL | 56,758 (6.9%) | 66,154 (6.8%) | 47,946 (4.7%) | 44,731 (3.8%) |
| | CL | 29,094 (3.5%) | 35,646 (3.7%) | 8,002 (0.8%) | 3,623 (0.3%) |
| Telugu | AL | 24,234 (2.9%) | 25,619 (2.6%) | 21,027 (2%) | 18,802 (1.6%) |
| | CL | 17,634 (2.1%) | 15,364 (1.6%) | 6,437 (0.6%) | 2,169 (0.2%) |
| Marathi | AL | 16,553 (2.0%) | 20,412 (2.1%) | 17,730 (1.7%) | 16,587 (1.4%) |
| | CL | 12,036 (1.5%) | 12,420 (1.3%) | 7,535 (0.7%) | 1,888 (0.16%) |
| Gujarati | AL | 2,028 (0.2%) | 1,707 (0.2%) 531 | 2,181 (0.2%) | 1,975 (0.2%) |
| | CL | 403 (0.05%) | (0.05%) | 290 (0.03) | 241 |

*Source:* Population Census Reports, 1972, 1983, 1990, 2000, CSO, Mauritius.

Creole, but also the other Indian languages which are part of the sociolinguistic landscape of Mauritius. The presence of Arabic as from 1983 is in relation to Urdu and will be discussed below.

The 1983 census marked a clear departure from the 1972 edition on various counts including language concepts and categories, like for example the acknowledgement of Creole and Bhojpuri as languages. The pre-selected list of languages that used to be included in the census form was removed and the choice of the ancestral and the current language was left to the respondent. A more radical change was the removal of the question relating to one's ethnic community. This created a dilemma for the census authorities because of the established link between linguistic group, ancestral language and ethnicity. The instruction given in the census form at 'C 11 Religion' is an indication of the degree of confusion that this led to: "The language of forefathers of the person should also be specified when it is necessary to clearly establish the religious domination of that person". Press announcements published by various socio-cultural associations gave instructions on how to reply to census questions on religion, linguistic group and language usually spoken. Minority language groups recommended the respective languages as responses to the three questions. The Indo-Mauritian Catholic Association for its part asked its members to define themselves as Tamil, Hindu, Telugu or Marathi Catholics, while the Mauritius Arabic Language Teachers and Students Association invited its members to write Islam under religion, Arabic for linguistic group and Creole as language usually spoken.

The 1990 census added yet another innovative feature with the option given to include two ancestral languages, expressed as follows: "If the language of the paternal forefathers is different from the language of the maternal forefathers, write both". Many respondents interpreted this option as also applicable to the language currently used at home, as a result of which the census report also contains interesting comparative data on Bhojpuri and Creole coupled with another language of interest to the present study. While data on current bilingualism are most welcome in a multilingual context, ancestral bilingualism questions the one to one relation between ancestral language and linguistic group. The 1990 census also re-introduced the literacy language category, which had been removed in 1972.

The most notable finding of the 1983 census report is the emergence of Bhojpuri as a linguistic entity. It comes very close to Hindi as "ancestral language" (Bh: 18.7%; H: 21.6%), and obtains a higher score as "current language" (Bh: 15.2; H: 11.5%) The figures for Hindi do not correspond to actual reality and can only be explained by reference to its prestige or to the fact that people tend to identify Hindi in the first sense used by Barz, that is, the Hindi family of Indian dialects and languages. This is confirmed by its drastic decline in 1990 and its almost non-existence in 2000.

The displacement of Hindi by Bhojpuri in the census returns no doubt reflects the historical and sociolinguistic reality, but it also illustrates a very significant change in language attitude. Bhojpuri was traditionally looked down upon as the low language with Hindi fulfilling all the functions of the high language. Hindi still functions as the language of reference but more as a cultural construct and identity marker in a multicultural context, whereas Bhojpuri is re-established as a historical fact and a linguistic reality subjected to the dynamics of language in society. The Hindi-Bhojpuri shift may also be attributed to the impact of modernity. Hindi and the values associated with it used to be transmitted through the traditional community network of *baithkas* and socio-cultural organizations. Now it is taught in the formal context of the modern school and sustained through the media and Bollywood.

The *baithkas* no longer exist or function as such, and Hindi has almost completely lost its status of a constructed ancestral language. But the loss has in a way been compensated by its status of literacy language to which I will refer later.

The trend observed in the case of Hindi also applies to the other Indian languages, but not to the same extent, except for Urdu and Gujarati. The latter has lost its historical importance, noted earlier as the language of the small group of merchants and traders. Its function as an ancestral or current language is more residual than real. The other minority languages, Tamil, Telugu and Marathi, still function as ancestral languages, which is a fact of history, but much less as currently spoken languages. They do however possess strong symbolic value as markers of group identity. The fate of Urdu, which is almost non-existent in the 2000 census, is somewhat different. Historically, the language of the Bihari Muslims was Bhojpuri, but the linking of Bhojpuri with Hindi and Hinduism led to its replacement among the Bihari Muslims by Urdu as the ancestral language, with Creole and Bhojpuri as the spoken languages. Then, in 1983, Arabic suddenly became their first ancestral language (6.8%, compared to 5.7% for Urdu). This unexpected radical shift can only be explained by referring to the then emerging new international context of Arab inspired pan-Islamic solidarity. However, in the subsequent censuses of 1990 and especially 2000, Arabic disappeared altogether, thus confirming an artificial status based on religious ideology rather than historical consideration. Emrith (1994: 181) adds an economic explanation to the religious factor by stating:

> In the seventies, with the rise of the oil-rich states in the Middle-East and the many job opportunities that became open to Mauritian workers, Arabic, which had hitherto been studied by Muslims for religious purposes, suddenly generated a new and vigorous interest among Muslims, who saw the language as more

> than just the language of the Holy Qur'an. (...). Understandably, some Muslims began to question the relevance for Muslim boys and girls to continue to study Urdu in the schools and began a campaign to dump Urdu in favour of Arabic. (...). The controversy it generated was futile and, for a while, literally split the Muslim community on an issue that touched the core of their culture and heritage.

To obtain the overall ancestral language situation of the Muslims at the last census, we have to add the figures of Urdu (2.9%) with the ancestral bilingualism categories of Bhojpuri+Urdu (0.32%) and Creole+Urdu (0.95%), which amounts to a bare total of 4.2 per cent. It is therefore tempting to conclude that the concept of ancestral language for the majority of the Muslim population of Mauritius no longer functions as a marker of group identity.

As could be expected, the dominant pair in Table 2 is Bhojpuri-Hindi, but the figures for both ancestral and current bilingualism show a significantly regressive trend. The figures for ancestral Bhojpuri+Urdu and for Bhojpuri+Tamil-Telugu-Marathi (the latter have been combined because of their numerical marginality) may be considered to relate to the historical though limited role of Bhojpuri as a link language. But a comparison with Table 3 reveals a striking contrast: it is Creole, rather than Bhojpuri, which emerges as the dynamic and progressive component of any bilingual combination with an Indian language. More surprisingly, this is more systematically apparent in the ancestral bilingual combinations. Here again, it is not the figures as such that count but the pattern that they reveal. Language and social dynamics in multicultural Mauritius favour those languages which have the highest coefficient as Languages of Wider Communication (LWC): Creole, at the home and national level; French and English, at the national and global level, acquired by the majority of learners through the medium of the school.

The community-based mode of acquisition and transmission of standard Indian languages has virtually disappeared. Being literate in Indian languages only would mean traditional literacy acquired through non-formal modes and within the community. That belongs to the past. The school has now taken over the function of teaching Oriental languages (that is, Indian languages, modern Chinese and Arabic), alongside English and French.

**Table 2**

*Bilingualism. Bhojpuri + Another Indian Language*

| | *Ancestral Bilingualism* | | *Current Bilingualism* | |
|---|---|---|---|---|
| | *1990* | *2000* | *1990* | *2000* |
| Bhoj + Hindi | 32,917 (3.2%) | 22,977(1.9%) | 20,976 (2.0%) | 7,298 (0.6%) |
| Bhoj + Urdu | 3,553 | 3,842 | 603 | 166 |
| Bhoj + Tam-Tel-Mar | 1,366 | 1,983 | 351 | 151 |
| Bhoj + Other Indian L | 163 | 407 | 23 | 30 |
| Total | 37,999 (3.7%) | 29,209 (2.5%) | 21,953 (2.1%) | 7,645 (0.6%) |

**Table 3**

*Bilingualism. Creole + an Indian Language*

| | *Ancestral Bilingualism* | | *Current Bilingualism* | |
|---|---|---|---|---|
| | *1990* | *2000* | *1990* | *2000* |
| Creole + Bhoj | 34,356 (3.4%) | 65,868 (5.6%) | 48,574 (4.7%) | 64,105 (5.4%) |
| Creole + Hindi | 2,281 | 5,222 | 3,426 | 4,572 |
| Creole + Urdu | 10,116 | 11,164 | 6,478 | 3,536 |
| Creole + Tamil | 5,981 | 7845 | 5,312 | 3,274 |
| Creole + Telugu | 1,163 | 2201 | 1,797 | 2,841 |
| Creole + Marathi | 1,088 | 1809 | 1,779 | 1,656 |
| Creole + other Ind L | 1,207 | 2877 | 1,701 | 1,881 |
| Total | 56,192 (5.5%) | 96,986 (8.2%) | 69,067 (6.8%) | 81,865 (6.9%) |

*Source:* 1990 and 2000 Census Reports.

The census definition of being literate in a language means "the person can, *with understanding,* both read and write a simple statement" in that language.

The literate population is calculated as from the age group of 12, a cutting point which reasonably assumes that basic literacy has been acquired at the end of primary schooling. Literacy in Oriental languages only is lowest in the 12–14 age group (only 190 respondents) and highest in the 65+ age group (4,053), which confirms the traditional mode of acquisition. In the case of Creole and Bhojpuri, the fact that they are predominantly spoken languages, coupled with their exclusion from the education system, explains their marginal status as literacy languages.

**Table 4**
*Literacy Languages Read and Written*

| | *1990* | *2000* |
|---|---|---|
| Total Population (aged 12 and over) | 7,85,063 | 9,10,616 |
| Oriental languages (OL)* | 24,257 (3.1%) | 22,278 (2.4%) |
| European languages | 4,09,396 (52.1%) | 5,46,927 (60.0%) |
| European and Oriental languages | 1,69,723 (21.6%) | 1,70,975 (18.8%) |
| Creole | 28,632 (3.6%) | 29,690 (2.9%) |
| Bhojpuri | 2,938 (0.4%) | 2,212 (0.2%) |
| Creole and Bhojpuri | 4,138 (0.5%) | 3,392 (0.4%) |
| None | 1,44,762 (18.4%) | 1,31,073 (14.4%) |

* Oriental languages (OL) = Indian, Arabic, Chinese.
*Source:* 1990 and 2000 Census reports.

English, French and Oriental languages are offered right from the first year of primary education. The European languages are learned by all the pupils but Oriental languages are chosen on the criteria of ancestral linguistic group. The figures in Table 4 show that literacy in the European languages is on the rise, which is not the case for European and Oriental languages combined. On the basis of the general trend noted, it may be assumed that literacy in the Oriental languages is on the decline.

That said, the school has a crucial responsibility in the maintenance of the Indian languages, a fact highlighted by the government decision reached after a prolonged struggle to give them equal status with the European languages for examination, certification, and selection purposes at the end of primary schooling and for entry to the secondary level. This is reflected in the latest statistics on the OL school population presented in Table 5.

Oriental language enrolment at primary level shows an almost perfect correlation, language wise and globally, with the demographic size of population of Asian origin. The problematic situation of Urdu and Arabic noted earlier is here resolved with the two languages reaching a total of more than 16 per cent which corresponds to that of the Muslim population of Mauritius. Another interesting feature of the primary OL enrolment is its even distribution from year 1 to year 6 of the primary schooling, thus reflecting the enhanced status of Indian languages. At the secondary level, however, a sudden and significant fall in OL enrolment is noted:

**Table 5**

*Number of Pupils Studying Oriental Languages at Primary and Secondary Level in 2005*

| | *Primary* | *Secondary* | | | |
|---|---|---|---|---|---|
| Total Pupils | *(6 years)* *1,18,737* | *Year 1* *17,415* | *Year 5* *18,091* *('O' level)* | *Year 7* *8,207* *('A' level)* | *Total pupils* *(Y 1–7)* *1,06,805* |
| Hindi | 50,208 (42.3%) | 5,377 (30.9%) | 2,014 (11.1%) | 659 (8.0%) | 21,063 (19.7%) |
| Urdu | 14,310 (12.1%) | 1,188 (6.8%) | 259 (1.4%) | 101 (1.2%) | 3,954 (3.7%) |
| Tamil | 7,160 (6.0%) | 380 (2.2%) | 64 (0.3%) | 20 (0.2) | 1,306 (1.2%) |
| Telugu | 2,583 (2.2%) | 143 (0.8%) | 12 (0.1%) | 11 (0.1) | 479 (0.4%) |
| Marathi | 1,880 (1.6%) | 113 (0.6%) | 14 (0.1%) | 5 (0.06%) | 350 (0.3%) |
| Arabic | 6,705 (5.6%) | 1,349 (7.7%) | 120 (0.7%) | 17 (0.2%) | 4,103 (3.8%) |
| Chinese | 1,871 (1.6%) | 115 (0.7%) | 5 | 0 | 304 (0.3%) |

*Source:* Digest of Educational Statistics, 2005, (CSO Report, January 2006).

from 50 per cent in year 1 to only 13.8 per cent in year 5 for the 'O' level examinations and a mere 10 per cent for the terminal 'A' level examinations. While being more in line with the social trend, the OL enrolment pattern at secondary level also reflects the lack of incentive to learn OL and the absence of perspective in terms of career prospect. In the same vein, it may be argued that the mission of the primary school is to lay the foundations in the various subjects considered necessary and important by society and that in the case of OL, knowing the basics is sufficient for the purpose they serve.

In summary, the various languages accounted for within the Mauritian context may be categorized into three distinct domains, as follows:

- The home/private, non-formal/public domain of oral use occupied by Creole, and to some extent by Bhojpuri, especially in the countryside.

- The domain of symbolic reference and cultural identity covered by the Oriental languages and Bhojpuri, and now progressively in association with Creole.
- The domain of education, information, career prospects and advancement, which is the realm par excellence of English and French.

There is thus a significant degree of complementarity among the languages and the language categories discussed, which would explain to a large extent why the politics of linguistic and cultural pluralism, as practised within the Mauritian context, have up to now been generally successful.

**Conclusion**

Of the three languages that Mauritius has inherited from Bihar, Hindi and Urdu have survived with varying fortunes under the combined influence of internal forces and external factors such as the independence and partition of India and later, in the case of Urdu, the rise of Islam and the Arabian world. The spectacular incursion of Arabic into Urdu's ancestral territory has meant that with these two richly endowed languages of culture and religion, the concept of ancestral language or linguistic group has become meaningless for the Bihari Mauritian Muslims. Hindi for its part now extends beyond Bihar as the generic language of greater India, thus leaving the ancestral territory free for Bhojpuri to be established in its historical rights as the original language of the Bihari Mauritian Hindus.

In 1947, when the first modern constitutional reform extended voting rights to all adults who could show proof of basic literacy in any of the languages in use in Mauritius, Hindi and Urdu played an important role as instruments of political change, decolonization and democracy. Creole was among the languages listed in the second schedule of the 1947 constitution, even though nobody paid attention to "the Creole patois in use in the Colony". But Bhojpuri was left out in favour of Hindi, listed as "Hindustani". And yet that was the language in use among hundreds of thousands, at home and in the sugarcane fields. They were the ones who bought the parcels of barren land that the sugar estates decided to get rid of in the late 19th century. Out of each "little acre of love"[10] they produced green gold. Then one day the sugar-mill owners refused to crush the canes from their little acres of land, on the grounds that they were too coarse for their new sophisticated machines and their sugar content too low. That was in 1937.

On 13th August of that fateful year, thousands of small planters and labourers assembled on the Union-Flacq estate of Rajcoomar Gujadhur, one of the few Indo-Mauritians who owned sugar estates and mills in those days. They defied the estate's armed employees and marched on, shouting "*mare salah*", according to the police report quoted by Hazareesingh (1976). The armed employees opened fire on the marchers, killing four of them and wounding several others. That single event triggered a series of historical developments which culminated in the making of modern Mauritius, the Mauritius that India would like us to make of Bihar.

The history of sugar and the small planters is known, though not fully. That of Mauritian Bhojpuri, historically the first language of protest and redress, is being written thanks to the dedicated contribution of Sarita Boodhoo and Suchita Ramdin. Some essential chapters still need to be added, revisited or completed. Others may be lost without translation or publication. The announced Bihar day celebrations in Mauritius, the first of its kind outside India, would be an appropriate historic occasion for the launch of a Mauritius-Bihar Bhojpuri project.

## Notes

1. webindia123.com, New Delhi, January 08, 2007.
2. Press Trust of India, January 07, 2007.
3. PatnaDaily.com, Patna, January 21, 2007.
4. Ramessur Ory wrote the first Ph.D. study on Mauritian Bhojpuri, which he submitted in 1970 to the Varanaseya Sanskrit University in Banaras. In his acknowledgement, he refers to his impressive collection of folk stories and songs and to a brief study of Mauritian Bhojpuri included in his survey of language in Mauritius in view of obtaining his "Mahopadhya". In the early 1980s, I initiated a project at the MGI for the thesis of Ory to be translated in English. Unfortunately, it did not go beyond the first pages.
5. Roy, J.N. *Mauritius Me Hindi Bhaashaa Kaa Sanshipta Itihaas*, New Delhi, 1970. Quoted by M. Chintamunee, in H. Unmole, (ed.) Proceedings of the National Seminar on the Language Issue, University of Mauritius, 1984, p. 184.

6. Mewasingh, P., "The Role of Bhojpuri in Mauritius", in Unmole (1984), p. 278.
7. Gambhir, S., "Mauritian Bhojpuri: An International Perspective on Historical and Sociolinguistic Processes", in U. Bissoondoyal and S.B. Servansingh, (eds.), *Indian Labour Immigration*, MGI, Mauritius, 1986.
8. Bahadoor, D., "The Role, Function and Contribution of Hindi in Mauritius", in H. Unmole (ed.) (1984).
9. Sooriah, P., *Telegu Migrants in Mauritius*, 1977, quoted in Rao, G.S. and Sharma, R., *Sociolinguistic Survey of Mauritius*, 1989, CIIL, Mysore.
10. The story of the Indo-Mauritian labourer and peasant and his anchorage in the new homeland is depicted in a number of novels by Abhimanyu Unnuth, including *Ek Bigha Pyar* (1972) and *Lal Pasina* (1977), published by Rajkamal Prakashan, New Delhi.

## References

Baker, P. and Ramnah, P. 1985. "Mauritian Bhopuri: An Indo-Aryan Language Spoken in a Predominantly Creolophone Society". *Papers in Creole Linguistics*, No. 4. Canberra: Pacific Linguistics.

Barz, R. 1980. "The Cultural Significance of Hindi in Mauritius". *The Indian Cultural Review*. MGI, Mauritius.

Bhuckory, S. 1988. *Hindi in Mauritius*. Mauritius: EOI, 2nd edition.

Boodhoo, S. 1999. *Bhojpuri Traditions in Mauritius*. Mauritius: MBI.

Carter, M. 1999. *Across the Kala Pani: The Bihari Presence in Mauritius*. Mauritius: CRIOS.

Central Statistical Office. "Digest of Educational Statistics", 2005. Mauritius.

——. *Population Census Reports* (1972–1990). Mauritius.

Domingue, N. 1971. "Bhojpuri and Creole in Mauritius: A study of Linguistic Interference and its Consequences in Regard to Synchronic Variation and Language Change". Ph.D. thesis, University of Texas at Austin.

Emrith, M. 1994. *The History of Muslims in Mauritius*. Editions Le Printemps, Mauritius, 2nd edition.

Gambhir, S. 1986. "Mauritian Bhojpuri: An International Perspective on Historical and Sociolinguistic Processes". In U. Bissoondoyal and S.B. Servansingh (eds.), *Indian Labour Immigration*. MGI, Mauritius.

Hazareesingh, K. 1976. *History of Indians in Mauritius*. London: Macmillan.

Hookoomsing, V.Y. 1986. "Creole and the Language Situation in Mauritius". In E. Annamalai et al. (eds.), *Language Planning: Proceedings of an Institute*. Mysore: CIIL.

—. 1986. "Langue Et Identité Ethnique: Les Langues Ancestrales à Maurice". *Journal of Mauritian Studies*, No. 2, Vol. 1.

—. 2003. "Preserving Pluralism in the Context of Development and Modernisation: The Case of Mauritius with Particular Reference to the Indo-Mauritians". In R. Sharma and E. Annamalai, (eds.), *Indian Diaspora: In Search of Identity*. Mysore: CIIL.

Neerputh, N. 1986. *Le Système Verbal Du Bhojpouri Mauricien*. Paris: l'Harmattan.

Ramdin, S. 2007. A Linguistic and Cultural Study of the Evolution of Bhojpuri in Mauritius' Ph.D. thesis in progress, University of Mauritius.

Ramyead, L.P. 1985. *The Establishment and Cultivation of Modern Standard Hindi in Mauritius*. Mauritius: MGI.

Unmole, H. (ed.). 1984. Proceedings of the National Seminar on the Language Issue. Mauritius: University of Mauritius.

# 2

# Urbanism and Death of Religion

## Strategies of Religious Manifestation in Modern Society

P. PRATAP KUMAR

Much of the discussion on survival of religion and secularization is based on the distinction between religious belonging and religious practice (Davie, 2000; Martikainen, 2006). Religious belonging assumes that people may belong to a religion and may not practice it and hence do not actively pass on those beliefs and practices to the next generation. Such an assumption ignores the possibility that even though one does not practice religion, they may make resources available for public transmission of their beliefs and practices. The proliferation of temples and organizations among Hindus in South Africa is an example of this tendency. Even in the European context, studies in religious pluralism in the diaspora context reveal that in the last decade of the 20th century a substantial number of Muslim organizations were established in Finland (Martikainen, 2006). The example of the Festival of Chariots in Durban is a case in point to suggest that not everyone who comes to the festival is a keen devotee or not even interested in the religious aspect. Some simply come to enjoy the spectacle. Such festivals not only achieve religious goals of devotees, but more importantly serve to generate social awareness of the religious group's presence. In the multicultural societies, such desire to create awareness among the outsiders is not to be considered by any means less important. It is often a form of looking for social acceptance and legitimating. It is for this reason the involvement of government officials and politicians in the various ceremonies is noteworthy.

In the following, I shall identify two strategies that Hindus in South Africa have used to perpetuate their old worldview. First is the invention of homogeneity and the period of the discussion is set in an earlier period in the history of Hindus in South Africa (mid-19th and early 20th century) and the second is the public performances which are held today in the modern context of South Africa. I make use of these two examples from different time periods to suggest that there is continuity in the religious transmission among Hindus in South Africa.

**Inventing Homogeneity as a Strategy**

In what follows, I shall demonstrate how Hindus in South Africa[1] have perpetuated their traditions by finding innovative ways. One important clarification needs to be made at the outset. That is, the people whom we refer to as 'Hindu' did not come to South Africa as a homogenous group. Rather they came from a variety of locations, mainly rural areas and with a variety of traditions and cultural beliefs. I do not need to make the point here that the category 'Hindu' came from the outside as much scholarly literature exists on this issue. The people whom we as scholars as well as the practitioners themselves refer to as Hindus are characterized by their heterogeneity in that they practiced seemingly diverse beliefs and rituals as is evident in the context of South Africa. There are mainly four linguistic groups identified in South Africa—Tamil, Telugu, Hindi and Gujarati speakers with their denominational, sectarian and cultural beliefs. Generally, Tamil people are identified as worshippers of Shiva and his cognate gods, the Telugus have been worshippers of Vishnu and his cognate deities although they have become integrated into the Tamil community overtime by assimilating the beliefs and practices of the Tamils. The Hindi speaking people generally practiced Vishnu and to be more accurate Rama who is considered an incarnation of Vishnu.

The Hindus who came from various villages in India in the 19th century had a certain homogenous worldview belonging to their respective village traditions. So, when they left India and their homogenous life world and boarded the ships to reach Natal, even while they were in the ships, their so-called homogeneity began to disintegrate as they had to mix and live among other Indians from north and south with their different linguistic, cultural and religious beliefs. For the first time their sense of being other began to dawn on them. When they eventually reached Natal, the plantation owners selected the Indian labourers not on the basis of their linguistic and cultural unity, but rather on the basis of their ability to perform on the farms using their knowledge of the sugarcane growing. As such they lived on the farms not as homogenous communities but making new alliances and bonds with other Indians who did not necessarily speak the same language and perform the same rituals.

When they freed themselves from the indenture contract, they began to regroup on the basis of same language and culture and this time in the proximity of urban locations. They began to buy small landholdings nearer to the urban areas in order to be able to reach town easily and sell the fruits and vegetables that they started growing on those small farms. And this is the beginning of their desire to forge their new identity in the new land. It seems to me that fundamental to this new identity is a sense of homogeneity that they began to invent. Since their original homogenous life world had collapsed, it was incumbent upon them to find new ways of finding this new homogeneity. This meant that it had to be invented. And they did so through the religious, cultural and linguistic institutions that they began to build. Their original village based and language based cultural identity began to give way to a broader sense of being either a south Indian or north Indian. The Tamils and Telugu speaking people began to oscillate towards becoming integrated into one cultural group and in a similar process the north Indian linguistic communities eventually became integrated into what is commonly known today as the Hindi-speaking community.

This meant that, for instance, the south Indian communities integrated their various village based ritual practices in their new temples and shrines that they began to build from as early as 1870s. The rituals associated with Kavadi, fire walking, and Mariamman worship became part of their new programme of homogeneity. The temples began to integrate different worship patterns and deities within the same complex. In other words, the inclusion of shrines with the images of Vishnu, Shiva or Muruga and Mariamman or Draupadi has become the norm to cater to the different ritual traditions of south Indians. Mixing of such diverse ritual traditions in temples and shrines in India is rather uncommon, but in South Africa it became a tool to be deployed to reinvent a new homogeneity for south Indians. But by the second and third generation, even north Indian communities began to assimilate such new ritual traditions to the extent that today they have become a pan South African Indian ritual traditions. As each temple developed its own character around the priests, elders and families that worshipped in it, new rules of ritual procedures, conventions and even local legends as to how a temple came to be in that location had to be invented. For instance, unlike in the case of India, a Brahmin can be any one who knew how to perform rituals and not necessarily the one who belonged to the caste of Brahmins with all its sub-groupings (Kumar, 2000: 35). Why a coconut cannot be broken in the temple as it happens in temples in India had to do with the local health restrictions and less to do with ritual procedure and it is something that they had to invent to accommodate local municipal laws. Over a period of time, the new rules and conventions became norms.

As the caste rules that guided their social life could not be observed any more in the new context due to their inability to live as single and homogenous caste groups, a new social structure began to emerge. Some quickly acquired higher caste status by acquiring new caste names and by observing new rituals. Cognate caste groups began to enter into marriage alliances which gave rise to a new social organization in which caste for all intents and purposes gave way to a loose linguistic and broad cultural unity. In this process of homogenization of different ritual practices and caste identities, it provided them a sense of being a new community. As such, discovering a new way of finding homogeneity was fundamental to their survival in a new place. They dug deep into their old cultural and religious practices and integrated them in ways that would make sense to their own context. The succeeding generations followed suit. For the new generations, the old inventions, assimilations and integrations became a tradition that they could call South African Hinduism. These are expressed in their many religious institutions that they had built during the last one and a half centuries in South Africa. Their proclivity for building temples and religious institutions or organizations is a part of their ongoing homogenizing strategy. Baumann in his study of the South Asian diaspora in Germany pointed out that religious institutions are the most commonly built social organizations among the diaspora (Baumann, 2002: 95–98). And this in my view is an attempt to pass on their ancient beliefs and practices to the next generation. Such an invented homogeneity did not always mean that Hindus did not pursue their specific forms of worship. The three different festivals outlined below indeed reflect such diversity within the Hindu groups.

**Public Performances as Transmissions of Beliefs**

As part of this strategy, I focus on three festivals that occur around the same time every year at the present time period. During the Easter weekend in the greater Durban area, three festivals associated with Hinduism take place. While the three on their own may not have anything in common, the three festivals represent different social groups within the Hindu society, who wish to ensure their beliefs and practices are transmitted to the future generations. These festivals are—the Festival of Chariots of the ISKCON, the Mariamman Festival, and the Fire Walking Festival dedicated to the worship of Draupadi as Hindu goddess.

The case of the ISKCON in South Africa is an example to point out how a religious institution could use its public dimensions such as festivals in ensuring their beliefs are spread widely as well as continued into the next generation. For the last eighteen years, the Hare Krishnas in Durban have been organizing the annual Festival of Chariots (*rathayatra*) on the beachfront. The selection of the beachfront during the Easter season beginning on Good Friday is interesting. The beachfront becomes the hive of many sporting activities sponsored by the major cell phone industries in the country. The television coverage on these events is extensive. Right in the middle of these material activities, the ISKCON locates its festival of chariots in an effort to bring to the people what they call Krishna Consciousness. It boldly advertises on the billboards the focus of their festival. On the one side of the banner it says—Yoga, Mantra, Astrology and philosophy. On the other side of the banner it says—food, fashion, Vedic art and meditation. The classical and the ancient on one side, the modern and contemporary on the other side seem to indicate their ability to make themselves relevant to the contemporary society. It is a blend that reflects in their opening dance performances which included the classical Indian dance form with the modern fusion dance and the African rhythm. Various stalls are set up to cover a range of activities from spiritual aspects to material products—stalls for meditation, arts on Krishna, question and answer sessions, devotional music stall, stalls for food and drinks, eastern wear (dress), gifts and souvenirs, Krishna Seva stall (service to Krishna) and free food service—all of these are seemingly put together to produce a heightened consciousness of Krishna. The sacred chant of "Hare Krishna and Hare Rama" is boldly announced on the banners at the entrance and it is chanted continuously to the accompanying music.

The festival begins on the Good Friday evening with the gathering of some of the high ranking monks of ISKCON from around the world. Their spiritual addresses are followed by a politician's (the local Minister of Arts and Culture) speech in which he strongly identifies himself as a follower of the movement. Amidst various activities and celebrations, the crowds that are continuously pouring in are entertained. Some are hard core devotees, some are visitors, some are tourists who happen to be on the beach and some are homeless people who come for the sake of free food. Everyone is encouraged to partake in the free food offered in the name of Krishna.

**Figure 1**

*Hare Krishna devotees dancing during the festival of chariots' procession on the beachfront in Durban. Photograph by Pratap Kumar*

On the following Saturday, the procession carrying the chariot of Krishna begins at the City Hall with the City Manager opening the event. The procession's route is marked out and the local police and the traffic department are on hand to ensure that the procession

**Figure 2**

*The Head of the ISKCON in Durban Chanting the Hare Krishna Mantra During the Procession. Photograph by Pratap Kumar*

proceeds smoothly. The chariot is decorated with the symbols associated with Krishna worship and the image of Swami Prabhupada is seated in the chariot. Singers and dancers accompanied by hundreds of devotees pull the chariot across the streets of the city in the demarcated route. Ahead of the main chariot is a smaller cart carrying the image of Lord Chaitanya, who began the movement of Krishna devotion in Bengal back in the 15th century. Many centuries later, Swami Prabhupada in the mid 1970s took the movement to the west and reinvented it as a popular and modern one known today as the International Society for Krishna Consciousness. The massive success and popularity of the movement is attributed to its ability to transmit their philosophical and religious ideas throughout the world through festivals and public chanting of the name of Krishna. In the last two decades of its existence in South Africa and especially in Durban, the movement has managed to raise enormous resources, both human and material, to become one of the most successful religious organizations in the modern world.

The Mariamman festival takes place in a number of local temples solely dedicated to the worship of Mariamman. The most

**Figure 3**

*Devotees of Mariamman Usually Make Offerings to Mathuraiveeran, a Male Guardian Deity Located Outside the Main Shrine of Mariamman. Photograph by Pratap Kumar*

famous being the one that is organized in the south of Durban at an Indian suburb called the Isipingo Township. The other one is organized at the more than hundred year old temple built in the Sugar estate at Mt. Edgecombe, another Indian suburb. There are two older temples built here—one is for the worship of Mariamman, a village goddess still worshipped in many parts of south India. The other one is a small shrine of Kali. The Kali shrine might have been established by the Hindi speaking north Indian Hindus, but now is appropriated by the Tamils. The red Flags, which are usually associated with the Hindi speaking Hindu practice, hoisted at the Kali temple betray its earlier association. While the Mariamman temple has a male non-Brahman priest, the Kali temple has a female non-Brahman priest. Both temples are also marked with the presence of the anthill, which is usually associated with the village goddess worship in India. At both places, worship includes both vegetarian and non-vegetarian offerings such as chicken, eggs and goats or sheep. Some devotees slaughter the animals and prepare food and distribute to the devotees that come to these temples during the festival period. In general, there are no outsiders who

**Figure 4**

*Devotees of Mariamman Making Offerings to Lakshmi. Photograph by Pratap Kumar*

come to this festival as it is highly regulated and restricted through various ritual rules. At the Mariamman temple, however, as part of the festival the organizers this year (2006) felt it appropriate to have a debating contest for the youth. The theme of the debate is "Public Speaking and Critical Thinking". The festival is organized in cooperation with the local African National Congress members. Mrs Ela Gandhi, the granddaughter of Mahatma Gandhi was the guest of honour. The debate was participated by both African and Indian youth.

The other one is the festival of Fire Walking. It is celebrated at the temple in the old suburb known as Cato Manor on the banks of the Umgeni River. This former township was inhabited initially by indentured Indians and later joined by the African people and subsequently under the Group Areas Act of the apartheid government it was taken over from these groups. However, it was never resettled by the whites although that was the intention. As such, the township became a vacant land until recently when it was gradually occupied by squatters. The temple that was built for the

**Figure 5**

*Devotees Making Offerings to Mariamman [Main item offered is a porridge made of sour milk and rice]. Photograph by Pratap Kumar*

worship of the goddess Draupadi remained untouched along with the small shrine of the goddess Gangamma on the roadside of Bellair road which is the main road to reach Cato Manor. The festival of fire walking is an annual ritual that takes place at the Draupadi Amman temple. Devotees take vows in the times of their various needs, such as financial crisis, family crisis, health and psychological crises and so on. They undergo fast for a period of ten days before the fire walking ritual. The fast mainly refers to abstaining from non-vegetarian foods, alcohol, cigarettes, sex and other activities that are considered non-conducive to their spiritual growth. On the Good Friday, the festival of Fire Walking takes place during which devotees put themselves through extreme painful procedures of piercing their bodies with sharp hooks. Some pull festival carts with their hooks. The devotees are said to enter into a trance state and do not feel the pain. The festival culminates in the final event of walking on the hot coals that have been burning during the day. The devotees who have taken vows are the only ones allowed to walk on the fire to the exciting loud and thundering roars. One of the devotees interviewed by the local journalist says, "[y]our state of mind is altered and all you focus is the Mother. Your body is numb and you do not feel any pain when you are pierced, or when you are crossing the fire." (*Sunday Tribune*, April 16, 2006). The attendance at

**Figure 6**

*Draupadi Temple in Cato Manor Area of Durban [It Depicts the Appropriation of Draupadi as Goddess within the Shaivite Tradition]. Photograph by Pratap Kumar*

this festival is mainly by the devotees but it does attract a fair number of visitors, tourists and casual Hindus who come to see the spectacle rather than to participate in the ritual of walking on the fire.

Although like the Hare Krishna Festival of Chariots, these festivals also attract a great number of devotees, they are characterized by the specific groups of Hindus who attend these rituals and festivals and they are located within the temple complex unlike the Festival of Chariots which ventures out on to the beach. Such public manifestation of religious ceremonies and festivals, albeit driven by religious devotion, are clearly organized ways to ensure their survival into the future. The Festival of Chariots, Mariamman and Kali worship and the fire walking ritual may not have much in common from a theological point of view, but they do represent the multifaceted Hinduism that we find in the diaspora.

A caveat needs to be made. It is perhaps assumed that everyone who attends these festivals is a religiously inclined devotee. The various activities provided at the Festival of Chariots do not necessarily attract only devout Hindus, but a whole range of people—from curious ones to serious ones. So, the modern urbanized transmission strategies of religious groups attract all walks of people. There is also no evidence to suggest that every one following the rituals is doing so for spiritual nourishment. Some may be participating in them for material and psychological reasons and others might have simply accompanied families as an outing.

In order for the secularization thesis and the accompanying transmission thesis to be conclusively proved, the instances that I have cited above need to be taken into account. The continued relevance of these rituals in the lives of people depends on their motivation to pass them on to the next generation as values from their past. It is unlikely that this sense of the past will simply vanish in the increasingly scientific and modern world despite the many options that they might present. If at all, returning to such simple ritualized life from time to time may seem romantic as modern life becomes more and more complex. Heelas et al. have suggested a subjectivization thesis which can account for the decline of religion ("life-as religion") on one hand and growth of spirituality ("subjective-life") on the other. They have argued that the Durkhemian principle which says, "people are more likely to be involved with forms of the sacred which are 'consistent with their ongoing values and beliefs' than with those which are not" is the basis of their subjectivization thesis (Heelas et al., 2004: 78). This would mean that people do not subscribe to beliefs if they are not related to their daily life. My own study indicates that people do not necessarily relate their religious beliefs to their everyday life. They can easily compartmentalize their lives and live their modern lives and at the same time follow their age old rituals because that is what their previous generations have passed on to them. With the exception of a few devout Hare Krishnas, the majority who participate in their rituals do not necessarily structure their lives in accordance with the beliefs of the Krishna Consciousness philosophy. Similarly, the Mariamman and Druapadi goddess worshippers do not necessarily live their everyday life trying to make sense of their activities in line with their rituals that they perform at these festivals. Nonetheless, they participate in them and perpetuate them, for it is these rituals and practices which give them a sense of who they are and where they came from. And they pass them on to their next generation to keep their memory alive. In an idealized world people may be found to be practising what they experience spiritually. Even Shankaracharyas have been found to be wanted for criminal activities. Therefore, my study indicates that both transmission thesis and the subjectivization thesis are problematic in explaining the survival of religion in modern society. Religion will survive not because people can or cannot follow what they preach, but rather in their ability to separate their idealized beliefs from their daily working lives.

## Significance and Future Directions

The significance of some of the findings that I present here in this paper, I believe, have to do with how religion is going to be perceived and addressed in contemporary discourse. The increasing attention given to religion in social sciences and especially with the rise of studies on the diaspora, and the emphasis placed on religion within the context of the diaspora studies, it is imperative to come to terms with the fact that religion as a phenomenon will remain with us and perhaps will become a much more complex social issue than we social scientists had envisaged. It is in this context, I believe, my overall argument that religious transmission in modern society may take place in more complex ways than it was in the traditional societies is valid. I, therefore, suggest the following areas for future research: the role of religion in shaping the identity of immigrants and transnationals abroad; the extent to which the context of religious practice has significantly changed as people carry their religious beliefs to new places from their homelands; and finally sociology of religion as a discipline takes a new look at the importance of religion for theorizing society.

## Note

1. Hindus in South Africa today belong to 4th and 5th generation. Their forebears came in 1860 and thereafter as part of the indenture system of labour.

## References

Baumann, Martin. 2002. "Migrant Settlement, Religion and Phases of Diaspora". *Migration: A European Journal of International Migration and Ethnic Relations*, 33/34/35: 93–117.

Berger, Peter L. 1998. "Protestantism and the Quest for Certainty". In *The Christian Century*, August-September, pp. 782–796.

Bruce, Steve. 1988. *The Rise and Fall of the New Christian Right: Conservative Protestant Politics in America 1978–1988*. Oxford: Clarendon Press.

—. 1989. *God Save Ulster: the Religion and Politics of Paisleyism*. Oxford: Oxford University Press.

—. 1990. A *House Divided: Protestantism, Schism, and Secularization*. London: Routledge.

—. 1996. *Religion in the Modern World: From Cathedrals to Cults*. Oxford: Oxford University Press.

—. 2002. *God is Dead: Secularization in the West*. Malden, Mass.: Blackwell.

—. 2003. *Politics and Religion*. Cambridge: Polity Press.

Davie, Grace. 2000. *Religion in Modern Europe: A Memory Mutates*. Oxford: Oxford University Press.

De Santa Ana, Julio. 1995. "Culture in Tension and Dialogue". *International Review of Mission*, Vol. LXXXV, No. 336: 93–102.

Heelas, Paul and Woodhead, Linda et al., 2004. *The Spiritual Revolution: Why Religion is Giving Way to Spirituality*. Oxford: Blackwell.

Kumar, P. Pratap. 2000. *Hindus in South Africa: Their Traditions and Beliefs*. Durban: University of Durban-Westville.

Luckmann, T. 1967. *The Invisible Religion: The Problem of Religion in Modern Society*. New York: Macmillan.

—. 1983. *Life-World and Social Realities*. London: Heinemann Educational Books.

Martikainen, Tuomas. 2006. "Immigrant Settlement and Religious Organisation: The Case of Finland". In P. Pratap Kumar (ed.), *Religious Pluralism and the Diaspora*, pp. 335–351. Leiden: Brill.

Martin, David. 1978. *A General Theory of Secularisation*. Oxford: Blackwell.

—. 1995. "Sociology, Religion and Secularization: an Orientation". *Religion*, 25: 295–303.

Staal, Frits. 1979. "The Meaninglessness of Ritual". *Numen: International Review for the History of Religions*, Vol. 26: 2–22.

—. 1983. *Agni: The Vedic Ritual of the Fire Altar*. Vol. 1 and 2. Berkeley: Asian Humanities Press.

# 3

# Ethnicity, Class, State and Conflict

## The 'Indian Question' in Natal, South Africa

BRIJ MAHARAJ

There is a significant degree of coalescence between race, class and ethnicity in South Africa, where the apartheid state had defined and maintained ethnic categories, and structured inter-ethnic relations through discriminatory regulations and institutional practices. The subject of ethnicity, however, has generally been avoided in South African scholarship. This neglect can be partly ascribed to the attempts of the apartheid state to manoeuvre ethnic groups in order to reinforce white domination. Hence, scholars were concerned that analysis of ethnicity was likely to legitimize state agendas (Bonner and Lodge, 1989; Bozzoli, 1987). Moreover, the most acute differences were between whites and non-whites so that this difference became the main vector along which political activism and academic agendas were mobilized. There was also a tendency among South African scholars to view the experiences of ethnic minorities as 'mere appendages, worthy of mention but really peripheral to the mainstream of historical developments' (Bhana, 1985: 3). However,

> [e]thnic cultures and identities possess a reality in South Africa which it would be myopic to ignore ... Ethnic identities ... need to be confronted and understood, both as instruments of manipulation from above and as modes of accommodation and adjustment from below. (Bonner and Lodge, 1989: 11)

However, the collapse of Eastern Europe and the Soviet Union, and the resurgence of ethnicity in these regions, forced even the African National Congress to reconsider the significance of ethnicity in South Africa (*The Leader*, 4/10/91) and to integrate minority experiences 'in the mainstream synthesis' (Bhana, 1985: 3). With this in mind, this paper focuses on the Indian ethnic minority and its experiences prior to the formal ending of apartheid rule in the early 1990s. The 'Indian community' in South Africa can be viewed 'as the product of state definition as well as the manner of accommodation and resistance to the state and its agenda' (Singh and Vawda, 1988: 3). This paper attempts to present a historical perspective on the nature of conflicts experienced by Indians in Natal in their quest for recognition as South African citizens. While racism is traditionally associated with the Afrikaners, Indians experienced rabid forms of discrimination at the hands of the English in Natal. "It was in Natal, not in Bloemfontein, that as late as 1946, European clubs carried the sign 'Indians and dogs not allowed' " (Reddy, 1986: 3).

For the purposes of this paper 'ethnicity refers to a subjective perception of common origins, historical memories, ties and aspirations' (Chazan et al., 1988: 102). An ethnic group is defined as a 'community conscious of sharing similar characteristics such as a distinct language, a religion, a culture, or a historical experience of its own and is conscious of its differences with other communities by virtue of these same characteristics' (Harik, 1972: 303). The formation of ethnic identity is, however, always influenced by struggles. Firstly, there is struggle within the ethnic group for control over its 'material and symbolic resources'. This will determine the group's boundaries, and the conditions which will ascertain inclusion or exclusion. Secondly, there is struggle between ethnic groups as they compete for resources, rights, and privileges. Finally, there is struggle between the state and the groups which dominate it, and the other ethnic groups in the country (Brass, 1985: 1). Moreover, the negotiation of ethnic identities is influenced by historical and geographical specificities, and is therefore dynamic and changing (McAllister and Sharp, 1993: 9).

About three quarters of the Indian population in South Africa lives in Natal, with two-thirds living in the Durban metropolitan region. Although generally perceived as a homogeneous ethnic group, the Indian community is stratified on the basis of class, religion and language. About 70 per cent are Hindus, 20 per cent Muslims and the remainder Christians. Although English is the first language of the present generation, Tamil, Hindi, Telegu, Gujarati and Urdu are the dominant vernaculars. In spite of high levels of urbanization and modernization, Indians have maintained their cultural identity, and this has been facilitated by apartheid regulations that required Indians to perform their ethnicity. This has been read by other South Africans as 'proof of their "unassimilability", and by Africans as their being racist and discriminatory against the indigenous population' (Moodley, 1975: 256). For more than a century Indians were also regarded as aliens in the country of their birth. A consistent policy of all South African governments during this period was that Indians should ultimately be repatriated to India. Indians thus constitute a vulnerable ethnic minority, 'sandwiched' between the dominant white[1] ruling class, and the African majority.

This paper is divided into six sections. It commences with a brief analysis of the indentured labour system in Natal, followed by a discussion of the emerging class cleavages in the Indian community. In the third section, the white response to Indian prosperity in Natal is examined. The interaction between the central and local states in imposing segregation measures upon Indians is discussed in the fourth section. This is followed by an analysis of the Indian response to repression and segregation. In the fifth section, the nature of Indian-African conflict is explored. The final section briefly reflects on anxieties in the post-apartheid era.

**Indentured Labourers: Coolies and Half-slaves**

The origin of South African Indians can be traced back to the agricultural labour requirements of colonial Natal in the mid-nineteenth century.[2] During this period, sugarcane had been identified as the most profitable commercial crop suited to the climate of this region. However, a major shortcoming was an apparently unsatisfactory labour supply. Successful cultivation of sugarcane required a high labour per hectare ratio. Furthermore, the labour had to be semi-skilled, especially for harvesting and milling activities. Indentured labourers were vital to the economy of Natal because they could be exploited with long working hours, and low wages which were further reduced through massive penalties for petty offences. By the 1880s, when unskilled wages in the country were between 3 to 4 pounds, Natal continued to have cheap labour, still only paying between 10 shillings and 1 pound per month for men and 5 shillings for women, a fair proportion of whom were skilled (Meer, 1985: 46).

The local state of Durban supported the local sugar planters in their motivation for indentured labour because the success or failure of the colonial economy depended 'solely on the constant supply of labour' (*Natal Mercury*, 25/7/1855). The first batch of Indian labourers arrived in Natal in 1860, and they continued to arrive until 1866, when immigration was temporarily halted because of the economic depression and the glut in the world sugar market. During this period, Indian labourers contributed significantly to the wealth and prosperity of Natal. In 1863, sugar worth 26,000 pounds was exported, and in 1864, 1,00,000 pounds (Joshi, 1942: 46). By 1866, 6,445 Indian men, women and children were in Natal (Brain, 1985: 202).

The initial period of indenture in Natal was 5 years. At the end of this period, they received a certificate of discharge which they had to always carry with them. They could return to India at their own expense or remain in the colony as free labourers.[3] However, at the end of the first five years most labourers had accumulated numerous fines for petty offences which could only be repaid through another period of re-indenture (usually another 5 years). Re-indentured labourers toiled under more arduous and formidable conditions, as employers drew up their own contracts, which offered no protection to employees (Meer, 1985). At the end of 10 years of continuous residence in Natal, the Indians were entitled to a free passage to India. In terms of Law 2 of 1870 passed by the Natal government, this could be exchanged for a free grant of Crown land valued the same as the cost of the return trip.

The first batch of repatriates arrived in India in 1871 and informed the government of the abuses and exploitation in Natal e.g., flogging, inadequate medical treatment, excessive fines for minor offences, and pay deductions for absenteeism.[4] The Indian government responded by prohibiting further recruitment of indentured labour until employment conditions improved. Meanwhile, in Natal by 1871, there was an increased demand for Indian labour. During this period, Natal planters were experiencing severe labour shortages which was affecting productivity and profits, and many estates were liquidated (Brain, 1985). In order to allay fears of the labourers and appease the Indian government, the Natal government established the Coolie Commission of Inquiry, which reported in 1872 that except in isolated cases, Indians had not been subjected to ill treatment or persecution by their employers. [5]

However, the Commission recommended that a Protector of Indian Immigrants, who understood Indian languages and culture, be appointed. Also, labourers who had completed their period of indenture should be offered land grants[6] in lieu of a free return passage to India because 'the advantages of retaining in this country a race of men of individual habits and skill can scarcely be doubted' (Thompson, 1952: 63). In 1874, the Indian Government sanctioned the continuation of indentured labour to Natal under the new, improved working conditions. The Indian population in Natal increased from under 10,000 in 1875 to about 1,00,000 by the year 1900 (Davenport, 1987: 117). By 1885, the Indian occupation structure was more complex. The majority (95%), however, remained working class indentured labourers, who were controlled by laws which encouraged massive exploitation by employers. There was also an emerging petty bourgeoisie, comprising the passenger Indian and the ex-indentured (Ebr-Valley, 2001; Vahed, 2001, 2002, 2003).

## Class Cleavages: The Development of Petty Bourgeoisie Indians

An emerging group was the 'free' Indians, who played a key role in the economy of Natal. Although the law permitting the exchange of the free passage to India for crown land was cancelled in 1890, many enterprising ex-indentured Indians purchased or rented plots of land, and through their industriousness, soon became successful cultivators (Freund, 1991). In 1877, the Protector of Indian Immigrants reported that all the 'fishing and nearly all the market gardening and hawking of fruit and vegetables are in the hands of Indians' (Brain, 1985: 211). Little or no capital was required for engaging in such petty enterprises (Swan, 1984: 241). At the turn of the century, Indians were also engaged in skilled and semi-skilled activities in industry and commerce. In fact by the time indentured labour was stopped in 1911 all sectors of the economy of Natal were dependent to some extent on Indian labour.[7]

Another group, which was very evident by 1910, was referred to as the 'new elites'. These were the offspring of indentured or ex-indentured labourers, who were differentiated from their class roots in terms of their superior positions in the occupational hierarchy, made possible by their advanced educational qualifications. They included highly trained professionals such as lawyers, accountants, teachers, bookkeepers and clerks (Kuper, 1956; Swan, 1985).

The late 1870s saw the arrival of a new class of Indians—the so-called 'passenger' Indians (because they paid for their own passage), who were mainly traders, and were often referred to incorrectly as Arabs. They differed in terms of caste, occupation and linguistic groups from the indentured Indians. This group was relatively homogeneous, comprising mainly Gujarati Muslims who had similar economic interests (Swan, 1984; Padayachee and Morrell, 1991; Hansen, 2003). They made every effort to distinguish themselves politically, socially and economically from the indentured labourers, and regarded themselves as part of a commercial bourgeoisie rather than the working class or peasantry (Ginwala, 1974).

Initially, the passenger Indians were primarily engaged in supplying the consumer needs of the Indian community. Gradually, they began to diversify, and also served white and black customers in Natal, Transvaal and Orange Free State. Their success was phenomenal, and can be attributed largely to their determination to work hard and succeed; business acumen; ability to identify markets, which ranged from the urban to rural trading outposts; maximum exploitation of their connections with India; and utilization of family labour. These factors, cumulatively, contributed significantly to the ability of Indians to compete successfully against white traders, and lead to increasing conflict between the two groups.

### Anti-Indian Imbroglio: Ethnic or Class Conflict?

The general economic success and prosperity of the immigrant group, generated a great deal of envy, bitterness and anti-Indian sentiments amongst whites. The whites in Natal were more concerned about the 'Asiatic menace' than the 'Native problem'. Natives were perceived as a passive threat, but Indians were regarded as a 'sophisticated and active menace to their own position in colonial society, competing for space, place, trade, and political influence with the imperial authority' (Swanson, 1983: 404). Whites displayed racial prejudice against Indians, feared their economic competition, and were also concerned about their rapid population expansion which was perceived as a political threat. Additional complaints against Indians were that they did not pay income taxes or do military service; small white farmers were being displaced by market gardeners; and that they were displacing blacks and whites in the labour market (Henning, 1989).

The emerging Indian bourgeoisie also appeared to pose an increasing threat to white domination of capitalist enterprise. 'Editorials declared the "Asiatic trader" a "parasite", "dangerous and harmful", "the real cancer that is eating into the very vitals of the community"' (Wyley, 1986: 16–17). The conflict between white and Indian capital thus provides at least part of the explanation for the tension that was usually expressed in racial and ethnic terms. During this period, trade was a significant economic activity of local white South Africans, and was also a symbol of social status. Indian merchants challenged white economic hegemony and status. Durban whites retaliated to this threat in racial terms, treating wealthy Indian merchants 'in the same way as other racially distinct groupings in colonial Natal, the African and Indian labouring poor' (Wyley, 1986: 46).

As the anti-Indian imbroglio increased, the government was forced to appoint a commission of inquiry in 1885 to investigate the various allegations. The Indian Immigrants (Wragg) Commission reported that the overwhelming white opinion was that Indians should remain under indenture for the duration of their stay in Natal. However, the Commission concluded that the competition offered by the free Indians was legitimate, and had been welcomed by the general community. The Commission was also keen to protect the vested interests of agricultural capital, especially to ensure that there was an abundant supply of cheap labour. The evidence presented by prominent whites to the Commission acknowledged the contributions of Indians to the economy of Natal. Sir Henry Binns (former Chairman of the Indian Immigration Trust Board and Prime Minister of Natal) stated that if Indian immigration was permanently stopped, it would lead to unemployment among whites as tropical cultivation would be impossible without these labourers (Joshi, 1942).

In spite of the findings of the Commission, the anti-Indian agitation continued and culminated in a three-fold legislative programme which was chiefly conceived to curb the economic and political force of the Indians, and ultimately to promote their repatriation to India (Meshthrie, 1985). The first part of the programme was an attempt to disenfranchise Indians in terms of the Franchise Act of 1896. Interestingly, only 3 Africans and 251 Indians had the vote in Natal (Meer, 1961). Secondly, in terms of Law 17 of 1895, a poll tax of 3 pounds was imposed on all Indian heads of households who did not reindenture or return to India. Failure to pay the tax could result in deportation or imprisonment. In 1903, this tax was extended to all members of the family (Bradlow, 1970).

Finally, in terms of the Dealers Licenses Act No. 18 of 1897 local authorities could refuse trading licenses to Indians without fear of them having recourse to the courts.[8] This Act was passed in response to the 'strong public feeling which was being expressed, both through the local press and in the form of public demonstrations, at the ease with which increasing numbers of Asiatic could obtain licences in Durban' (Gabriel, 1938: 21). This resulted in an absolute decline in the number of Indian traders. In 1897, licensed Indian traders comprised 55 per cent of the total in Natal (523 out of 941). In 1900, they were 27 per cent, (472 out of 1,578) (Swanson, 1983: 416). The Licensing Officer for Durban was to later remark:

> I use my discretion as to whether an Asiatic should trade in any particular street or area .... A European licence is granted almost as a matter of course; whereas the Indian licence is refused as a matter of course.[9]

These constraints on the economic activities of Indians were underpinned by a consistent policy of residential segregation, pursued most vociferously by the local state in Durban, which often went against central state initiatives.

## Segregation and Apartheid: The Role of the Local State

The local state of Durban, representing the white ruling class, was at the forefront of calls for segregation of Indians. In 1871, the Durban Town Council adopted a policy to create separate Indian locations. It represented the 'first concerted attempt at group area segregation in Durban and one of the first in a major South African town' (Swanson, 1983: 405). The scheme failed because the Governor refused to consent to it.

Local agitation for the segregation of Indians continued into the twentieth century. However, in 1920, the state-appointed De Lange Asiatic Inquiry Commission stated that 'indiscriminate segregation of Asiatic in locations and similar restrictive measures would result in eventually reducing them to helotry' (Joshi, 1942: 104). Rather, it advocated a system of voluntary segregation, which, if possible, should be mutually agreed upon. The central state attempted to facilitate this via the Lawrence Committee and the Pretoria Agreement (Maharaj, 1995). This process would have been facilitated if municipalities laid out suitable residential and commercial areas, with satisfactory public services and amenities to attract Indians. However, the Durban City Council (DCC) continued to neglect Indian areas. This resulted in professional and business class Indians moving into white areas, and a resultant white outcry against 'penetration'. Following the outcome of two state appointed commissions into penetration,[10] the central state was forced to respond to the mass hysteria of Europeans in Durban, who 'threatened racial riots if Indians were not restricted from acquiring landed properties' (Choudree and Pather, 1946: 6). Furthermore, the Natal Post-War Works and Reconstruction Committee had reported that the "Indian of the labouring, peasant and employee class is serving a useful purpose, but the Indian of the more affluent classes is a menace to European civilisation in Natal" (Cooppan and Lazarus, 1955: 7).

The state response came in the form of the 'Pegging Act' (Trading and Occupation of Land—Transvaal and Natal—Restriction Act, No. 35 of 1943) which 'pegged' the racial pattern of land ownership in the Durban municipal area for three years as determined by the Second Penetration Commission as at March 1943. However, the central state conceded that Indians in Durban had convincing and justifiable demands for improved housing and civic amenities (*Daily News*, 4/4/43).

Three years later, pressure from the whites and the local state of Durban for statutory segregation had increased. Smuts announced on 21 January 1946 that the Asiatic Land Tenure and Indian Representation Act would replace the Pegging Act (Singh, 1946). Prime Minister Smuts, previously sympathetic to the complaints of the Indian community, now revealed that he had been swayed by local white agitation in Natal:

> The Europeans of Natal were very restless and there was grave disquiet. They feared that they were going to be undermined. They were afraid of the Indian's economic competition. The Government had to face the facts and therefore these proposals were going to be enacted as a matter of policy.

Unlike the Pegging Act, this new legislation (dubbed the 'Ghetto' Act by the Indian community) was to apply to the whole of Natal and Transvaal, permanently. The Act created two kinds of areas—uncontrolled and controlled or exempted areas. In the uncontrolled areas there were to be no restrictions on ownership and occupation of property. These areas were generally owned and occupied by Indians. The controlled areas were reserved for European ownership and occupation only. Predictably, the DCC claimed that this Act represented a sincere attempt to solve a perplexing and intricate endemic problem, 'and to provide a means whereby two races fundamentally different in character and tradition may dwell together in peace and harmony'.[11]

Following the ascent to power of the National Party (NP) in 1948, the Ghetto Act provided the foundation for the Group Areas Act (GAA) of 1950, which exercised nation-wide and comprehensive controls over urban land with respect to ownership, occupation, residence and trading. During this period, there was a collusion and close collaboration between the NP and the DCC with regard to the planning of the group areas legislation. The NP claimed that the GAA was a response to the calls from Durban, Pietermaritzburg and practically the whole of Natal to act against Indian penetration and expansion (Maharaj, 1992, 1997). The Mayor of Durban, Percy Osborne, stated that the GAA was the "life-line whereby the European City of Durban will be saved".[12] The DCC's collaboration with the government resulted in the group area proclamation of 6 June 1958, in terms of which Durban was zoned a 'white' city. As a result, about 75,000 Indians and 81,000 Africans were uprooted from settled communities.[13]

Indians, however, largely resisted attempts by the state to dispossess them. They were opposed to any form of statutory segregation and measures which denied them their rights as law abiding citizens. As a disenfranchised and voiceless group, Indian aspirations were articulated at different times by the various political organizations.

## Protest and Resistance: Accommodationists versus Confrontationists

The development of political consciousness among Indians is normally associated with Mohandas Gandhi, a barrister, who arrived in Pretoria in 1892 to represent an Indian merchant in a lawsuit. After experiencing personal racial insults, and spurred by a concern about the plight of Indians, he stayed on for 21 years, fighting for the rights of his fellow Indians.[14] Gandhi was responsible for the formation of the Natal Indian Congress (NIC) on 22 August 1894 and served as its first secretary (Swan, 1985; Bhana,

1997). Gandhi was well-known for his policy of passive resistance or 'Satyagraha' (Keiser, 1981; Bhana and Meshthrie, 1984).

The NIC, however, served the interests of, and was controlled by, the affluent merchants. Furthermore, with a membership fee of three pounds per annum, only the wealthy could afford affiliation. The various restrictions in Natal curbed the expansion of the bourgeoisie and threatened the very existence of the petty bourgeoisie. Therefore, although the merchants sometimes included the complaints of the working class in their political representations, they were primarily concerned with their own problems (Ginwala, 1974: 183). The working class was thus not regarded as an important constituency. In fact, the only tangible associations between the elite and the "underclasses were the essentially exploitative patron-client relationships formed by money lenders, shopkeepers and the owner-operators of the Durban produce market" (Swan, 1984: 244).

Since the 1930s, it was evident from participation in the Colonization Commission, Lawrence Committee and the Pretoria Agreement, that the moderates were prepared to accept some form of voluntary segregation, as long as their vested commercial interests were not adversely affected (Pahad, 1972; Bhana and Meshthrie, 1984; Maharaj, 2003). Working class Indians would be most affected by residential segregation, and the moderates were prepared to offer this group as the 'sacrificial lamb' (Ginwala, 1974: 418).

The Colonial Born and Settlers Indian Association (CBSIA) was formed in 1933 to oppose the elite ideology of the NIC (Padayachee et al., 1985). In 1939, a new generation of more militant political activists began to contest leadership positions in the NIC. As a result, the majority in the NIC and the CBSIA merged to form the Natal Indian Association (NIA). However, the more conservative elements continued to operate under the NIC banner, lead by A.I. Kajee.[15]

In an atmosphere of increasing hostility and intolerance these organizations utilized peaceful measures, which included recourse to the law, passive resistance and appeals to India and the United Nations, to expose the injustice and violation of human rights in South Africa (Haines, 2001). However, although they claimed to represent the Indian community, there was very little evidence of mobilization of the working class. Political action mainly "consisted of constitutional protest: letters, petitions and deputations" to government officials in South Africa or India (Swan, 1987: 192). The major players in Durban, the NIC and NIA, had access to central state structures, and both adopted accommodationist strategies of negotiating with the state to protect their commercial, residential and investment interests. Hence, political action was determined by economic status and the extent to which specific interests were threatened (Ginwala, 1974). The NIA had served on the Lawrence Committee, and the NIC was party to the abortive Pretoria Agreement. Significantly, both attempts at voluntary segregation and co-operation were destroyed by the local state (Maharaj, 1995, 2003).

After a great deal of grass roots mobilization of working class Indians, 'there was a distinct shift in the predominantly accommodationist, merchant dominated class politics of the pre-1945 NIA/NIC, to ostensibly more militant, aggressive and less accommodationist politics of the post-1945 period' (Padayachee et al., 1985: 156). With a more radical leadership, the NIC embarked on a massive passive resistance campaign to protest against the Ghetto Act. The campaign was launched on 13 June 1946 and suspended on 31 May 1948. Resistance took the form of occupying properties in defiance of the Act. The state responded by arresting the resistors, and many prominent Indian leaders were sent to prison. The state also auctioned the properties of passive resistors to defray fines. [16]

However, there was very little evidence of mass working class support for the passive resistance campaign, as this group was not immediately affected by the Ghetto Act. The Ghetto Act seriously affected "those Indians capable of purchasing land in white areas for either residential or investment purposes. It did not immediately affect the majority of less affluent Indians who had no plans for either living or investing outside existing Indian ghettos" (Johnson, 1973: 78). In fact the question of housing for the underclasses "living in shackland settlements was not raised with any force by either the NIC or NIA, since elements within the Indian merchant class were extensively involved in rack-renting to the Indian and African working class" (Bailey, 1987: 48). However, there were repercussions for the working class as rents and property prices escalated in predominantly Indian areas. The poor were forced into high density 'slums and near slums', and landlords demanded outrageous 'key money' or 'goodwill' for the right to rent a single dilapidated room (Swan, 1987: 191).

By 1945, political organizations had barely attempted to address working class problems such as low wages, shoddy working conditions, and housing shortages. Under such circumstances, it would have been unreasonable 'to have expected any greater empathy or committed support for these political struggles from the newly proletarianised and poorly educated working class' (Padayachee et al., 1985: 156). The main reason for this was because segregation affected different classes of the Indian community in different ways. It reduced opportunities for investment and commercial expansion for the wealthy, and there was also a possibility of financial losses. The less affluent of the elites faced the possibility of moving into working class neighbourhoods. Segregation represented a double-edged sword for the underclasses—with increasing rents and slum clearance some would become homeless, while others could possibly be rehoused in municipal housing schemes (Swan, 1987).

The accommodationists, under the leadership of A.I. Kajee, formed the Natal Indian Organization (NIO) in 1947. Divisions between the NIC and NIO were directly related to class. Membership of the NIO consisted largely of businessmen, attempting to obtain concessions from the government by 'constitutional' and 'legitimate' means (Johnson, 1973: 68). While opposing segregation, it was also against the more militant strategies of the NIC. Although the NIO was more acceptable to, and entered into dialogue with, both the central and local states, it was unable to obtain any major concessions (Maharaj, 2003).

Although the NIC had greater grass roots support, it failed to effectively mobilize this support. Leadership was sterile, and it often resorted to rhetorical slogans when there was a need for immediate action. This was partly due to the fact that leaders were frequently arrested and harassed by the police. The majority of Indians were low income labourers who were afraid of being arrested, and the consequent loss of jobs, earnings and family support associated with political activism. A telling indictment against the political leadership of the period was the failure to mobilize across racial barriers:

> A study of the working class areas of Durban would surely reveal that even by the 1930s there was a considerable intermingling of African and Indian workers. Much of this was superficial—on the race track, in the cinema, or in the bus—but some was more

> durable, in terms of worker or home relationships. This urban intermingling might have become the basis for a political movement, if the Indian leaders had not remained so completely middle class, whether they were moderates or radicals in their ideology. (Tinker, 1973: 525)

**Ethnic Conflict: Indians vs. Africans**

It has been conventionally argued that the abundant indigenous Zulu labour in Natal was inadequate and unsuitable for sugar plantations. However, on the contrary, the local Zulus comprised a proficient labour force and were 'by no means disinclined to labour, or unwilling to render it to the planters, but upon their own terms and at their own times' (*Daily News*, 13/11/1960). There is adequate evidence which reveals that while Natal was arranging for the introduction of indentured labour, the Zulus were working diligently in both the skilled and unskilled sectors of the economy (Meer, 1985; Richardson, 1986; Dhupelia, 1982). So the difficulty facing the planters was not a shortage of labour, but rather a lack of a plentiful supply of cheap labour. The cost of Indian labour was high, especially in terms of costs of recruiting and travel to Natal. This had the effect of lowering the wages paid to Africans, which was one of the reasons for introducing indentured labourers (Ginwala, 1974). The indenture system was compared with attempts to control African labour (Ginwala, 1974):

> The indenture system also had much in common with methods of controlling African labour that were in the process of evolution elsewhere in South Africa—such as the pass laws and compound systems for general African workers and mine workers. Workers were regarded as transients requiring to justify their presence outside the confines of their place of employment, they were not entirely free to choose employers or type of work. They were housed in compounds and their movements were controlled. (46)
>
> The anomaly arose when an Indian sought a place within the established pattern, and unencumbered by an indenture contract was not subject to the special labour laws, either because he was a passenger Indian or because he had completed his indenture. Had the system of control of African labour been worked out and established prior to the arrival of Indian labour, then it is arguable that free Indians would have been placed into that system as was foreign African labour. African labour control grew on an *ad hoc* basis and by the time mineral discoveries and exploitation brought

into being its distinctive and more rigid pattern, the indenture system was already established for Indian labour in Natal. (47)

For the first twenty years after the introduction of indenture, Indians constituted one of the poorest section of the Natal population. During this period, Africans were the main suppliers of basic foodstuffs such as maize, vegetables and kaffir corn. However, by 1882, these products were being produced almost entirely by Indians in the Natal coastal region. Hence, as the relative material circumstances of Indians improved, the African population became more impoverished. Thus, by the end of the nineteenth century, Africans replaced the Indians as the most indigent at the bottom of the economic hierarchy (Ginwala, 1974). As a result of the relative advantages enjoyed by the Indians and their relative material progress vis-à-vis the Africans, Indo-African relations in Natal were characterized by incipient tension and conflict.

The wealth and business interests of the trader group were envied by whites as well as Africans. The limited number of African traders in urban areas resulted in Indian traders becoming very conspicuous. African leaders argued that preference should be given to African traders in African areas. Ethnic differences between Africans and Indians became more evident as Africans believed that all Indians had more privileges and opportunities than them (Kirk, 1983).

However, what was often obscured was the fact that the majority of Indians belonged to the working class. Surveys revealed that over 70 per cent of the Indians were desperately poor. Being semi-skilled and unskilled workers, their wages were low. In addition, many of them had a large number of dependents (Kirk, 1983). Hence, a significant proportion of Indians did not benefit directly from the comparative advantages enjoyed by Indians as an ethnic group. Their economic conditions were not much different from those of African workers (Ginwala, 1974). In addition, there were various institutional factors which limited the employment opportunities of Indians and Africans.[17]

Indians and Africans competed for jobs in the urban labour market. The main area of competition was in secondary industry, where there was a large demand for unskilled labourers. Indians had a comparative advantage over Africans in that they were more highly urbanized. With their experience, Indians dominated in the semi-skilled and supervisory jobs which whites rejected. However, except in the area of employment, the benefits which accrued to Indians were mainly in the interest of the bourgeois and petty bourgeois groups (Kirk, 1983).

Both Indian and African political organizations did not do much to foster inter-group relations. However, this began to change in the post-1945 period. In 1947, a pact was formed between the South African Indian Congress (SAIC)[18] (lead by Dr Y. Dadoo), the NIC (lead by Dr G.M. Naicker), and the African National Congress (lead by Dr Xuma), to form a united front in opposing segregation and oppression. The pact did not receive much support, especially from the African petty-bourgeoisie. Selby Msimang, executive member of the Natal ANC stated that the 'pact reflected a spirit of co-operation only at leadership level', and that to the best of his knowledge, Dr Naicker had not done anything to promote co-operation (Mesthrie, 1989: 42).

The tensions and conflicts which characterized Indo-African relations were vividly played out in Cato Manor.

## The 1949 Cato Manor Riots

Cato Manor, an evocative name in Natal, has powerful connotations with the history of the dispossessed in South Africa, and represents 'a living monument to the heartbreak and destruction wrecked' by apartheid (*Herald*, 27/4/88). After completing their period of indenture, many pioneering Indians settled here and began developing the area. With the passage of time, the area grew by leaps and bounds. This was not unrelated to the fact that being located outside the jurisdiction of the DCC, they were able to erect substandard dwellings at low cost. With the extension of the city's boundaries in 1932, Cato Manor was incorporated into Durban. However, it remained a chronically neglected area in terms of services and facilities, with overcrowding, inadequate health and sanitation services, and rampant disease (Edwards, 1983, 1989).

In addition to Indians, the area had a large African population. Africans began to move into Cato Manor in the early 1940s as they were ejected from areas like Overport and Puntans Hill by the DCC. Many Indian farmers realized that they could make more profits by allowing Africans to build shacks on their lands, and many of them became 'shacklords' (Edwards, 1983; Maharaj, 1994). Often Indians would let a huge plot of land to an African for a nominal site rent. The tenant would then sub-lease to hundreds of others who would build shacks and pay rent. As a result, a large class of African 'tenant-landlords' came into being, who had a vested interest in the continued existence of Cato Manor. This group also operated 'shackshops' in Cato Manor, and experienced a great deal of insecurity and competition:

> They lead an insecure, harassed existence squeezed by the authorities on one side and by competition with Indian traders on the other. These illegal traders and 'tenant-landlords' form the social soil for the anti-Indian attitudes that one finds in the area. (*Fighting Talk*, August 1959: 3)

However, while the interaction between African workers and the Indian petty bourgeoisie was primarily exploitive, Indian businesses in Cato Manor provided opportunities for African workers and their families to escape from the austerity of direct local state control:

> Indian traders provided the basic infrastructure of the squatters' slums: the bus services and retail outlets—the services which could be provided because of the particular position of Indian people as a 'buffer group' in the racial hierarchy of urban segregation. (Hemson, 1977: 103)

The incipient conflict between Africans and Indians in Cato Manor burst into the open with the January 1949 riots.[19] Africans sacked and looted Indian stores. After two days of bloody rioting 50 Indians and 87 Africans were killed, and 503 Indians and 541 Africans were injured. Thousands of Indian stores and dwellings were destroyed or damaged (Ladlau, 1975). The state viewed the violence as a racial conflict between Indians and Africans, and argued that this justified its policy of racial separation.[20] This view was reinforced by evidence submitted by individual Africans to the Van Den Heever Commission of Inquiry:

> They all expressed a deep and widespread resentment of the Indians, complaining of being overcharged in Indian shops, of ill-treatment on Indian buses, [and] of rack-renting. Resentment was expressed at the virtual Indian ... monopolisation of those branches of trade and transport serving African areas, while complaints with regard to the superior position of the Indian in industry and in the trade-union movement were also voiced. (Ladlau, 1975: 18–19)

However, while there was Indian-African tension, the riot was a 'complex phenomenon, fed by white prejudice and Government policy as well as by the aspirations of an embryonic African bourgeoisie' (Ladlau, 1975: 19). While the riots appeared to be unplanned, structurally, they were predetermined by the nature of the South African social formation:

> The differential incorporation of the various racial groups, enjoying different levels of rewards, set the stage for seeking a scapegoat and revenge for long-suffered misery. Indians were perceived by Africans as most obviously benefitting from this situation precisely because they occupied a 'middleman' role. These stereotypes provided a focal point for quick mobilisation of Africans. (Moodley, 1980: 231)

Hilda Kuper, a social anthropologist, argued that like Jews in other countries, Indians were being used as 'scapegoats' by the dominant ethnic groups:

> Sufficiently wealthy to serve as a bait for greed, too few to be feared and, in the main, ideologically opposed to counter aggression with physical violence, their ethnic difference and cultural diversity serve as excuses for discrimination and oppression. (*The Star*, 4/6/79)

It was rather unfortunate that prominent African leaders in Natal have from time to time attempted to threaten Indians by referring to the 1949 riots (Moodley, 1980). Indo-African tensions burst into the open again in 1985 with the Inanda riots. The prevailing circumstances and causes of the riots were somewhat similar to that of the 1949 riots. However, there were also important differences: the state used the 1949 riots to justify its ideology and policies of segregation. 'The conflict of 1985 is an end product of that process' (Hughes, 1987: 354).

**Anxieties in the Democratic Era**

As the momentous democratic elections approached in April 1994, historical events coalesced with the more immediate to reinforce the feeling of vulnerability and fear so characteristic of middlemen minorities, especially in periods of political change. The Indo-African riots of 1949 in Cato Manor and 1985 in Inanda, continued to weigh heavily on the memories of Indians. This was reinforced by the expulsion of Indians in post-colonial Kenya and

Uganda. The Natal region also created its own insecurities with the area through much of the 1980's, convulsed in internecine violence between Inkatha and the United Democratic Front (Desai and Maharaj, 1996).

In the immediate build-up to the elections, many in the Indian community were unsettled when Africans invaded 779 houses earmarked for Indian occupation in Cato Manor. Media attention around the occupations was intense, and the fact that it happened in Cato Manor served to heighten anxiety (Johnson and Zulu, 1996). The ANC approach only served to exacerbate fear and suspicion. Mandela initially appealed to the African squatters to move out, but subsequently appeared to backtrack (Gigaba and Maharaj, 1996).

These developments highlighted feelings of vulnerability especially in the large working class Indian townships of Phoenix and Chatsworth, which are contiguous to African residential areas, Kwa Mashu-Inanda and Umlazi, respectively. Over the past few years, African squatters from Inanda have sporadically entered Phoenix and looted households. In some areas of Phoenix that border Inanda and Ntuzuma, houses have been abandoned after consistent attacks. In recent times, African squatters have taken to occupying vacant land in Indian suburbs, producing new sources of tension. It is these perceptions which appeared to gain currency as the elections approached. Fear and vulnerability became the pervasive phenomenon. As much as physical security was an issue, security at the level of the job market was a major concern for Indians. Affirmative action was seen as a major threat.

Though a large proportion of Indians belong to the lower classes, their average socio-economic situation is above the South African one. Some Indian entrepreneurs succeeded in taking advantage of the post-apartheid black-empowerment deals. It has been argued that 'affirmative action policies in the 1990s have expanded the commercial and professional opportunities available to (Indians), resulting in their slice of national income expanding exponentially in the decade after 1994' (Habib and Naidu, 2004: 2).

However, the poorest sections of the Indian community have been adversely affected by the 'simultaneous application of an affirmative action policy with a neo-liberal economic programme' (Habib and Naidu, 1999: 189). Those Indians with low levels of skills and training are vulnerable and can be easily replaced by Africans when companies are forced to change the demographic profile of their employees (Habib and Naidu, 2004). The government response was that Indians also ought to be favoured by affirmative action, and that any attempt to exclude them from such programmes was a deliberate misinterpretation of the legislation.

In terms of their economic status by the end of the 1980's, Indians had come to occupy what has been referred to as an in-between character (Freund, 1995). There was a general tendency for Indians rather than Africans to move upwards into skilled occupations (Bell, 1983). An important factor in the Indian propensity for upward mobility was that the level of educational attainment of the economically active Indian population was substantially higher than that of Coloureds and Africans, facilitated at least partially by community education projects initiated by the Indian community.

However, there is also a proportionally large Indian working class (60%) in South Africa (Desai, 1996: 124). Many of these workers have little in common with affluent Indians as far as lifestyle is concerned (a function of vastly different consumer capacities)—yet they too identify and are identified with middle and high income earners. Many Indian workers are singled out as a minority in the middle because of the semi-skilled or supervisory positions inside of the factory plant assigned to them by the white bosses. Often Indian workers also enjoy dissimilar access to education and training inside the company (Desai and Maharaj, 1996). While those in the business and professional sectors thrived in the post-apartheid era, working class Indians increasingly feel disillusioned and marginalized in the rainbow nation.

## Conclusion

The main theoretical proposition of this paper was that the formation of ethnic identity was influenced by struggles within groups, between groups, and between the state and its various ethnic populations. In this context, this paper presented a historical perspective to the struggles of Indians, a major ethnic group in Natal, in their quest for recognition as South Africans. In this process, they engendered tensions and conflicts among themselves, with the white ruling class and the African majority, as well as the local and central states. In any society where racial discrimination is predominant, racist ideology will be enunciated by the state and economic structures at a number of levels (Sarre, 1989). Indians struggled against discrimination, poverty, and lack of political and civic representation. Given their initial indentured status, they were regarded as 'temporary sojourners' in the land of their birth for the greater part of a century. In 1961, they were accepted as South African citizens, albeit second class.

Indians managed to survive the economic and political onslaught primarily because of some locally specific configurations, along with a consciousness of themselves as an ethnic group based on some kind of identification with what they considered a rich cultural heritage. The ability to mobilize this ethnicity helped. According to Chazan et al. (1988: 102), 'ethnicity as a subjective basis for collective consciousness gains relevance to the political process when it spurs group formation and underpins political organisation.' However, Indians were not a homogeneous group, and experienced various divisions and tensions, particularly between the traders and the working class. There was increasing evidence that political organizations were used to articulate merchant interests, sometimes at the expense of the underclass. Certainly, it was only in the post-1945 period that working class issues became more prominent in Indian political agendas. This tradition of non-cooperation with the apartheid regime continued into the 1980s when more than 80 per cent of the Indian community rejected participation in the tricameral parliament.

Indian labour contributed significantly to the economic development of the Natal region. However, the commercial, merchant and professional groups were perceived as an economic threat to whites in Natal, and this was reflected in racial prejudices which were transformed into policies limiting their access to land and housing, as well as trading opportunities. Initially, these policies were confined to the local state, but as the pressure from the white electorate mounted, the central state was forced to introduce sweeping legislation which culminated in the Ghetto Act of 1946. Hence, the social and economic prejudices of whites against Indians were sanctified by legislation, and adopted as state policy.

Indians enjoyed a relatively privileged position compared to that of the African majority both because of community survival strategies and the relative privileges they enjoyed compared to Africans. In addition to dominating the trading sector, they also competed with Africans in the urban labour market. The nascent conflict between these two groups burst into the open with the 1949 riots, and has resurfaced periodically. The riots reflected a complex interaction between race, ethnic, political, economic, and social forces.

With the current political changes taking place, there has been concern that the cultural and religious interests of Indians may be jeopardized. At least for some, the Indian contribution to the socio-political transformation in South Africa should be the 'satyagraha' tradition, to 'demonstrate to the country and to the world that the principles of non-violence, democracy and racial tolerance will have a home in a future South Africa ... and a vigorously protected one at that' (*The Leader*, 18/9/91).

## Notes

1. The category 'whites' like the category 'African' is not a singular racial or ethnic group. Differences mark these categories too however, space precludes a longer discussion of the interpellation of these differences alongside the differences in the category 'Indian'. Moreover, the period for this study, the late 1800s until 1994 (the dismantling of the apartheid government), was marked by a relative consolidation and marking of racial difference along the major categories.
2. For an in-depth analysis of the arrival of Indians in South Africa, and their historical development, see Waiz 1927; Joshi 1942; Stein 1927; Calpin 1949; Joshi 1952; Thompson 1952; Palmer 1957; Pachai 1971; Pachai 1979; Bhana and Brain 1990; Desai 1996; Ferguson-Davie C.J. (n.d.).
3. Section 9 of Law 14 of 1859, cited by Ferguson-Davie, (n.d.), p. 11.
4. For some vivid examples of problems experienced by the indentured labourers, see Bhana, and Pachai, (1984) Meer, (1980); Sannyasi and Chaturvedi (1931).
5. Cited in Thompson (1952: 63).
6. Only 50 plots of land were granted out of 13,000 applications (see Ginwala, 1974: 426).
7. Report of the Protector of Indian Immigrants, 1901, cited in Brain, 1985, op. cit., p. 228.
8. A good analysis of the trading restrictions imposed on Indians is provided by Gabriel (1938) and Pachai (1978).
9. "The Truth about the Indian in South Africa", a reply to "Meet the Indian in South Africa", (The South African Government's Illustrated Brochure), issued by the SAIC, n.d., p. 11.

10. U.G. No. 39, 1941, Report of the Indian Penetration Commission; U.G. No. 21, 1943, Report of the Second Penetration (Durban) Commission.
11. "The Indian in Natal: Is He the Victim of Oppression?" Pamphlet issued by the DCC and the Durban Joint Wards Committee, 1946.
12. Minutes of Council-in-Committee Meeting of the DCC held with the Technical Sub-Committee on Race Zoning, 15/8/51.
13. Hansard, col. 1472, 5/8/58.
14. For a critical analysis of Gandhi's role in South Africa, see Swan (1985) and Naidoo (1989).
15. United opposition to the Pegging Act in 1943 saw the merger of the NIC and NIA as the 'newly formed' Natal Indian Congress in 1943.
16. Report of the Passive Resistance Council. Source: NIC Agenda Book, 1947.
17. These included restrictions on movement between provinces; the Colour Bar; Apprenticeship Act of 1944; and the 'Civilised Labour' Policy. See Naidoo and Naidoo (1955).
18. The SAIC was formed in 1923 and comprised the NIC, Transvaal Indian Congress (TIC, established in 1927) and the Cape British Indian Council. See Mesthrie (1989).
19. For different views on the riots see Meer (1969); Ladlau (1975); Kuper (1965); and Webster (1978).
20. UG 36-1949. Report of the Commission of Enquiry into Riots in Durban. Pretoria: Government Printer.

## References

Bailey, D.E. 1987. "The Origins of Phoenix, 1957–1976: The Durban City Council and the Indian Housing Question". Unpublished M.A. thesis, University of Natal.

Bell, R.T. 1983. "Growth and Structure of Manufacturing Employment in Natal". Report No. 7, ISER, University of Durban: Westville.

Bhana, S. 1985. "Girmitiyas in Search of History". Inaugural address delivered at the University of Durban-Westville.

—. 1997. *Gandhi's Legacy: The Natal Indian Congress, 1894–1994*. Pietermaritzburg: University of Natal Press.

Bhana, S. and Brain, J. 1990. *Setting Down Roots: Indian Migrants in South Africa 1860–1911*. Johannesburg: University of Witwatersrand Press.

Bhana, S. and Mesthrie, U.S. 1984. "Passive Resistance among Indian South Africans: A Historiographical Survey". *South African Historical Journal,* 16: 118–131.

Bhana, S. and Pachai, B. 1984. *A Documentary History of Indian South Africans*. Cape Town: David Philip.

Bonner, P. and Lodge, T. 1989. 'Introduction'. In P. Bonner et al. (eds.), *Class, Locality and Culture in 19th and 20th Century South Africa,* pp. 1–17. Johannesburg: Ravan Press.

Bozzoli, B. 1987. "Class, Community and Ideology in the Evolution of South African Society". In B. Bozzoli, (ed.), *Class, Community and Conflict: South African Perspectives,* pp. 1–40. Johannesburg: Ravan Press.

Bradlow, E. 1970. "Indentured Indians in Natal and the 3 pound Tax". *South African Historical Journal,* 2: 38–53.

Brain, J. 1985. "Indentured and Free Indians in the Economy of Colonial Natal". In B. Guest and J.M. Sellers (eds.), *Enterprise and Exploitation in a Victorian Colony,* p. 202. Pietermaritzburg: University of Natal Press.

Brass, P.R. 1985. "Ethnic Groups and the State". In P. Brass (ed.), *Ethnic Groups and the State,* pp. 1–58. London: Croom Helm.

Calpin, G.H. 1949. *Indians in South Africa*. Pietermaritzburg: Shuter and Shooter.

Chazan, N. et al., 1988. *Politics and Society in Contemporary Africa*. London: Macmillan.

Choudree, A. and Pather, P.R. 1946. *A Commentary on the Asiatic Land Tenure and Indian Representation Act and a short Survey of the Indian Question in South Africa*. London: SAIC.

Cooppan, S. and Lazarus, A.D. 1955. *The Indian as an Integral Part of South African Society*. Johannesburg: SAIRR.

Davenport, T.R.H. 1987. *South Africa: A Modern History*. London: Macmillan.

Desai, A. 1996. *Arise ye Coolies*. Johannesburg: Impact Africa Publishing.

Desai, A. and Maharaj, B. 1996. "Minorities in the Rainbow Nation: The Indian Vote in 1994". *South African Journal of Sociology,* 26: 118–125.

Dhupelia, U. 1982. "African Labour in Natal: Attempts at Coercion and Control 1893–1903". *Journal of Natal and Zulu History,* 5: 36–48.

Ebr-Vally, R. 2001. *Kala Paani: Caste and Colour in South Africa*. Colorado Springs, Colo.: International Academic Publishers.

Edwards, I. 1983. "Living on the 'Smell of an Oilrag': African Life in Cato Manor in the late 1940s". Paper presented in a workshop on

African Life in Durban in the Twentieth Century, University of Natal, Durban.

Edwards, I.L. 1989. "Mkhubane Our Home: Shantytown Society in Cato Manor Farm", 1946–1960. Unpublished Ph.D. thesis, University of Natal, Durban.

Freund, B. 1991. "The Rise and Decline of an Indian Peasantry in Natal". *The Journal of Peasant Studies*, 18: 263–287.

—. 1995. *Insiders and Outsiders: The Indian Working Class, 1910–1990*. Pietermaritzburg: University of Natal Press.

Gabriel, B. 1938. "Trade Licences (Natal)". Paper presented at the first conference of the NIC, 10–11 December, Durban.

Gigaba, M. and Maharaj, B. 1996. "Land Invasions During Political Transition: The Wiggins Saga in Cato Manor". *Development Southern Africa*, 13: 217–236.

Ginwala, F.N. 1974. "Class, Consciousness and Control: Indian South Africans 1860–1946". Unpublished Ph.D. thesis, Oxford University.

Habib, A. and Naidu, S. 1999. "Election '99: was there a 'coloured' and 'Indian' vote?". *Politikon*, 26: 189–199.

—. 2004. Transcending Race in the Fight for the 'Indian vote'. www.sabcnews.com/features/elections_2004/issues/ isiindians.html (accessed 18/2/05).

Haines, C.G. 2001. "The United Nations and the Challenge to Racial Discrimination in South Africa 1946–1950". *Africa Studies*, 60: 185–204.

Hansen, T.B. 2003. "We are the Arabs of Gujarat: The Purification of Muslim Identity in Contemporary South Africa". RAU Sociology Seminar. Available at www.rau.ac.za/

Harik, I.F. 1972. "The Ethnic Revolution and Political Integration in the Middle East". *International Journal of Middle East Studies*, 3: 303–323.

Hemson, D. 1977. "Dock Workers, Labour Circulation, and Class Struggles in Durban, 1940–59". *Journal of Southern African Studies*, 4: 88–124.

Henning, C.G. 1989. "The Indian South African (1860–1989)". In J.K. Motwani and J. Barot-Motwani (eds.), *Global Migration of Indians: Saga of Adventure, Enterprise, Identity and Integration*, pp. 11–36. New York: First Global Convention of People of Indian Origin.

Hughes, H. 1987. "Violence in Inanda, August 1985". *Journal of Southern African Studies*, 13: 331–354.

Johnson, R.E. 1973. "Indians and Apartheid: The Failure of Resistance". Unpublished Ph.D. thesis, University of Massachusetts.

Johnson, R.W. and Zulu, P. 1996. "Public Opinion in KwaZulu-Natal". In R.W. Johnson and L. Schlemmer (eds.), *Launching Democracy in South Africa*, pp. 189–211. New Haven: Yale University Press.

Joshi, P.S. 1942. *The Tyranny of Colour: A Study of the Indian Problem in South Africa*. Durban.

—. 1952. *The Struggle for Equality*. Bombay: Hind Kitabs.

Keiser, R.D. 1981. "The South African Indian's Challenge to the Union and Imperial Governments, 1910–1919". *South African Historical Journal*, 13: 78–95.

Kirk, S.L. 1983. "The 1949 Durban Riots: A Community in Conflict". Unpublished Master's dissertation, University of Natal, Durban.

Kuper, H. 1956. "Indian Elites in South Africa". Paper presented at the Social Science Conference, University of Natal, 16–22 July, Durban.

Kuper, L. 1965. *An African Bourgeoisie*. New Haven: Yale University Press.

Ladlau, L.K. 1975. "The Cato Manor Riots, 1959–1960". Unpublished Master's dissertation, University of Natal, Durban.

Maharaj, B. 1992. "The 'spatial impress' of the Central and Local States: the Group Areas Act in Durban". In D.M. Smith (ed.), *The Apartheid City and Beyond: Urbanisation and Social Change in South Africa*, pp. 74–86. London: Routledge.

—. 1994. "The Group Areas Act and Community Destruction in South Africa: The Struggle for Cato Manor in Durban". *Urban Forum*, 5(2): 1–25.

—. 1995. "The Local State and Residential Segregation: Durban and the Prelude to the Group Areas Act". *South African Geographical Journal*, 77: 33–41.

—. 1997. "Apartheid, Urban Segregation and the Local State: Durban and the Group Areas Act in South Africa". *Urban Geography*, 18: 135–154.

—. 2003. Co-operation ... Consultation and Consent': The failure of voluntary residential segregation in Durban in the 1940s'. *South African Geography Journal*, 85: 134–143.

McAllister, P. and Sharp, J. 1993. "Overview: The Ethnic Taboo". *Indicator SA*, 10(3): 7–10.

Meer, F. 1969. *Portrait of Indian South African Indians*. Durban: Avon House.

—. 1985. "Indentured Labour and Group Formations in Apartheid Society". *Race and Class*, 26: 46–60.

Meer, I.C. 1961. "The Franchise in the Republic of South Africa". Paper presented at the Natal Conference on Municipal Franchise, 23 July, Durban.

Meer, Y.S. 1980. *Documents of Indentured Labour: Natal 1851–1917*. Durban: Institute of Black Research.

Mesthrie, U. 1989. "Indian National Honour vs. Trader Ideology: Three Unsuccessful Attempts at Passive Resistance in the Transvaal, 1932, 1939 and 1941". *South African Historical Journal*, 21: 39–54.

Mesthrie, U.S. 1985. "Reducing the Indian Population to a `Manageable Compass': A Study of the South African Assisted Emigration Scheme". *Natalia*, 15: 36–56.

Moodley, K.A. 1975. "South African Indians: The Wavering Minority". In L. Thompson and J. Butler (eds.), *Change in Contemporary South Africa*, pp. 250–279. Berkeley: University of California Press.

—. 1980. "Structural Inequality and Minority Anxiety: Responses of Middle Groups in South Africa". In R.M. Price and C.G. Rosberg (eds.), *The Apartheid Regime: Political Power and Racial Domination*, pp. 217–235. Berkeley: Institute of International Studies.

Naidoo, B.A. and Naidoo, J. 1955. *Economic Opportunities and Mode of Living of the Indian Community*. Johannesburg: SAIRR.

Naidoo, J. 1989. *Tracking Down Historical Myths*. Johannesburg: A.D. Donker.

Pachai, B. 1971. *The South African Indian Question 1860–1971*. Cape Town: C. Struik.

—. 1978. "South African Indians and Economic Hostility". In B.M. du Toit (ed.), *Ethnicity in Modern Africa*, pp. 271–280. Boulder: Westview.

—. 1979. "Aliens in the Political Hierarchy". In B. Pachai (ed.). *South Africa's Indians: The Evolution of a Minority*. Washington: University Press of America.

Padyachee, M. et al., 1985. *Indian Workers and Trade Unions in Durban 1930–1950*. Durban: ISER.

Padyachee, V. and Morrell, R. 1991. "Indian Merchants and Dukawallahs in the Natal Economy, c1875–1914". *Journal of Southern African Studies*, 17: 71–102.

Pahad, E. 1972. "The Development of Indian Political Movements in South Africa, 1924–1946". Unpublished Ph.D. Thesis, University of Sussex.

Palmer, M. 1957. *The History of Indians in Natal*. Cape Town: Oxford University Press.

Reddy, E.S. 1986. "Significance of African and Indian Joint Struggle", *Mainstream,* (28 June).

Richardson, P. 1986. "The Natal Sugar Industry in the Nineteenth Century". In Beinart, W. et al. (eds.), *Putting a Plough to the Ground: Accumulation and Dispossession in Rural South Africa 1850–1930,* pp. 129–175. Johannesburg: Ravan Press.

Sannyasi, B.D. and Chaturvedi, B. 1931. A Report on the Emigrants Repatriated to Indian under the Assisted Emigration Scheme from South Africa and on the Problems of Returned Emigrants from all Colonies. Bihar: Pravasi Bhavan.

Sarre, P. 1989. "Race and the Class Structure". In C. Hamnett, L. McDowell and P. Sarre (eds.), *Changing Social Structure,* pp. 125–132. London: Sage Publications.

Singh, G. 1946. *The Asiatic Land Tenure and Indian Representation Act of South Africa: A Brief Survey of its Background, Terms and Implications.* Council for Human Rights: Durban.

Singh, M. and Vawda, S. 1988. "What's in a Name?: Some Reflections on the Natal Indian Congress". *Transformation,* 6: 1–21.

Stein, Z.A. 1927. "A History of Indian Settlement in Natal from 1870–1893". Unpublished Master's dissertation, University of Cape Town.

Swan, M. 1984. "The 1913 Natal Indian Strike". *Journal of Southern African Studies,* 10: 239–258.

—. 1985. *Gandhi: the South African Experience.* Johannesburg: Ravan Press.

—. 1987. "Ideology in Organised Indian Politics, 1891–1948". In S. Marks and S. Trapido (eds.), *The Politics of Race, Class and Nationalism in Twentieth Century South Africa,* pp. 182–208. London: Longman.

Swanson, M.W. 1983. " 'The Asiatic Menace': Creating Segregation in Durban, 1870–1900". *International Journal of African Historical Studies,* 16: 401–421.

Thompson, L.M. 1952. "Indian Immigration into Natal (1860–1872)". *Archives Year Book for South African History,* 2: 1–76.

Tinker, H. 1973. "The Politics of Racialism: South Africa's Indians". *Journal of African History,* 14: 523–527.

Vahed, G. 2001. "Race or Class? Community and Conflict amongst Indian Municipal Employees in Durban, 1914–1949". *Journal of Southern African Studies,* 27: 105–125.

—. 2002. "Constructions of Community and Identity Among Indians in Colonial Natal, 1860–1910". *The Journal of African History,* 43: 77–93.

—. 2003. "Deconstructing 'Indianness': cricket and the Articulation of Indian Identities in Durban, 1900–32". *Sport in Society*, 6: 144–168.

Waiz, S.A. 1927. *Indians Abroad*. Bombay: Imperial Indian's Citizenship Association.

Webster, E. 1978. "The 1949 Durban Riots: A Case Study in Race and Class". In P. Bonner (ed.), *Working Papers in Southern African Studies*, pp. 1–38. African Studies Institute, University of Witwatersrand, Johannesburg.

Wyley, C.H. 1986. "The Natal Dealers Licences Act of 1897 and the Conflict between Indian and White Capital in the Borough of Durban 1897–1909". Unpublished Honours thesis, University of Natal, Durban.

# 4

# The Relevance of Life History Writings as a Methodological Technique of Social Inquiry

## The Autobiography of Munshi Rahman Khan in Understanding the Indian Diaspora

MOHAN K. GAUTAM

Since the last quarter of 20th century, the life histories are becoming the important methodological mode in understanding the historical perspective and the structure of the Indian diaspora. The available sources have often been limited to one-sided colonial reports, travellers and missionary writings and the so-called historical records. Unfortunately, the disciplines of social sciences have not given sufficient importance to the life histories. Moreover, there has been no attempt to discover those emigrants, who would have gone to the colonial plantation colonies and might have written the life histories on the basis of their experiences in the plantation colonies. This is also a known fact that the colonial masters did not want to send/import educated workers. They were only interested to send those workers who had sufficient knowledge in working in the fields. That is an evident fact the *arkatis* (recruiters) recruited only those people who did not know anything about the colonies at all. In the eastern part of Uttar Pradesh (formerly Oudh and North West Province) and the western part of Bihar (Bhojpur region), people always went for seasonal migrations owing to the fact of their poor

First appeared in *Man in India: A Quarterly Journal of Anthropology*, Vol. 87, Nos. 1 and 2: 13–25 (2007). 

conditions, administrative and political persecution (remnants of 1857 sepoy mutiny) and unknown natural famines in form of excess in drought or rains. When recruiters told them about rosy future in the colonies they accepted the offer and in this way they got trapped in their sweet talks. However, there were very few people who were educated but fell in the trap for dreamy higher daily wages. This was the case of Munshi Rahman Khan, a man of 24 years, a teacher in Bundelkhand, who once upon a time went to see the Ram Lila open theatre (based on the life of Lord Rama, the Hindu incarnation of Vishnu) in Kanpur. While coming back to catch his train from Collectorganj railway station he was trapped by two Muslim recruiters. Since he used to write his daily diaries, he wrote:

> "While I was standing on the bridge of the canal and looking at the water, two Muslims, who later proved to be moneyminded devils, came to me. Thinking them to be sympathetic gentlemen I greeted them. Because they were wearing clean and fine dresses, they were looking nice. They replied my greetings and asked me from where I was coming. I said, "I am coming from an inn (Sarai) of the Parade grounds". Then they asked me where I was going. I told them, by the train of 8 'o clock I am going to Chandpur. They asked again, "Would you like to have a job?" I said, "What kind of job?" They said it is a government job. Then they asked, "Are you educated?" I said, "Yes". "I have passed the middle school". They happily told me. "Then you could become a sardara (headman) and receive a salary of 12 annas per day (formerly before the independence of India a Rupee had 16 annas and 64 paisas). The work has to do with sugar". "Hearing, such tempting words I became very happy. I just forgot my own self, got separated from my own family and fell into the trap of my luck".

He went to Surinam and afterwards got settled there. In 1943, he compiled his diaries and made his autobiography *Jeevan Prakasa*.

It is a fact that the autobiography of Munshi Rahman Khan is a unique personal life history, a document of rich experiences of an Indian emigrant. Though, he was not a trained writer he wrote honestly about his daily activities in his diary. It could be an important methodological tool for the student of Indian diaspora to understand the historical activities of his life and its connection with the neighbourers, government officials and the administration and infrastructure of the plantation. During the 1950s, he also wrote another small text, another version of the chapter of emigration of his autobiography 'Dharma aura Kali samvada', where it seems he has given very general information and sometimes seems to be biased. He came to Surinam by a ship known as "Avon" which had 750 emigrants and 150 black African workers. After landing in Surinam at the fort all the emigrants were sent to 19 plantations. Munshiji was sent to Lust en Rust plantation of Mr Hoorst together with 5 more persons (5 men and 1 women; 2 Muslims and 4 Hindus). The languages which the emigrants belonged were Bhojpuri, Avadhi, Bihari, Braj and Bundeli and rest from Rajasthani, Telugu, Punjabi, and Bengali. Eight emigrants returned to India after their termination of the contract and a few moved to Guyana. There is always a doubt that how a single person could have observed the activities of all the emigrants. In his other manuscript which is based on the chapter on emigration, his accounts of the Hindus seem to be an overstatement and might be a personal bias which he could have developed during the Hindu Muslim tensions of 1930s in Surinam. Before I tackle these points I should also like to give some sociological importance of the life history approach. How far the life history approach can be useful in understanding the Indian diaspora? The oral history narrated by others about him should also be given some thought as a cross-reference for the reliability of the information as it deals directly to the cultural milieu and experiences in historical perspective of Munshi Rahman Khan.

Munshi Rahman Khan (1874–1972) wan an emigrant from India who came to Surinam in 1898 under a five year contract of the indenture labour system to work on plantations. After the termination of the contact he took another five years contact. In the mean time he got married and children were born. Afterwards he settled and became a Dutch citizen. In 1970s, I discovered his manuscripts through his grandson Albert Rahman Khan, a teacher in a school in The Hague. Afterwards I introduced his autobiography *Jeevan Prakasa* to the wider public through my scientific writings in international journals. It is a very important work because it is written by an emigrant about his experiences right from his recruitment, his stay in the sub-depot in Kanpur, travel to Calcutta, stay in the main depot at the Garden Reach harbour in waiting for the ship, ship "Avon's" three month journey to Surinam, his five years' contract to work in the plantation of Lust en Rust, his marriage, birth of children, buying house, teaching Hindi to fellow Indians, etc. (Gautam, 1986, 1995, 2002, 2003). Unfortunately, not many emigrants wrote their experiences in form of autobiographies. In Fiji, Totaram Sanadya wrote his experiences which were helped and published by Banarsidas Chaturvedi in India (1973). In Mauritius, some information was given but not in detail by Pt. Kashiram Kistoe (Ramburn, 1984). In Trinidad, there were no emigrant writers but a very nice diary was published about the clipper ship "Shiela" by Capt. W.G. Angel (Ramchand and Samaroo, 1996). Only recently a few articles have been published in Trinidad about the life histories by Samaroo and Shamshuddin. Munshi Rahman Khan's autobiography with comment has also been printed in a very limited number by Gautam (1997) and Sinha-Kerkhof, Bal and Singh (2005).

Recently, in 2006 another manuscript containing 27 pages was discovered by Gautam (2007) which is known as Dharam aura Kali samvad (Discussion between Dharma and Kali about the emigration of Indians from India to Calcutta). It is written in Hindi with devnagari script. Possibly, this manuscript was written after 1953 (year is not mentioned, but should be in 1953–1954) and was based on the chapter of emigration of his autobiography. It is a strange phenomena that unlike his autobiography, the narratives seem to be not very authentic. It has added many things which are not in his emigration chapter of *Jeevan Prakasa*.

## Life Histories in Social Sciences

In anthropology and sociology, the role of methodological technique in using the personal documents and oral testimonies has always been considered as the secondary source in studying the social realities. During the 17th and 18th century, the process of the discovery of the new territories for trade expansion and colonization, anthropology developed through sporadic travellers who wrote diaries and collected objects of the non-European cultures. These written accounts were based on personal experiences and in an unsystematic manner.

With the growth of European museums and the academies, there started some sort of systematization in researches and the written reports. The researcher conducted his field work to describe and record the forms and nature and the extent of some sort of social order in human life. Similar to the natural sciences, anthropology also built social models to observe an ongoing structure of the people and the system of social life. The observation techniques were used to get an authentic image of the society. It was the start of empirical inquiries where the field worker did not give or add any comment and evaluation on the collected information. In 1874, *Notes and Queries,* a manual of research instructions for scientists was published with the joint cooperation of many anthropologists including Pitt-Rivers. In 1895, Putnam and his assistant Boas organized the World Columbian Exposition (Collier and Tschopik, 1954). Boas emphasized that accurate and detailed monographic descriptions be made in the field during field research. This followed a battery of trained field workers who did researches in Mexico, North West Coast of America, Siberia and the South Pacific.

In Europe, the findings of Malinowski (1932) and Radcliffe Brown (1933)—themselves influenced by Durkheim—led to functional approach in anthropological research (Gautam, 1969). The foundation of Museum de L'Homme (Museum of Man, Paris, France) was the direct outcome of their findings. Anthropology became a full-fledged subject which "grew out of expeditions and museums" (Kroeber, 1954). Malinowski, was first pioneer, who for the first time used the participant observation (1940), was an outstanding field worker. His study on the Nuer society provided a fusion between theory and description (Barth, 1966). The explanatory model being the representation of the interrelated set of assumed factors explained the observed phenomenon. With the ideas of Boas (1907) and Malinowski, new researches became *monographs,* describing the bizarre details of the observed people. The "wholistic" approach covered everything, i.e., the socio-economic, religious, political and cultural aspects of the people as the social reality. The written monographs provided the cross-cultural translation in a functional-structural model with quantitative method by using statistics for comparative studies. Most of the conducted research was an accumulation of some sort of case studies.

When new colonies were discovered by the European colonizers they required people to colonize the colonies and workers to work for the colonizers. Since the countries were very big, Europeans migrated to new territories of North America and Caribbean countries. In order to work hard and prepare the land for cultivation, the slaves were collected from African countries mostly from West Africa and sold in open markets in England (Charlotte and Plimmer, 1973). It is only in the first two decades of the 19th century when in the colonies a movement started against the slavery in England. The slaves were treated inhumanly. At last in 1832–33, slavery was abolished in British Empire but continued in France and

Netherlands. The plantation suffered enormously because the so-called free citizens (the slaves) either ran away to the forests or started their own work. The economy of the plantation suffered heavily and production almost came to a stand still. In order to boost the economy of the plantations, the new labour force was found in India. Under the five year contract of indenture labour system, the first ship of emigrants landed in Mauritius in 1834. The Caribbean has also suffered economically. In 1838, the next assignment of export of Indian labourers was for British Guyana when two ships *whiteby* and *Hesperus* landed with a cargo of 396 Indians including 22 women.

Later on the supply of Indian labourers filled the gap in other Caribbean countries (Trinidad in 1845) and in East and South African countries. During the period of emigration (1834 to 1916), 1.2 million Indians were sent to work on plantations while from Europe 36.3 million Europeans migrated to North America (Barz and Siegel, 1986; Tinker, 1974).

The first account of the life history writings started by Thomas and Znanieck, in their five volumes (1918–1920) on the Polish immigrants to the United States of America, based on personal records in the form of letters, diaries, life histories and oral testimonies. During the 1920s, the Chicago School of Sociology used personal narratives extensively, but considered them as generally exploratory tools only (Bruce Shaw, 1980). The Leiden school published a book for the researchers in conducting their field inquiries (Brouwer, 1922) and was used not only in natural sciences but also in social sciences.

However, in social psychology, the use of life histories became a "must" for the diagnosis of emotional disorders. Freud worked on individual psychological case studies. During the 1930s, the social scientists described their representativeness of the subjects and the adequacy, reliability and validity of their work. Dollard (1938) commended and emphasized the use of life histories in community studies approach. He wrote that the life history is often a "deliberate attempt to define the growth of a person in a cultural milieu and to make theoretical sense of it". During the 1940s, the life history approach became more critical and gave an extensive explanation (Simons, 1942) in a situational analysis. Thus, life histories became prominent with the subject's experience through situational analysis for building an explanatory model. After Allport's work (1942), Gottschalk, Kluckhon and Angel (1945) emphasized the need in using personal records and documents. As the time passed, new critical elements were added. Redfield (1960) and Oscar Lewis (1961) revived the life history approach. For a decade, the methodology remained generally silent. Denzin (1970) showed the advantages in social research through life histories. In the later years, it was made clear that the oral histories are as important as the documentary material. According to him, a life history "presents the experiences and definition held by one person, group, organization interprets those experiences". Vansina (1965) stated that what is "false" and what is "truth" always required qualification. It was due to an emerging dispute between historians and folklorists. Geertz (1975) and Worseley (1964) both argued that the value of the oral literature can neither be discarded nor be accepted without having the cross-references. Reliability of observation often depends upon the cross-references. Vansina argued three categories which have to be thoroughly checked up "those made in defense of private interests, those made under the influence of cultural values and those to personal idiosyncrasies". These sources of biases can be checked through the test of general credibility, honesty, narrative's plausibility related to the past experiences and general test of internal consistency (Allport, 1942). If there is an available documentary evidence of other kind it can also be used.

Having seen the sociological development with the study of life histories, one thing becomes clear that the autobiography of Munshi Rahman Khan certainly is an important work as it is based on his personal experiences during the time of emigration and his settlement in Surinam.

## Evaluation of Munshi Rahman Khan's Dharma and Kali Discussion

In this article I am not looking at the *Jeevan Prakasa* of Munshi Rahman Khan but his other book which is a form of discussion between the King Kali (from points of view of Hinduism a mythological king at the inception of Kaliyuga started more than 5000 years ago) and the protector of Dharma (code of conduct and moral values of the Hindu society), personified as Dharma. King Kali asks Dharma, "why are you so sad today. Please tell me your problems". Dharma replies, "In the beginning in India there were Hindu kings who were efficient and did take care of their subjects and followed Hindu dharma. They were protectors of Hinduism. After the arrival of Muslims in India Hindu kingdoms were finished. But they did not destroy the Hinduism. But due to conflicts between these two communities the English got benefit and gradually took the administration of India from Muslims. But they did destroy neither Islam nor Hinduism". When in 1832, slavery was abolished in the plantation colonies the shortage of labourers was felt. African slaves (who got name as Creole) ran away to the forests or started their own work, mostly under the same owners of the plantation. The new labour supply was found in India. During the 19th century, English sent Indians to the plantation colonies to work for a period of five years under the contract of indenture labour system. The Brahmin caste was not allowed to emigrate. But many Brahmins changed their names and got recruited as Girmitiyas. They even changed their names in the caste of Ksatris (Singh). This Kshatrization process was necessary to go to the plantation colonies. In the beginning in the sub-depots, Hindus and Muslims cooked their food separately. They were promised better day wages. Later on in the main Depot in Calcutta, in ship journey, Depot in Surinam and finally in the plantation, the caste system gradually disappeared and according to Munshi Rahman Khan the so-called Hindus became non-Hindus. Munshi Rahman Khan means that they did not follow the code of the Hindu caste system based on restrictions in touching, eating, and marriage. When the girmitiyas reached Calcutta, they were both Hindus and Muslims. But next day according to Munshi Rahman Khan, all the recruitees were asked by two Bengali Brahmins, who were wearing calf leather shoes to bath in the Bhagirathi River (Ganges). They washed their bodies with soap and oil but during the process of bathing, they gave up their Hindu religion by throwing their sacred threads and rosaries into the river and said to Ganges, "O Ganga mother, we surrender our pure Hindu religion to you and having become Shudra we go to Surinam. When we return after crossing the black water (*kalapani*) we will become Hindu and bear the sacred thread". They were given the yellow uniform, a tin plate and a clay mug. These utensils were multipurpose and functional. During their stay, there were some sort of courtships between the sexes. Before boarding the ship, the order was announced that they should be pairs as husband and wife. Many high caste Hindus got married to low caste women and did not follow the Hindu ideals. In the ship as a protection from rough sea, the doctor and compounder gave them medicine in the same glass which was not even cleaned for everyone. That destroyed the

Hindu hierarchy and stratification of low and high castes. In Surinam, many high caste people also got married to low castes. During the ship journey, they were given a common food (even the meat was given to them) and they ate nicely. In the plantation, the accommodation was a single small room in a long barrack but it was meant for two persons to live together. Munshiji gave a rosy image of the plantations. It is possible that his plantation Lust en Rust was different than other plantations. But, in fact, there were a lot of restrictions. Without a pass one could not go out of the plantation even to meet a friend. There were also brutalities. If the people were ill, either they were not given the medicine or forced to work. The treatment was almost like slaves. There were also protests by Indians and the plantation owners called police who used firing and killed many people. The case of Zoelen plantation is a living memory in the minds of emigrated Indians and is boldly written in their history of emigration.

The other handwritten manuscript *Dharma aur Kali Samvad's* copy, discovered in the heaps of old papers at the house of Albert Rahman Khan, grandson of Munshi Rahman Khan belongs to the son of Munshi, Dildar Khan. It is a rewritten version of the chapter of emigration in his autobiography and will be discussed in this article. Perhaps he wanted to write this manuscript in a form of discussion between two characters. It becomes clear that the character of Dharma is actually Munshi Rahman Khan who is narrating the events. The descriptions of three parts of this manuscript are Munshiji's narration to the emigration right from the recruiters' (arkatis) bluffs and traps in getting the potential labourers for colonial plantation colonies to stay in the plantation in Surinam. He also describes in detail the events in the main Depot in Calcutta's Garden Reach harbour, including medical check up and eating food together. The second part deals with the ship journey and the depot in Surinam. The last part is about the five years' contract in the plantation. The plantations according to their size and work required from 10 to 150 workers. They were given accommodation in the barrack rooms. Their supervision was in the hands of manager, and his assistants. For first three months, free ration was given. They were also given utensils and the agricultural implements (shovels, cutters, etc.). Medical care was very nice. If an emigrant was ill he was provided a free medical care, bed and free medicines. The pregnant women after seven months got three months' leave. This is a rosy description of his plantation but in reality the plantations were not interested in extensive medical care. There were no provisions for three months' leave. Even after the delivery if the woman was weak then medical doctor recommended more leave. In the plantations, cacao, coffee, bananas, sugar, etc., were produced which were not produced in India. In the beginning, training was given about the care of new crops. It was also told that if the work is good then more wages or bonus can be expected. After three months when free ration stopped, the emigrant's family side by side also started doing extra work for their own livelihood. According to him, the hard work of Indians gave them good results and better money. They saved money and even remitted to their homes in India and eventually when they left for India took the money with them. Munshi Rahman Khan also remitted money to his family in India several times. Those who settled in Surinam bought the land and became agriculturists. Those who did not have sufficient money they were given seven years' grace period (no payment of revenue) by the government and afterwards became agriculturalists. During the 1960s, according to him, the children of the emigrants had achieved tremendous progress. They had become doctors, engineers, politicians, businessmen, teachers and established temples, mosques, orphan homes, schools, etc.

The first two parts of the second text, if compared with the chapter of autobiography, certain facts are inconsistent:

1. Munshi Rahman Khan states that those Indians (high castes) who emigrated to Surinam had changed their caste names. It seems he is just generalizing it. In his ship there were only three Brahmin families, one from Avadh region, Gonda district (father and daughter), other from Banda district, Bundelkhand (brother and sister) and the last one from Punna, Madhya Pradesh (mother with two children). These persons retained their names as Brahmins, There is no evidence that caste names were changed. The second high caste group was of Thakurs, who also maintained their original names. One can find these facts in the ships and the government of Surinam's register of records in Paramaribo. When the names were registered in the sub-depot and in the government register, they were the same as told by the recruitees. That is why the names in the government register are found, like Phool Chand, Dubari, Tulia, Budhna, Sukhia, Puran, Beni, Binda, Janaki, Etwari,

Somvari, etc. These persons have no surnames because they belonged to Kurmi, Chamar, Kori, Ahir, Lodh, Ahir, Hajjam, Karar, Musahir, Pasi. However, it is a fact that the names were not written correctly because the clerk was not used to their pronunciation. The spellings were not correct. The names were changed only after 1930s, of the people who did not have surnames in Surinam when, structurally speaking, the issue of marriage became a problem. According to the registration records only 8 families of the ship "Avon" changed their caste names. It is also a known fact that women were very few hardly 30 per cent. The process of Ksatrization, similar to sanskritization started and the low castes changed their names into high castes, such as, "Singh" (belonging to Kshatriya caste). They also adopted high caste ideals and followed the rules of dieting with other castes.

2. In the second text, Munshi Rahman Khan narrates the condition in the main Depot and gives a title, "Caste, dharma (code of conduct), karma (practical and thought out actions), inter caste relations and behaviour all destroyed". It is a very general statement. He says that after taking a bath in the river all got the same yellow coloured uniform, tin plates and clay mugs which were already used by the earlier emigrants whose caste and religion were unknown. Here again Munshiji is giving a very general statement because for going to Surinam the ship journey took three months and the return journey again took three months. That means, it took about 7 months and one cannot think practically that the same utensils were used by the various emigrants. He further says that the hierarchy was destroyed among the Hindu emigrants. All people of high and low castes sat together and ate together. Moreover, men and women talked together. The untouchability was kept aside and this destroyed the caste system. The fact is that in Surinam, the emigrants always followed the rules of hierarchy and caste system in the form of varna category (Hindu society is divided into four varnas, Brahmin, Kshatriya, Vaishya and Shudra and the caste system has come out of these categories) in their family rituals.
3. For example, in his autobiography in the chapter on emigration, there is no mention of giving order at the main depot in Calcutta before embarking the ship to the emigrants to

join as husband and wife, which was done by high caste Hindus with very low caste women. One has to ask what was the proportion of men and women in his ship "Avon". There is no information in its records that there were marriages.

4. Similarly, in the ship the jamadar (headman) did ask the emigrants by saying bhakti ha, bhakti ha, that vegetarians should make their own line separately to receive their food which is not mentioned in the second text. It means there were also vegetarians in the ship who were given food separately. How many were vegetarians is not known.
5. While talking about the medicine given by doctor and his assistant to the emigrants in the same glass is not mentioned in the chapter of autobiography. Only it says that some sort of lemon juice was given and he presumes that it was mixed up with meat juice. This medicine was lemon juice to protect them from dizziness and vomiting when the sea was rough.
6. In an other example in the second book, Munshi Rahman Khan says that when the ship reached Surinam there also many people got married and this relationship took place between high caste men and low caste women. This account is not mentioned in the chapter in his autobiography. The ship has not registered such information.
7. In another episode, Munshiji says that the utensils which the people possessed consisted of only a tin plate and clay mug which were used in drinking, cleaning face and cleansing the body. It is possible that the clay mug was there but if it was broken how it was replaced? Here the text is silent. It is known fact that the majority of the emigrants took with them a copper tharia (plate) and a copper lota (mug) which are the identity symbols of the emigrated Indians not only in Surinam but in all the Caribbean countries. Why these two utensils are not mentioned?
8. Finally, as it is mentioned in his autobiography when his group of 6 people was taken by boat to the plantation of Lust en Rust, according to him his boatman was a Brahmin, carrying a religious book *Ramayana* to the plantation. If the high castes had lost their Hindu hierarchy in Calcutta's main Depot then why he found the Brahmins in Surinam. Moreover, especially the Hindus do have an orange/red flag known as Hanuman jhandi in front of their houses. It is said that it is the symbol of their Hindu-cum-Indian identity.

All these points question the reliability of the second book. It seems right that after the 1930s' Hindu-Muslim conflict, Munshiji must have taken his stand in favoured Muslim community and perhaps this was the only way to state his ideas against the Hindus in Surinam. Since he could not mention it in his autobiography, he stated it in the second book. In the second book he writes, "Now the guardian of Hinduism should think about the caste and food (restrictions) traditions and the boycott which they planned against the Muslims." This Hindu, Muslim tension was started in the 1930s when Hindus created a 20 point programme to boycott the Muslims and opened their own shopping centre. Muslims were isolated and took help of the government of Surinam. Similarly, during those years a one act play 'Vir Hakikat Rai' was organized and played in various cities in Surinam by an Arya Samaji, Pt. Sukh Lal (Hindorie) which was banned by the Dutch Surinam government because it did hurt the Indian Muslims.

Considering all these questions and inconsistencies, it can be said that Munshiji mugged many ideas as he became pro Muslim and condemned the Hindu system of the emigrants.

Under the methodological tool, it would give us some explanation that why Munshiji deviated from his first autobiography's text and added new ideas in the second book. Perhaps we should check the facts by consulting the cross-references. This article is not focused on the detail analysis of Munshi Rahman Khan's autobiography but on his last version of the chapter on emigration of Indians to Surinam. However, it is a fact that the second book of discussion is actually the personal experiences of Munshi Rahman Khan. He says very clearly:

> Bharatvasi gaye bahu karan naukari heta
> Dipu aura jahaja ka hala kahun saha ceta
> Bharati ho main bhi gaya Dutch Gayana desha
> Jasa bita bhaga men lakha kaha na aura
> (Many Indians went (to Surinam) for the sake of service
> Consciously I tell the condition of the Depot and the ship
> I also got recruited for Dutch Gayana country
> As I experienced in my luck I have told that only.

The main question arises why Munshi Rahman Khan changed or added new things in this text of the second book. Why did he not keep the same facts which he has already narrated in his autobiography? Perhaps as it is said there were problems within

Hindu-Muslim relations. Munshiji took advantage of Hindu caste system, untouchability and hierarchy and used it against the Hindu system of the Surinami Hindus. On the other hand, he does mention the Constitution of independent India where untouchability has been abolished. This news he quotes from the excerpt of a newspaper, *Venketeshwar Samachar* of 26 January and 6 February 1953. In his discussion with king Kaliyuga, Dharma says, "O Kaliyugaji please think for a moment that great country India together with freedom has abolished untouchability and fulfilled the last ritual of samskar (cremated the untouchability)." He further says, "When there is no untouchability then there is no caste system, and when there is no caste system then where is no dharma, and when there is no dharma then there is no God and when there is no God then where is the deliberation (moksha) and when there is no deliberation then the world is without feelings and completely dead".

> "Jaba chua-chut nahin taba jati kahan jaba jati nahin
> taba dharma kahan jaba dharma nahin taba isha kahan
> jaba isha nahin taba moksha kahan jaba moksha he nahin
> taba samsara nirasa athva sarva nashta hai"

(*Dharma aur Kali Samvada*, p. 19)

## References


Allport, G.W. (1942). "The Use of Personal Documents in Psychological Science", *Social Science Research Council*, Bulletin No. 49, New York.

Barth, F.W. (1966). "Anthropological Models and Social Reality", *Proceedings of the Royal Society B*, Vol. 165: 20–34.

Barz, R.K. and Siegel J. (eds.). (1988). *Language Transplanted: The Development of Overseas Hindi*. Otto Harrassowitz Wiesbaden.

Boas, F. (1907). "Some Principles of Museum Administration", *Science New Series*, Vol. 25: 920–33.

Brouwer, H.A. (ed.). (1922). *Practical Hints to Scientific Travellers*. Leiden: E.J. Bril.

Bruce, Shaw. (1980). "Life History Writing in Anthropology: A Methodological Review", *Mankind*, Vol. 12, No. 3: 226–33.

Chaturvedi, B.D. (1973). *Fiji Dvipa Men Mere 21 Varsha*, (based on the experiences of Totaram Sanadya). 4th edition, Varanasi.

Charlotte and D. Plimmer (1973). *Slavery: The Anglo-American Involvement*. David and Charles: Newton Abott.

Collier, D. and H. Tschopic. (1954). "The Role of Museum in American Anthropology", *American Anthropologist*, Vol. 56: 768–79.

Denzin, N.K. (ed.) (1970). *Sociological Methods: A Source Book*. London: Butterworths.

Dollard, J. (1938). "The Life Histories in Community Studies", *American Sociological Review*, 3: 724–37.

Evans-Prichard, E.E. (1940). *The Neur*. Oxford: Lasrendon Press.

Gautam, M.K. (1986). "Maintenance-Mechanism of Indian (Hindustani) Ethnic Identity in Surinam and The Netherlands", In U. Bissoondoyal and S.B.C. Servansingh (eds.), *Indian Labour Review*, pp. 265–288. Moka: Mahatma Gandhi Institute Press.

—. (1995). "Munshi Rahman Khan (1874–1872): An Institution of Indian Diaspora in Surinam". Unpublished paper presented at the ISER-NCIC Conference on Challenge and Change: The Indian Diaspora in its Historical and Contemporary Contexts, The University of West Indies St. Augustine, Trinidad and Tobago.

—. (1997). *Munshi Rahman Khan, Reconstruction of a New History of East Indian Emigrants in Surinam Through his Autobiography*. Lucknow and Delhi: Indo-European Publishers.

—. (1999). "The Construction of Indian Image in Surinam: Deconstructing Colonial Derogatory Notions and Reconstructing of the Indian Identity", In M. Gosine and D. Narine (eds.), *Sojourners to Settlers: Indian Migrants in the Caribbean and the Americas*. New York: Windsor Press.

—. (2003). "Munshi Rahman Khan", *Pravasi Samsar*, No.1: 1. New Delhi.

—. (2003). "Ethnic Identity of the East Indians in Surinam", In R. Sharma and E. Annamalai (eds.), *Indian Diaspora: In Search of Identity*. Mysore: Central Institute of Indian Languages.

—. (2007). *Munshi Rahman Khan ki Eka Nayo Hasthlikhita Pustika: Dharma Aura Kali Samvada*. New Delhi: Hindi Jagat.

Geertz, C. (1975). *The Interpretation of Culture*. New York: Basic Books.

Gottschalk, L.G. Kluchkhon, and R. Angell (1945). "The Use of Personal Documents in History, Anthropology and Sociology", *Social Research Council*, Bulletin No. 53, New York.

Kroeber, A.L. (1954). "The Place of Anthropology in Universities", *American Anthropologist*, Vol. 56: 293–311.

Lewis, O. (1961). *The Children of Sanchez*. Harmondsworth: Penguin.

Malinowski, B. (1932). *Argonauts of the Western Pacific*. New York: E.P. Dutton.

Ramburn, S. 1984. *Pt. Kashinath Kishto: Kashinath Ratnavali,* Mahatma Gandhi Institute Press, Moka.

Ramchand, K., and Samaroo, B. (eds.). (1995). *A Return to the Middle Passage: The Clipper Ship 'Sheila'*. Port of Spain: Caribbean Information Systems and Services Ltd., (originally published by Capt. W.H. Angel).

Radcliffe-Brown, A.R. (1933). *The Andaman Islanders*. Cambridge: University Press.

Redfield, R. (1946). 'Forward', in Gottschalk, L., Kluckhon, C. and Angell, R. *Social Research Council,* Bulletin, No. 53, New York.

—. (1960). *The Little Community and Peasant Society and Culture*. Chicago: University of Chicago Press.

Shaw, B. (1978). Indigenous Perspective: Recording Aboriginal Australian Life Histories, *Australian Anthropological Society Conference Paper,* August, Sydney.

Simons, L. (1942). *Sun Chief: The Autobiography of a Hopi Indian*. New Haven: Yale University Press.

Sinha-Kerkhof, K., Ball, E. and Singh, A.D. (2005). *Autobiography of An Indian Indentured Labourer Munshi Rahman Khan (1874–1972): Jeevan Prakash*. Delhi: Shipra.

Tinker, H. (1974). *New System of Slavery: The Export of Indian Labour Overseas 1830–1920*. Oxford: Oxford University Press.

Thomas, W. and Zannieck, F. (1927). *The Polish Peasant in Europe and America,* Gorham Press, Boston, Vols. I and II, 1918, Vol. III, 1919 and Vol. IV and V, 1920.

Vansina, J. (1965). *Oral Tradition: A Study in Historical Methodology*. Harmondsworth: Penguin.

Worseley, P. (1964). *The Third World*. London: Weidenfeld and Nicolson.

# 5

# The Indian Diaspora in the West Indies/Caribbean

## A Cultural History of Triumphs and Tribulations

KUMAR MAHABIR

The abolition of slavery in the early 1830s in the British, French and Dutch colonies of the West Indies/Caribbean led to a severe shortage of labour in the sugarcane plantations. The ex-slaves had exercised their right of freedom of choice to discontinue working on the sugarcane plantations even for a wage. The subsequent shortage of labour served as a catalyst for the introduction of a system of imported contract labour. The British first introduced labourers from India to the Caribbean through a semi-slave system of contract labour known as indentureship. In 1838, Britain sent the first Indian labourers from the port of Calcutta to British Guiana (now Guyana) based on the success of the system in Mauritius.

Initially, the Caribbean initiative met resistance since accusations were levied at the harsh treatment of the newly-arrived workers. Nevertheless, with lobbying by John Gladstone and other British planters, the system continued and expanded. It was later extended to Trinidad and Jamaica (1845) and then to other Caribbean islands like St. Lucia (1856), St. Vincent (1856), Grenada (1857) and St. Kitts (1861). The system was also adopted by the French and Dutch who took Indians to Martinique (1853), Guadeloupe (1854), French Guyana (1855), St. Croix (1862) and Surinam (1873). By the time the indentureship system ended in 1917, about 400,000 Indians came to the Caribbean colonies, most of whom chose to settle in the islands.

Most of the indentured immigrants to the Caribbean came from north India, primarily Uttar Pradesh and Bihar, while lesser numbers from south India. The majority of immigrants to the French territories originated from south India and spoke Telugu and Tamil. Northern Indian immigrants spoke the Hindi dialects of Bhojpuri, Urdu and Bengali. The vast majority of these immigrants were Hindus with about 10 per cent Muslims. Many factors in India encouraged migrants to leave and seek their fortunes elsewhere. Severe famine in India was one such factor. Describing the living conditions of peasant farmers, Dutt (1969: 12) writes:

> The appalling poverty and joylessness of his life under such conditions cannot be easily pictured .... It is literally a fact and not a figure of speech that agricultural labourers and their families in India generally suffer from insufficient food from year's beginning to year's end. They are brought up from childhood on less nourishment than is required even in the tropics, and grow up to be a nation weak in physique, stunted in growth, easy victims to disease, plague and famine.

The land revenue system which benefited the land-owning classes and the colonial rulers of India compounded the problem for peasants in India. Bajpai (2001: 5–8) writes:

> The state was seen to connive with the exploitative elements of the agrarian society of Uttar Pradesh which was engaged in siphoning off the products of the peasants' toil ... the agrarian crisis deepened in these decades with indebtedness becoming widespread as well as deep, as the debt was passed on to succeeding generations.

The exploitative nature of the relationship between peasants and landowning classes is aptly reflected in numerous, seemingly arbitrary taxes. Examples include *dhururai* or dust cess, for dust raised as cattle passed the landlord's estate; and payment of presents, called *nazar*, in festivals such as Dusshera, Holi and Eid; *neota* or invitation cess, when villagers were asked to join in celebrations. There were also taxes for the variety of cane produced. *Nazarna* was payment due for permission to build or modify existing houses. The term *nazarana* was also used to describe an extra rent premium which was taken as a gift payment. So severe was the system of taxation that the practice of *kanya vikray* (sale of daughters, typically very young girls, to be married to much older men) developed to enable peasants to withstand conditions of extreme deprivation. These factors reflect the economic and social circumstances of India in the years of indenture. They served as push factors to encourage migrants to depart their homeland in search of a better future.

In the early days of indenture, when the passage from India to the Caribbean took at least three to four months, conditions on the ships were deplorable, resulting in high mortality rates. Caste endogamy broke down on the plantations as well as on the board of ships which traversed the Middle Passage. Due to the harsh conditions that Indians faced, they became united in their struggle for survival. Despite these cruel living conditions, Indians eventually produced a middle class of small farmers and shop owners.

By the time indentureship ended in 1917, many Indians did not exercise their option to return to India. They chose, instead, to remain as permanent settlers in the Caribbean where they got, bought and rented land to do agriculture and rear cows. By the end of World War II, those who chose to settle in the colonies easily constituted about half the population of Guyana, Surinam, and Trinidad and Tobago. They also formed the largest minority in Jamaica, Grenada, St. Vincent, St. Lucia and St. Kitts. Today, they constitute over 1.5 million in the region, settling in the territories of the Caribbean from Cuba and Jamaica in the northwest to Guyana and Surinam in the southeast. They form a visible ethnic group who has changed the face and form of culture, religion, music, food, architecture, politics and the economy in the Caribbean.

The social circumstances of the early years were exceedingly difficult. Not only were Indians moved thousands of miles from the land of their birth, but also they faced an apprehension and sometimes hostile host community of non-Indians and non-Hindus. Despite the loss of many valuable traditions through the death of the elders and the inability to resist the dominant Afro-European culture, several aspects of Indian cultural heritage have survived. The growing presence of Indians saw the rise of racial, cultural and religious trends that has contributed to the creation of a uniquely cosmopolitan Caribbean society at the beginning of the twenty first century. Notwithstanding their impoverished means and limited opportunities, the Indian presence has demonstrated steady social advancement in every field of endeavour, including literature, law, medicine, science, business and politics.

**Indians in Trinidad and Guyana**

The record of achievement of Indians in Trinidad and Guyana is as far as it is wide. In 1953, Dr Cheddi Jagan, an Indian of Guyanese birth, a dentist by profession and leader of the People's Progressive Party (PPP) was elected the first Premier of the Republic of Guyana. However, he was not to last, and given the social and racial instability of Guyana, was deposed. He wandered in the political wilderness until he was elected President of the Republic in 1995. Upon his death, Dr Jagan was succeeded by his wife Janet Jagan. Currently, Bharat Jagdeo, a PPP member since the age of twelve, is President of Guyana.

Like Guyana, the glass ceiling to political power was shattered in 1995, when Basdeo Panday, a trade unionist and opposition leader with more than 30 years in public life, became the first Indian to be elected as Prime Minister. His party, the United National Congress (UNC), deriving its support mainly from the Indian community, accomplished the seemingly impossible through an alliance with the Tobago-based National Alliance for Reconstruction (NAR) to form the government during 1995 to 2001. Additionally, during the term of office of the UNC, Kamla Persad Bissessar served with distinction as the first (Indian) woman to be appointed as Attorney General.

However, let it not be said that changes in the Indian diaspora have been circular and the same. In the last five years, Trinidad has undergone a paradigm shift engendered by a change in political fortunes of the UNC under Basdeo Panday. Whereas the reign of the Panday administration was driven by a consolidation of the Indian community, this has waned considerably. At this time in 2006, the only Indian to achieve the status of Prime Minister in the Caribbean next to Bharat Jagdeo of Guyana has suffered two electoral defeats. In making his way from the political scene, the diaspora will again revisit one of its most enduring deficiencies—a vision for place and space for the future. Perhaps the only person who has brought international recognition to the Indian presence in the Caribbean is the novelist, V.S. Naipaul. He won almost every major literary award in English in the world, and in 2001, won the prestigious Nobel Prize for Literature. Perhaps his most popular novel is *A House for Mister Biswas,* which is based on the author's early life in Hindu Trinidad.

In Trinidad and Tobago, the Indian heritage had become an integral part of the country's lifestyle, and has added significant content and colour to the nation's social and cultural mosaic.

For example, the Hindu festival of Light, Divali (or *Deepawali*) is a national public holiday, and despite the difference in theological origin, the celebration finds favour with the majority of the island's ethnic groups. Hindus form the second largest religious group after the Roman Catholics in Trinidad, and Divali is the second largest national festival in the country after Carnival. It is not surprising therefore that majestic mandirs adorn the landscape of Trinidad and Guyana. The off-shore temple in the sea at Waterloo, for example, built by one man with a bicycle, has become a world-famous tourist attraction. Temples in Guyana have the most varied architectural designs. They range from ancient single-chamber models made of timber to octagonal shapes made of concrete, and pagoda patterns fashioned after the classical era in India.

Eid-ul-Fitr, the Muslim celebration of Prophet Muhammed (uwbp) is also a public holiday, enjoying similar national acclaim. Every year, Shi'te Muslims commemorate the death of the grandsons of the Holy Prophet Muhammed by observing Hosay/Murraham. Participants wheel colourful, glitzy and ornate papier-mâché floats through the streets as part of a solemn procession. Tassa drums are played in a military style and moon dances are performed during the night procession. Large numbers of Hindus and Africans participate in this commemoration. In Jamaica, Hosay is one of the largest national cultural events.

Trinidad is the only Caribbean island with the distinction of celebrating Indian Arrival Day as a public holiday. The heritage day is observed in commemoration of the arrival of the first batch of immigrants who arrived on 30 May 1845. The day is marked with speeches, songs, music and dances and the re-enactment of the historic landing of the first batch of weary band of pioneers, who had sailed for six months over half of the world.

The region's diet is a culinary menu that draws heavily on Indian dishes and spices. Curry is a popular preparation of almost every kind of dish, and *roti* (pizza-like bread) has become a standard staple even in Jamaica. "Doubles," which is a *bara* sandwich made of chick pea and chutney, is indigenous to Trinidad. It is eaten hot and fresh by everyone who buys it from wayside vendors selling from shops, stalls and bicycles.

At present, seven of the country's twenty-five radio stations broadcast Hindi films and Indian music. "Radio Jagriti" is the last to be launched by the Maha Sabha Hindu religious organization. The Maha Sabha plans to produce the region's first Indian television station before the end of 2007. The Indian cultural identity has also been preserved by the importation of movies from Bombay, which is the largest film-producing country in the world. Indians in the Caribbean still flock with their families to see these movies at the local theatres that are largely owned by Indians. Many forms of Indian music have been maintained over the last four generations in the Caribbean. Some have been lost and others have taken new directions. Chutney is a musical cross-cultural genre which has been produced and popularized in Trinidad and exported to the Caribbean diaspora the world over. More than calypso and soca, chutney represents a fusion of various cultural influences and musical rhythms. Chutney and chutney-soca shows are held in the heart of the Carnival season in south Trinidad. Cultural connoisseurs see chutney as a Carnival fete with a curry flavour, and an attempt by Indians to affirm their identity by staging their own style of Carnival as a complement to the Afro-dominated parties in Port of Spain.

The most strident voice in the national community is that of the Sanatan Dharma Maha Sabha (SDMS). Founded in 1952, by Bhadase Sagan Maharaj, the SDMS is a pioneer in the field of education and organized religion of the Hindu masses. From 1952 to 1956, the SDMS was able to establish over 40 primary schools with its own building resources. The SDMS now has a temple in every community on the island. Indeed, the visionary Bhadase, who was equally revered as he was reviled, was tireless in his quest to lift the status of the Hindu community. Today, the SDMS is on par with its other denominational counterparts in the field of secondary education. The Lakshmi Girls High School is the flagship, standing shoulder to shoulder with other denominational colleges. With the revision of the Education Concordat, the SDMS has been successful in establishing three other high schools in the country.

The vociferous Muslim voices include the Anjuman Sunaat ul Association and the Trinidad Muslim League. Both Islamic bodies have successfully married education and religion for decades, and their mosques and schools are considered among society's highly respected institutions. Muslim, Hindu and Presbyterian children excel at all levels, and they dominate the professions of law, medicine, engineering and computer science. Hinduism was the dominant religion of the immigrants, and Islam accounted for a lesser percentage. But over time, Christianity has made significant inroads into the Hindu heartland. In 1868, Canadian missionary Rev. John Morton founded the Canadian Presbyterian Mission for the purpose of converting immigrants to the Christian fold. During the 1980s, the baton for prosetylization and conversion was taken over by the Pentecostal/Evangelical movement. Today, both the Presbyterian and Pentecostal churches count East Indians in significant numbers among their believers.

In the whole diaspora, individual efforts of the Hindu community have confirmed Trinidad's place on the Hindu pilgrimage map. In central Trinidad, devotees of the Dattatreya Yoga Centre consecrated an 85 foot/25 metre *murti* [statue] of Lord Hanuman. This astonishing achievement is unmatched in the Western hemisphere and is a first for Trinidad and Tobago. The soaring marble murti of the Hindu Monkey God is intended to symbolize the tower of strength that is the Hindu faith. By its height, the world was signalled a message that the Hindu spirit is indomitable and would grow to meet any obstacle. The unveiling was attended by the country's prime minister and president and many other national figures who, over time, have come to recognize and respect the place and space occupied by the Indian community.

Hindu women in the diaspora have also mounted a serious challenge to their male counterparts in the religious arena. In July 2003, after generations of male domination in the sphere of *Ramayan* recitation, a full panel of women narrated the scriptural epic in verse and song. The panel consisted of Gita Ramsingh, Mayanti Maharaj, and Shakuntala Jangbahadoor, who are well-known for their cultural and devotional activities. Such a formidable feminist gesture is a clear indication of the strength of Indian women who refuse to be suppressed by the barriers of gender.

Indians have contributed a fair share to the region's flora and fauna. Hindus in particular, cultivate consecrated trees in sacred groves to protect the species from destruction and extinction. Plants like the tulsi/basil (*Ocimum sactum*), neem (*Azardiracta indica*) and papal/peepar/banyan (*Figus religiosa*) are cultivated near the *jhandi* (yard shrine) as *in situ* germplasm preservation/collection centres to sustain individual and communal needs. Domesticated cattle and the water buffalo were brought by the British to work as traction animals during Indian indentureship in the Caribbean. The small mongoose was also imported from India to Jamaica, at first, and then to other Caribbean islands to control rats that infested the sugarcane plantations.

Many fourth and fifth generation Indo-Caribbeans are tracing their ancestral roots and are visiting their fore-parents' homes/villages in India. Those who are running away from their identity seem to have forgotten that others define them as Indians, and no matter how they call themselves in the cosmopolitan Caribbean, they cannot escape the fact that they are seen as distinct people.

## Indians in the Smaller Caribbean Islands

### *St. Vincent*

Immigration of indentured labourers became legal in St. Vincent in 1860. Two years after, the first ship to bring Indians to St. Vincent, the *Travancore,* arrived with 260 people. In all, there were eight shiploads of Indians to St. Vincent over this period. The first originated from Madras while the other seven ships left from the port of Calcutta. In all 2,475 Indians, mostly Hindus from the north-western provinces of Bihar and Oudh, were brought to St. Vincent while 1,050 received return passages to India (Register of Immigrants: Immigration Office of St. Vincent, 1861–1880).

Today, East Indians comprise only 5 per cent of the inhabitants of St. Vincent (Mahabir, 2003). While they are scattered in many villages, there are also some areas, notably Richland Park, Calder and Rosebank, where they are concentrated. Even though Indians in St. Vincent have lost all major aspects of their traditional culture like religion, kinship patterns, joint family and caste, they tend to form a separate, identifiable group. This is reflective of the historical separation of Indians from other races in the years of indentureship in the Caribbean. A respondent speaking to Mahabir (2003) of Indian-Black relations at that time notes:

> No, no, no, Black can't come near them. They wouldn't accept them at all. No. That time no Indian at all ever married a black. Negro find their rank; Indian find their own rank. All before that

> time, when we there in the estate, Indian people have nothing to do with Black, and Black people have nothing to do with Indian. You ah Indian, you keep to yourself; you ah black, you keep to yourself. No other people eh mix up with one another.

Race relations have changed dramatically since the earlier times. Indians interact with others on a daily basis in a tension-free manner and participate in the broader social and economic system. They still, however, maintain boundaries between themselves and others and tend not to engage in mixed race marriages.

This progression to more harmonious relations is seen in the writings of Mukdar Publications. The writings of 1974 indicate that higher levels of racial hostility existed even then. The authors write: "We always seem to get justified reasons for the hostilities directed against Indians. It is a pity that we, who have toiled in and for these places, giving our blood, sweat and tears, should be treated with such contempt." The authors explain that one reason for such resentment was related to the perception that Indians controlled a great amount of wealth and, hence, the economy of St. Vincent. However, in reality they state that "they do not control any means of production."

While many traditional aspects of Indian culture have faded as a result of missionary activity and Western influence, other aspects have remained intact. Traditional eating habits, and the affection for Indian foods and spices, have remained much the same as they were in the days of indenture (Stone, 1978). The love of jewellery by Indian women still carries with it the association with traditional culture (Mahabir, 2003).

While vestiges of Indian culture do exist in St. Vincent, more apparent is the adaptation of the original culture. This is due to the numerical insignificance of the Indian groups at specific time periods in the history of St. Vincent (Thomas, 1995). Upon completion of their indentureship contracts, many Indians chose to leave St. Vincent and return to India, or to go to other Caribbean territories like Trinidad, Guyana and Grenada. Large numbers continued to leave St. Vincent up to the 1890s. Additionally, a devastating hurricane which struck in September 1888, and the eruption of the Soufriere volcano in May 1902, had a devastating effect on Indians and their culture. The hurricane destroyed numerous sugar estates and houses of many Indians. The eruption killed over 2,000 people living on estates in the vicinity of the volcano, many of whom were Indians. The census of 1911 gave the Indian population as 377, while the census of 1921 indicated that there were only 265 (Thomas, 1995).

Given the small numbers of Indians in St. Vincent, it is understandable that much of their culture has been altered or even erased. For example, they do not marry according to Hindu or Muslim rites and prefer Christian-derived traditions (Mahabir, 2003). Funeral rites have also changed. Traditionally, where females would not attend funerals, both sexes now accompany the funeral procession. Likewise, the practice of shaving the head of male relatives and the cutting of women's fingernails at the death of a family relation is no longer practiced (Regisford, 1976). The *panchayat* system where community leaders settled disputes also no longer exists and has been superseded by the courts and legal infrastructure.

### *Cuba*

Indian immigration to Cuba, like much of the Caribbean, was stimulated by the labour needs of the sugarcane industry after the abolition of slavery. A notable difference, however, is that the majority of these Indian immigrants came from Jamaica, and only a minority from India. Sarusky (1989) estimates that 2,000 Indian immigrants arrived between 1905 and 1916 while 1,046 arrived between 1920 and 1931. Typically, these immigrants arrived without their families, and later explored the possibility of returning to Jamaica to take their families to Cuba.

Both men and women worked on the sugar plantations, with women receiving lower wages than men for equivalent work. In the early days of Indian arrival, men earned a salary of one peso per day and were required to work for approximately 12 hours. Indians lived in very modest wooden houses and had a harsh life. Additional difficulties were created by the language barrier which existed.

The harshness of plantation life simultaneously erased social and religious differences among the Indians while forcing them to learn Spanish and acculturate to Cuban norms. Despite these difficulties, Indians did strive to preserve some aspects of their cultural heritage. As obtained in other Caribbean territories, Indians were opposed to their daughters having relationships and marrying Cubans who were not of Indian descent (Sarusky, 1989). However, the same did not apply to Indian males, for whom there were no negative sanctions against marrying Cuban women. In so doing, they and their subsequent children acculturated to Cuban habits, culture and idiosyncrasies. The traditional reservation about mixed marriages has been relaxed in recent times, where at present "the majority of women descended from East Indians have married Cuban men" (Sarusky, 1989: 43). As such, economic, social and cultural conditions have resulted in large-scale Indian acculturation to wider Cuban norms.

The cultural practices of Indians in Cuba today reflect this acculturation. For example, on special occasions there may be traditional Indian foods; however, the food consumed by Indians on a daily basis does not differ from that of Cuban families. With respect to religion, ceremonies are carried out in a formalistic manner where very few participants understand the meanings of the various rituals employed. There, however, still persists nostalgia for the ancient customs. This is reflected in some of the retentions of their original culture. One example includes the performance of dance and music which reflect traditional Indian characteristics.

### *St. Lucia*

The 1980–1981 population census of St. Lucia showed that East Indians numbered 2,995 and comprised 2.6 per cent of the population. They are scattered all over the island but concentrations of them are to be found in Augier, Blaka, Marc, Belle Vue, Forrestiere, Vieux Fort, Cocoa and Odsan.

Prior to the introduction of Indians in St. Lucia, there were Africans, Caribs and Europeans. The Africans and Caribs denounced the introduction of East Indian labourers on the basis of economics and social relations (Rampersad, 1988). They maintained that indentured labourers created competition in employment for them. Indeed, jobs which would have originally gone to the Africans and Caribs were offered to the new immigrants. Like in the case of the other Caribbean territories, this was a strategy employed by the colonial administrators, who in this case, saw it fit to import Indian labour on a non-contractual basis to demolish the Africans' and Caribs' control of the labour market. The colonial officers even offered incentives such as land in lieu of a return passage to encourage the Indian labourers to stay in St. Lucia. As a consequence "a systematic campaign of harassment against East Indians was undertaken by Africans and Caribs" (Rampersad, 1988: 37). Even many years after, when it was recognized that the colonial imperialists were the common enemy "the African never showed any sympathy ... for the social transformation of East Indians' struggles in St. Lucia, but still bitterly and violently attacked East Indians" (Rampersad, 1988: 37). Additionally, Africans resented the fact that there was a limited amount of land, which they felt belonged to them, but which was being occupied by Indians. Indeed, one of the main issues which disturbed Africans was that while Indians were granted land under the Indentureship agreement, they did not get any when slavery was abolished. Unknown to Africans, this was a strategy used to encourage Indians to remain in St. Lucia. Rampersad (1988: 30) is, therefore, correct to assert that "Most of the evils Africans and East Indians in St. Lucia face, including ethnic conflict, have their historical roots in the colonial establishment of slavery, the indentureship system, and neo-colonialism."

In the past, while the vast majority of Indians were poor, the society did not make a distinction between the rich and poor Indian, and all faced many injustices and pressures from the wider society (*Mukdar*, 1974). It has been pointed out that "Indians could not even listen to the Indian radio programmes from Trinidad and Guyana in their own homes" (*Mukdar*, 1974: 9). These authors contend that such hostility should not have occurred, given that Indians did not constitute an economic, political or social threat. With such difficulties, it is understandable that Indians in St. Lucia have managed to hold on to only a few vestiges of their original culture. For example, a few people still practice, albeit infrequently, the art of cooking Indian food, singing Indian songs, and reciting Hindi prayers.

Apart from social and economic pressures, many other factors have resulted in the assimilation of Indians into the wider culture. The relatively small numbers who immigrated to St. Lucia, as well as their high rate of repatriation to India, and their relocation to other Caribbean territories are other factors. Joseph (2003), for example, notes that in the first three years of indenture, 1,535 labourers came to St. Lucia, while in the same period, 911 decided to be repatriated. The vast majority of Indians coming to St. Lucia viewed themselves as transient residents and came with the intention of returning to their homeland in India (Joseph, 2003). Additionally, the offer of £10 per adult or 10 acres of land was not sufficient to encourage Indians to remain in St. Lucia once their period of service was fulfilled. In all,

56 per cent of the immigrants were repatriated from St. Lucia (Roberts, 1891).

Additionally, the system of education, the status of the local economy, government's policy toward Indians, and their wide spatial distribution contributed to their assimilation. Joseph (2003) notes the rough terrain of St. Lucia and the underdeveloped transportation system precluded the frequent meeting of Indians. Indians were also scattered throughout the island over a wide spatial area. The small number of Indians on each estate, compounded with the erratic trend of immigration of Indians to the island, added to the difficulty in resisting assimilation. Indians in St. Lucia, therefore, never achieved sufficient population density to perpetuate and preserve their original cultural heritage. The poor state of the economy and the resultant low wages, as well as the unfriendly attitude towards Indians was also a contributory factor.

The proselytizing campaigns of the church also discouraged the communal spirit of Hinduism and Islam, considered then to be "heathen" Indian religions. "The proselytising work of the church demanded that Indians abandon their traditional beliefs and practices of Hinduism and Islam, and learn new beliefs, roles, habits, language, dress, attitudes and overall behaviour" (Mahabir and Maharaj, 1993: 236). The Canadian Presbyterian mission attempted to focus on the Indian community. Their efforts, however, were unsuccessful and resulted in the closure of a number of schools and churches. The withdrawal of the Presbyterian mission led Indians to attend churches and educational facilities that were used by the majority of the population, thereby accelerating acculturation. Mahabir and Maharaj (1993: 234) describe the situation of Indians in St. Lucia today as one of "almost complete biological and cultural assimilation".

What is significant about their assimilation is that they have not adapted their cultural heritage to the new setting, but rather have abandoned it in favour of a new identity and have adopted the culture of the wider, predominantly black community. Today, despite political participation and economic success by some Indians, there appears to be no systematic attempt to perform any function, even if discreet, to consolidate the Indian community (Mahabir and Maharaj, 1993).

### *Belize*

The authors of *Mukdar* (1974) indicate that in 1974 there were approximately 5,000 Indians in Belize. Several historians (e.g.,

Hosein, 1988) have also indicated that Indian "sepoys" (soldiers) were deported to Belize after the Indian mutiny in 1857. Estimates indicate that over 1,000 convicted rebels and their families were deported to Belize, then called British Honduras. Originally introduced to work on the sugar and citrus plantations, they still struggle to break free of the social and economic barriers of plantation confinement. Nevertheless, a few Indians in Belize have entered a number of professions, including teaching, shop-keeping, civil service employment. Others have even managed to enter high-level jobs through university education. The vast majority of Indians in Belize, however, represent a depressed minority who still live in rural villages.

While deculturation has taken place, Indians in Belize pride themselves on the cultural retentions which they have been able to retain. They have extended their friendship to Indians in other parts of the Caribbean with the hope of reviving their ancestral culture. At present, their contact with Indians in nearby Jamaica is their main means of sustaining their cultural heritage and traditions.

### *Grenada*

Though Indians number more than 9,700 in Grenada and form the largest minority group in the island, sociological and other writings have made only passing reference to them. One of the few systematic attempts to remedy this shortcoming includes a research paper by Kumar Mahabir (1994) entitled "East Indians in Grenada: A Study in Absorption". He writes: "The history of East Indians in Grenada is essentially a record of a relatively powerless ethnic group submitting without any organized resistance to an environment unfavourable to it in almost every sense." Disorganized and numerically small, Indians in Grenada have been unable to resist the pressure of homogenization to fit into the Black/African image.

Emigration of indentured labourers to Grenada was legalized in 1856, and 3,033 Indians were brought into the island between that time and 1878. Mortality rates were high, both in the Middle Passage and on the various estates. Neglect by those in charge was to blame for much of this misfortune (Mahabir, 1994). Surprisingly, the majority of Indians opted for the possession of land rather than the free return passage entitled to them after their labour contract.

As in other Caribbean territories, the Presbyterian missionaries attempted to 'educate' and 'civilize' Indian Hindus and Muslims in

Grenada. A notable absence of Indian priests hastened the rapidity of conversion to the Christian faith. The few *pundits* [Hindu priests] who existed at the time were insufficient to foster values which encouraged resistance to this conversion. Anglicization was made complete, and today there "is not a single community mosque or temple in Grenada" (Mahabir, 1994: 6). Indeed, by 1964, Fr. Devas noted that there was not a single Hindu or Muslim remaining in Grenada.

But despite the efforts of the church and the explicit aim of the state to bring about "the complete extinction of any survival of Indianness among the Grenadian Indians," there have remained, albeit in a modified form, some cultural retentions (Mahabir, 1994: 9). 'Borgh' is one such example. This ceremony consists of a function held on the second anniversary of a death, and is marked by fasting and the performance of Indian songs and dances. Additionally, Indian songs, musical instruments and dances have managed to survive, even if only in a restricted way. Another practice still observed is 'Mundan' or the shaving of a child's head within a year of birth, or on the second birthday. Indian cuisine including *roti,* curried goat and various forms of *tarkari* [cooked vegetables] along with many other traditional delicacies, still exist and have spread to the tables of many non-Indian families.

Race relations in Grenada appear to be among the most harmonious in the Caribbean (Mahabir, 1994). This obtained even in the days of indenture, perhaps because the sugar industry was on a decline, thus reducing the possibility of competition between Indians and ex-slaves for a limited number of jobs. While the initial phases of indenture still witnessed the characteristic separateness of both groups, eventually a healthy relationship developed to the extent that some Africans spoke Hindi and were allowed to sit on the *panchayats* (village courts). That race relations continue to be harmonious is indicated by the fact that the rate of inter-racial mixing in Grenada is the highest in the Caribbean.

### *Guadeloupe*

On December 24, 1854, the first group of Indians, numbering 344 in all, arrived in Guadeloupe on the ship "Aurelie". By the end of immigration in 1885, over 40,000 Indians had arrived on the island (Balram, 1988). Earlier immigrants had come illegally, both from India and other Caribbean islands. It was not until 1862 that the law forbidding emigration to the French colonies was repealed

(Jah, 1993). In India, immigrants came mainly from the ports of Pondicherry and Karikal in the south and were primarily Tamil-speaking. Approximately 80 per cent were from southern India and came mainly from Pondicherry, Madurai, Bangalore and Madras. This trend is in contrast to other Caribbean territories which received mainly Northern Indian indentured immigrants speaking Bhojpuri, Bengali, Urdu and Punjabi (Latchana, 1988a). Today, approximately 12.5–16 per cent of the population in Guadeloupe is of Indian origin (Schnepel, 1993).

As in the other colonial territories, ethnic and racial conflict seemed to be triggered by cultural and phenotypical differences between Indians and Africans. Economic tensions, in a split labour market organized along ethnic lines, appeared however, to be the factor of primary importance. "Even into the 20th century, the White planters played off this antagonism ... by using Indians as strike-breakers, transporting them to work in communities where there were labour disputes; thus, undercutting Blacks' struggle for economic and social justice" (Singaravelou, 1975: 184). Such tensions, together with the geographic isolation of the Indians (primarily in cane-producing rural areas such as northern and eastern Grande-Terre, Basse-Terre and Papaye-Mantouba) facilitated the continued separation of both groups, and precluded biological and cultural assimilation.

Other factors, however, worked against the maintenance of such divisions. Upon arrival, Indians were urged to assimilate, and by so doing, abandoned their native clothes and traditions, but more importantly their mother tongues (Sankarsingh, 2001). Religion, for Indians, shoulders the basic framework of their culture. Given that Hindi was the language of their holy scriptures and the medium through which they were taught, the loss of Hindi represented another significant blow to cultural retention. Additionally, in 1905, their practices suffered another blow with the introduction of a law in France which made Catholicism the religion of the state and, therefore, of its colonies. "Hindu ceremonies and marriages were not recognized by the state, and books such as the *Ramayana* and *Bhagavad-Gita,* were confiscated and replaced by the Bible" (Sankarsingh, 2001).

The passage of Departmentalist Law in March 1946 had the inadvertent effect of further eroding the cultural identity of Indians. The islands of the French Caribbean were transformed into an overseas department of France. All these laws facilitated the expansion of French institutions and integrated the colonial economies with the metropolis. Cultural assimilation was intensified with the expansion of the French education system and increased diffusion of the French language (Schnepel, 1993). With this came the imposition of the French cultural model to the detriment of the local island cultures.

The need to recognize the distinct cultural identity of the Antilles led the local Communist parties to initiate a debate in the late 1950s on the question of future political autonomy of the French colonies. With this debate came the forging of a national Afro-Creole culture which was decidedly different from French culture, and was reflective of the distinctiveness of Guadeloupian society. The derogatory image of the black slave was disbanded and replaced by a theory of resistance. Songs, dances and music of African or slave origins were revived and took on a new cultural, symbolic and political significance. These cultural expressions were an articulation of a legitimate Guadeloupian culture in direct opposition to the imposed French model.

Research by Schnepel (1993) indicates that the Indian community was not supportive of this Afro-Creole movement which members felt was exclusionary and neglected Indians as a distinct and contributory part of the Guadeloupian culture. Indians reacted to the way in which Creole, the 'product,' was packaged, to the message with which it was identified, as well as to the very groups promoting it. This new movement created feelings of insecurity among many Indians who were particularly sceptical of the nationalist ideology conceived by the Creole bourgeoisie and intelligentsia to serve their own interests.

With this Afro-Creole movement came the struggle of Indians for equal rights and recognition of their distinct cultural identity in Guadeloupe. In 1971, for example, the L'Association Guadeloupeane des Amis de L'Inde was formed with the aim of promoting knowledge of India, its civilization and culture. Other local associations were formed to teach yoga, Tamil, dance, and other creative arts, while new institutional ties were established with India. Additionally, an ambitious programme of cultural activities was mapped out. Museum exhibits, musical and dance productions, films screenings and public meetings were aimed specifically to promote Indian culture. More recently a journal,

*Le Soleil Indien: Regard et Contre-regards sur le Monde Indien,* has been established. It must be noted that there is a huge difference in Indian culture, traditions and customs in Guadeloupe and Martinique when compared to that of Indians in other Caribbean territories. This cultural difference reflects the domination of Southern practices over Northern Indian observances. This difference is also derived from the fusion of all Indian-derived religions into one by religious leaders shortly after 1905. This Indo-Creole creation was done as a strategy to preserve Indian cultural identity in response to religious persecution by the French authorities. This resurgence of interest in Indian identity was led largely by a class of elites of Indian background with important positions in business, the civil service, and the intellectual elite of the island. In essence, they have undertaken to become actively involved in re-discovering and re-claiming their Indian roots, and assisting other Guadeloupe Indians interested in a process of "re-ethnicisation" or "re-Indianisation" (Schnepel, 1993).

### *Martinique*

Martinique has received 25,509 Indians as indentured labourers out of which many of them had died or were repatriated. By the end of 1898, approximately 10,000 were counted (Japp, 1900). As in Guadeloupe and other French territories, these immigrants came primarily from Southern India. The early days of indenture were difficult for them. Nobel Prize laureate novelist V.S. Naipaul, quoting a Martiniquan, wrote that "they died like flies." Under the exploitation of French planters, coupled with the crippling economic climate, they were unable to escape the plantation and set up their own small farms through the purchase of land.

It is perhaps because of these struggles that Indians in Martinique have attempted to hold on to their traditional culture. The hard times created a network of relations of sufferers who shared a common experience and reinforced a feeling of cultural identity. Latchana (1988b: 25) notes that to this day "South Indian traditions have persisted, albeit modified, and in forms which have long died out in India." In Martinique, many temples can be found which are scattered throughout the island. These are the focal points of convergence for Hindu ceremonies which involve extensive decorations, food offerings, constant drumming and other features of traditional Indian practice. Additionally, the use of *kandyi* (a mixture of rice, coconut, onion and salt), the breaking open of a dry coconut, and the ritual use of limes, saffron, incense and camphor are all traditions derived from India. There are also elements reminiscent of Kali-worship in Southern India. These include spirit possessions, animal sacrifice, flag hoisting and fasting from salt. These ceremonies are typically followed by a feast.

Syncretisms can also be seen in many of the religious practices in Martinique. While many Indians are Roman Catholic, many religious ceremonies incorporate both Hindu and Catholic elements in their worship. For example, many of the deities in Hindu practice are associated with Catholic saints. The chief deity, Maldevidan, is also known as Vishnu, and in the Catholic pantheon is identified with Christ or St. Michael. Another major deity is Mariamman, and who is identified with the Catholic Virgin Mary. On Pentecost and Easter Sunday, elaborate ceremonies that resemble Kali-worship in Guyana and Trinidad are conducted. The Tamil language is often used in these religious practices.

Latchana (1988b) contends that such syncretisms reflect the need for adjustment by Indians in Martinique. Syncreticism was also brought about by the interplay of diverse sources of knowledge and the fusion of ritual elements from the many villages in Southern India from which immigrants came. Indians in Martinique faced less difficulty in retaining their traditional culture when compared to their counterparts in other Caribbean territories. Unlike Indians in the other smaller Caribbean islands, Indians in Martinique and Guadeloupe show great interest in re-discovering and re-claiming their culture of their forefathers in India.

## Conclusion

Indians have experienced much ridicule and hardships in the Caribbean, especially in the early days of Indentureship when they were despised by the newly-freed African slaves. Distrust existed because of phenotypical and cultural differences, and because the newly-introduced Indian immigrant labourers caused wages to decrease on the sugarcane plantations. Though both groups share a common history of colonial oppression, they have never been able to share a united cultural platform against the minority European elite that has controlled their destiny for centuries. In the odd moments when such a united platform was formed, Indians felt that they were marginalized even when they constituted half of the population of that society.

After 160 years in the Caribbean, Indian culture in Trinidad and Guyana has undergone change, adaptation, survival and triumph. In other countries like the smaller Caribbean islands (including Jamaica), Indian culture has been almost erased and replaced by the dominant Afro-European cultures of the territories which Indians have made their homes. In these countries, the numbers of Indians are so small that a resurgence of Indian culture seems improbable, and assimilation and absorption seems inevitable.

While today, Indians form a significant part of the Caribbean's cultural, social and economic landscape, their culture has received less recognition by the media and the government than it deserves. Institutional racial discrimination against Indians in Trinidad and Guyana has led to an increase in ethnic consciousness, and the development and affirmation of an Indian cultural identity that is unique to the Caribbean.

The recent resurgence of interest by Indians in their cultural heritage also indicates that they recognize that their cultural heritage was being threatened by alien practices and traditions. This alien culture was being imposed upon them—not to assist them as a community—but to make them subservient to the needs of the economically-dominant groups of the region. With greater economic independence, educational opportunities, communication networks, and travel to India, Caribbean Indians are attempting to revive the traditions which were brought by their forefathers from their ancestral land.

## References

Bajpai, G. 2001. "Colonialism and Emigration: The Movement of People from North India to Trinidad During 1870s and 1900". St. Augustine, Trinidad. Unpublished paper. Department of History, The University of the West Indies.

Balram, R. 1988. "Indians in Guadeloupe". In M. Latchana, and P. Hanoomansingh, (eds.), *East Indians in the Caribbean, 150th Anniversary, 1838–1988,* p. 22. Toronto, York University: Indo-Caribbean Conference Brochure.

Dutt, R. 1969, *The Economic History of India in the Victorian Age,* Vol. II. New York: August M. Kelley Publishers.

Hosein, J. 1988, "Ex-sepoys in Belize". In M. Latchana and P. Hanoomansingh, (eds.), *East Indians in the Caribbean, 150th Anniversary, 1838–1988,* p. 26. Toronto, York University: Indo-Caribbean Conference Brochure.

Jah, J. 1993. "The Immigration of Indian Labour to the French West Indies in the Second Half of the Nineteenth Century". In J.K., Motwani, M. Gosine and J. Barot Motwani, (eds.) *Global Indian Diaspora: Yesterday, Today and Tomorrow,* pp. 216–224. New York: Global Organization of People of Indian Origin.

Japp, J. 1900. *British Consul at Martinique to British Secretary of State for Foreign Affairs,* August 31, 1899, No. 16. Government of India, Bihar State Archives: Department of Revenue and Agriculture-Emigration.

Joseph, T.K. 2003. *An Invisible Existence: The Experience of Indians in St. Lucia, 1859–1979*. St. Augustine, Trinidad: Department of History, The University of the West Indies.

Latchana, Michael. 1988a. "Indian Immigration to the Caribbean". In M. Latchana and P. Hanoomansingh (eds.) *East Indians in the Caribbean, 150th Anniversary, 1838–1988,* p. 5. Toronto, York University: Indo-Caribbean Conference Brochure.

—. 1988b. "Indian Immigrants in Martinique". In M. Latchana and P. Hanoomansingh, (eds.) *East Indians in the Caribbean, 150th Anniversary, 1838–1988,* pp. 25–31. Toronto, York University: Indo-Caribbean Conference Brochure.

Mahabir, K. 1994. "East Indians in Grenada: A Study of Absorption". In M. Gosine, (ed.), *The East Indian Odyssey: Dilemmas of a Migrant People,* pp. 93–110. New York: Windsor Press.

—. 2003. *Indians of St. Vincent*. St. Augustine, Trinidad: Main Library, The University of the West Indies.

Mahabir, K. and Maharaj, A. 1993. "The Assimilation of a Minority Group: The East Indians of St. Lucia". In J.K, Motwani, M. Gosine and J. Barot-Motwani, (eds.), *Global Indian Diaspora: Yesterday, Today and Tomorrow,* pp. 234–250. New York: Global Organization of People of Indian Origin.

*Mukdar*. 1974. *Indians in the Caribbean*. Curepe, Trinidad: Indian Revival and Reform Association.

Rampersad, A. 1988. *The Colonial Legacy in St. Lucia: An East Indian Perspective*. Trinidad: Omega Bookshops Limited.

Regisford, M. 1976. *The Assimilation of East Indians into Vincentian Social Structure: A Comparative View*. St. Augustine, Trinidad: Main Library, The University of the West Indies.

Roberts, G.W. 1891. *The Population of St. Lucia*. Port of Spain, Trinidad: Publisher Unknown.

Sankarsingh, C. 2001. *Indians in Guadeloupe*. West Indies, Publisher Unknown.

Sarusky, J. 1989. "The East Indian Community in Cuba" in *The East Indian Community in the Caribbean*. Cuba: Latin American Continental Student Organization.

Schnepel, M. 1993. "The Creole Movement and East Indians on the Island of Guadeloupe, French West Indies". In J.K. Motwani, M. Gosine and J. Barot-Motwani, (eds.), *Global Indian Diaspora: Yesterday, Today and Tomorrow*, pp. 225–233. New York: Global Organization of People of Indian Origin.

Singaravelou. 1975. *Les Indiens de la Guadeloupe: Etude de Geographie Humaine*. Bordeaux: CNRS.

Stone, L. 1978. "East Indian Adaptations in St. Vincent: Richland Park". In T. Fraser, (ed.), *Windward Road: Contributions to the Anthropology of St. Vincent*, pp. 148–155. New York: Amherst.

Thomas, A. 1995. "Portuguese and Indian Immigration to St. Vincent (1885–1890)". *Journal of Caribbean Studies*, 14 (1 and 2).

# 6

# Transforming Diaspora

## Familiarity with Alien Terrains

KARTHIYAINI DEVARAJOO

Literary works by diasporic writers have been used extensively in diaspora studies recently. A study by Sandten explores Sujata Bhatt's literary works to examine how diasporic writers relate to the foreignness that they experience in their lives and are consequently able to reach out to other minority communities in the world. Sujata Bhatt, bicultural by birth and migration and tri-cultural by marriage, was born in Ahmedabad, India and when she was twelve her parents moved to the United States. She married a German writer and lives in Northern Germany. She had written in an autobiographical essay that her experience in life has given her the ability to comprehend in-depth other environments without being 'intimidated or overwhelmed by its foreignness' (quoted in Sandten 99). Diasporic writers, some who are in exile while others are later generations of immigrant communities, seem to have an ability to relate to other minority communities globally, the alien terrains. Sandten quotes Sujatha Bhatt's description of her own experience of exile:

> It is a power to comprehend, interpret and thus enter into the depths of almost any environment by writing about it imaginatively. It is also a power to control and give shape to any given environment in order not to be intimidated or overwhelmed by its foreignness. Ultimately, I believe that as a writer and a human being, the more languages and cultures that one intimately understands, the closer one comes to understanding the essence of life itself. (109)

I explore and chart the transformation in the Indian diaspora as documented in novels in English by Malaysian writers of Indian origin and the familiarity the writers of later generations of the diaspora strike with other minority communities globally, the alien terrains.

## Documentation of the Indian Experience

Writers of Indian origin worldwide have contributed towards the documentation of the Indian experience. They are prolific and have successfully made an impact globally by producing commendable writings that have gained global recognition. These include writers like Anita Desai, R.K. Narayan, V.S. Naipaul, Salman Rushdie, Arundhathi Roy, Jumpha Lahiri, Chitra Banerjee Divakaruni and Vikram Seth. Salman Rushdie states in the *The Vintage Book of Indian Writing (1947–1997)*, that "... this new, and still burgeoning, 'Indo-Anglican' literature represents perhaps the most valuable contribution India has yet made to the world of books"(x). I believe literature develops only in a settled and conducive environment. Compared to the Indians who migrated to the USA and the UK, the Indians who landed in Malaysia were the poverty-stricken peasants. Thus, the desire to document their experiences was delayed till they settled to a comfortable lifestyle.

An attempt to capture the Indian experience globally was also made through the publication of the *Encyclopaedia of Indian Diaspora* (2006) which was funded by Citibank. This encyclopaedia charts the growth of the Indian diaspora and aims to consolidate their achievements and contributions to global culture, business and arts. It also surveys the worldwide spread of the Indian communities that set out to maintain their 'Indian-ness' in a range of ways—through music, language, religion and dress.

Limited writings by Indians in Malaysia over the last 100 years confirm the lack of documentation of the Indian experiences in Malaysia, either through fiction or non-fiction. Currently, various NGOs are playing an active role in reprinting early documentations on Indians in Malaysia, which are no more in circulation in the public domain. In 2004, a 1938 non-fiction publication entitled *Indian Problems in Malaya: A Brief Survey in Relation to Emigration* (1900–1938) by K.A. Neelakandha Aiyer, which is not in circulation anymore, was reprinted by GOPIO, Malaysia for public consumption and as support for academic research on Indians in Malaysia and specifically Malaysians in general.

**Malaysian Writers of Indian Origin and their Novels**

After more than a century of making Malaysia their home, the Indians in Malaysia see a need to document their experiences in life. Of late there has been a sudden publication 'explosion' of literary works by Malaysians of Indian origin. Five Malaysian Indian women (Aneeta Sundraraj, Shoba Mano, Rani Manicka, Muthammal Palanisamy and D. Devika Bai and K.S. Maniam) within a span of four years, i.e., 2002–2005 published a total of seven novels in English. Two of these writers have already released their second novels, i.e., Rani Manicka and Shoba Mano. K.S. Maniam is an established Malaysian writer of Indian origin who has been publishing literary works since the 1980s. He is the "inaugural recipient of the prestigious Raja Rao Award" (September 2000, New Delhi) for his outstanding contribution to the Literature of the South (Author's Profile, *Between Lives).* Rani Manicka is a Malaysian writer of Indian origin based in the United Kingdom. Her *The Rice Mother* (2002), which was published in the United Kingdom, has been described as "A Malaysian Dynasty" because it portrays the lifestyle of one Indian family over four generations in Malaysia.

The 21st century also sees a rise in the number of Malaysian Indians writing in English and Bahasa Malaysia. Malaysians of Indian origin initially marked their contribution towards the development of Malaysian literature in English through Sybil Kathigasu. She wrote of the atrocities of the Second World War, especially the Japanese Occupation in Malaya in the early 1940s (Nor Faridah and Mohammad Quayum 2001: 13). Kathigasu is described as a woman ahead of her time and she faced much political struggle in the hands of the British with her husband and adopted son. However, her books are not available in the market now.

In the 1960s and 1970s, Lloyd Fernando's and K.S. Maniam's literary works caught the limelight. Until Rani Manicka's *The Rice Mother* (2002), the closest Malaysia got to a truly Malaysian story was Lloyd Fernando's novella *Green is the Colour* (1993). K.S. Maniam's first novel, *The Return,* a good text for a post-colonial reading, was first published in 1981 and then in 1993.

Marie Gerrina Louis published the next novel, her first, *The Road to Chandibole* (1994) and *Junos* (1995). Her first novel was set in Malaysia and the second in Calcutta and Singapore. Though I managed to read her first novel, there is not much information available on Louis as a Malaysian writer. Since 2002, however, there have been several novels: beginning with the publication of Rani Manicka's *The Rice Mother* (2002), *Touching Earth* (2004) and K.S. Maniam's second novel *Between Lives* (2003). Two other writers of Indian origin in Malaysia who have published novels in English include Aneetha Sundaraj (*Banana Leaf Man*, 2004) and Shoba Mano (*Love's Treacherous Terrain*, 2003, *Prodigal Child*, 2005).

During an interview, Mano revealed that she is already working on her third novel, *Echoes of the Angels*. Shoba Mano's second novel *Prodigal Child* was launched during the 2005 Book Exhibition in New York in June 2005. It has received impressive reviews since the launch. She is the first Asian to publish a romance novel in the United States. The Regent of Perak launched Aneeta Sundraraj's second book *The Autobiography of Tan Sri Dr Mahathevan* in 2004. The release of these books begins to fill the void that existed in the Malaysian literature scene. This publication augurs well for the local literary scene, especially for writings in English.

Another writer is Muthammal Palanisamy who wrote *Shore to Shore* (2004). She writes about her family's trials and tribulations during the pre and post-independence period in Malaysia. Issues of culture and tradition form the spine of this book. The writer chronicles the overwhelming effects of the 'imperial aggression' that split her family between two nations, Malaysia and India. The diaspora is in the making because the family connections are still strong and this link is financially supported through the family's firm economic grounding in Malaysia. Thus, the family is able to keep the physical links with India and they are not emotionally severed from their motherland. This novel seems to appeal to Indians in the sub-continent to quite an impressive extent. An interview with the author in October 2005 revealed that she has garnered interest to produce the same novel in Tamil and her fans organized an all paid for official launch of the Tamil version in Tamil Nadu in December 2005.

Another new writer is Devika Bai. Devika's debut novel, *The Flight of the Swans,* released in the US at the end of 2005, is her family saga on the Bhonsles. She is currently working on her second novel, also set in British India and Malaya.

Most literary studies in Malaysia are based on Maniam's works. Lesser known authors like Mano, Manicka, Sundararaj and Palanisamy have yet to receive sufficient critical attention in the field of literary study locally and abroad. Three Malaysian writers' works will be discussed here: K.S. Maniam, Shoba Mano and Rani Manicka. These three writers represent three different categories of Malaysian writers of Indian origin: Maniam is a senior writer residing in Malaysia, Mano is a junior writer residing in Malaysia and Manicka is a junior writer residing abroad.

**Transformation in the Writings**

Every community in the world strives to document its experiences and traces its past to be able to pave the path for its future. If members of a community do not dynamically reflect on their own status and contribution in today's fast-paced world, the community will face a natural death. It will be extinguished from the face of the earth like a flame and in years to come be forgotten and its future generations will be unable to trace their origins.

Writers can sustain the cultural heritage of their community through the production of interesting and appealing literary works. K.S. Maniam's vision[1] for the Malaysian novel to reach out and appeal to consumers in the global market was through a multicultural Malaysian setting. He toed the line in visioning the government's Malaysian national identity. However, the volatility of the diaspora consumes any form of patterned and structured predictions and identity formations for diasporic writers.

I perceive the diaspora as a volatile state because the diasporic individual, community or nation is constantly under pressure to evolve, to either integrate or assimilate. Historical facts support a general trend that French and Dutch colonies were under pressure to assimilate like in Mauritius and Indonesia, whereas the British colonies were under pressure to integrate like in Malaysia and India. Assimilation is a humiliation to the immigrant or native communities because they lose their ethnic identities through suppression of their racial, cultural, traditional and religious practices by the colonizers. As for integration, the immigrant and native communities are given the freedom to practice their racial, cultural, traditional and religious practices with due respect for other communities living together.

Hybridity is the catalytic element that supports the transformation of an individual or community from being a diaspora to being the citizen of the host country and to finally being a world citizen. Malaysia has always been a model of multiculturalism to the world and many Malaysians take the May 16, 1969 racial riots in their stride and admit that the incident was a learning experience for all Malaysians to be remembered but not stirred. It cannot be denied that it was a thought-provoking event in the history of Malaysia and even till today it triggers cautious responses from various quarters. And it also cannot be denied that Malaysia is still the best model the world has on peace and harmony in a multicultural, multiracial and multiethnic nation.

The transformation that the Indian diaspora in Malaysia undergoes is a gradual shift from one stage to another, seen through the works of these three different authors over a period of 12 years. Apart from tracing the change through the works of three different authors over a period of 12 years as reflected in the timeline in Diagram 1, this study also supports the transformation seen through the different novels by the same writer. The transformations observed are seen from two perspectives:

1. Novels by a senior writer as compared to novels by the younger generation of writers.
2. Different novels written by the same writer over a period of time.

The earliest published novel in this selection is by Maniam, *The Return* (1993), which revolves around an Indian family in pre-independence Malaysia. He highlights issues pertaining to the appropriation of the English culture and language by the protagonist Ravi and the state of being displaced as experienced by the character Periathai. Diaspora issues of divided allegiance and being ambivalent in the hostland are also addressed in this novel. Maniam's novel in 2003, *Between Lives,* discusses all the above issues in addition to issues pertaining to racial and cultural tolerance and integration in multicultural Malaysia. Unlike *The Return,* this novel supports a multicultural image of Malaysia with Malay and Chinese characters. This reflects the changes in the writings by the same author over a period of time. Maniam's personal experiences as a descendent of an immigrant Indian in Malaysia seem to colour the novel with issues of place and displacement which are significant themes by diaporic writers.

*The Rice Mother* (2002) by Rani Manicka and *Between Lives* (2003) seem to bridge the transformation from issues related to diasporas solely to multicultural Malaysia. As observed in *Between Lives,* Rani Manicka too highlights issues pertaining to diasporas initially and then moves on to issues that inflict Malaysians during the Japanese occupation and post-independence Malaysia. Widower Malaysian

Indian, Ayah gets married to Lakshmi and they both return to Malaysia to start a family. Lakshmi shares her longing for her homeland Ceylon with fellow diaspora, Mui Tsai, her neighbour. As the novel unfolds, Lakshmi discards her diasporic longing for her homeland and settles in the hostland, Malaysia.

The transformation in the writings of Malaysian Indian writers continue with Shoba Mano, who seems to be the first writer to move away completely from issues pertaining to the diaspora and portrays the Malaysian Indian as a citizen of the nation. The protagonists in *Love's Treacherous Terrain* (2003), Tanusha and Ashwin, are later generations of Indian immigrants who are citizens of the nation and issues highlighted in both these novels include racial tolerance, cultural integration with mix marriages as an issue in the lives of the characters. The writers, Rani Manicka and Shoba Mano, are themselves later generations of Malaysian Indians.

Both these young writers' second novels move away from issues pertaining to the Malaysian citizen to highlight concerns of other global minority communities. Rani Manicka's *Touching Earth* (2004), revolves around the lives of Balinese twins, Nutan and Zeenat who desperately try to make a living in London with other non-English characters who are themselves 'lost souls' in an alien terrain. Shoba Mano's *Prodigal Child* (2005), sympathizes with the Amerasians in Vietnam who are considered 'children of the dust'. Both the writers revert to issues that relate to diasporic communities such as displacement, longing for home and a quest for identity. Though all the characters in these two novels are non-Malaysians, both writers who are Malaysians of Indian origin provide a voice platform for minority communities with a familiarity that beckons some form of recognition and by doing so they function as citizens of the world. The above observations made can be projected on a timeline as shown in Diagram 1.

The themes and issues in the contemporary Malaysian novels in English are evolving over time. All the three writers showed a gradual shift in the themes and issues in their writing, i.e., from themes that support diasporic issues to national issues and finally to global issues. At the same time, themes and issues in each individual writer too seem to evolve from a diasporic to national as seen in K.S. Maniam's works or from national to global as seen in Rani Manicka's and Shoba Mano's works.

**Diagram 1**

*Evolving Themes and Issues in Novels by Malaysian Writers of Indian Origin*

| Diaspora<br>19th Century | Citizen<br>of a Nation | Citizen of the World<br>21st Century |
|---|---|---|
| | *Themes and Issues* | |
| Appropriation, displaced, allegiance | Racial and cultural tolerance/integration | Represent global exile, minority communities, ambivalent reach out to the world |
| | Novels | |
| *The Return (1993)*<br>*Between Lives (2003)* | *The Rice Mother (2002)*<br>*Love's Treacherous Terrain (2003)* | *Touching Earth (2004)*<br>*Prodigal Child (2005)* |

Being a diaspora is a temporary transitional phase in an individual or community. Members of a diasporic community are not diasporic generation after generation. After a few generations in the hostland, the later generations of a diasporic community seem to be no longer diasporic. They seem to assume stable national identities with an ability to later identify themselves with other minority or diasporic communities around the world. This transformation that the diasporic individual or community undergoes seems borderless for the themes, issues and characters transcend ethnic, racial, cultural, community, regional and national borders and boundaries. The later transformed writings of these Malaysian writers of Indian origin become the platform of various voices. Representations range from men, women, children, the rich, the poor, the powerful, the weak, the diasporic, the nationalist, the lost souls, the down-trodden, the Muslims, the Hindus, the Christians, the Malays, the Chinese, the Indians, the Malaysians, the Eurasians, the ChinIndians (children of Chinese and Indian mixed-parentage as found in Malaysia), Vietnamese, Amerasians, Americans, the clergy, Balinese, Italian, Spanish, English, drug addicts and prostitutes. If any creative writing can support the above range of representations, then it must be truly borderless and as such novels by Malaysian Indians can be categorized as transcending all the above borders to be considered international literature.

## The Success of Malaysian Novels

An interesting observation made is that the younger generation of Malaysian Indian writers were providing a voice platform for the minority communities around the world and their novels, such as *Touching Earth* and *Prodigal Child,* seem to achieve this by reverting to the diasporic themes and issues as discussed in early novels like *The Return* and *Between Lives.* Thus, Sujatha Bhatt's view that being a diaspora allows her to relate to the foreignness with ease seems to be true for our young Malaysian writers.

The twist in the international success of novels by Malaysian writers of Indian origin is that they do not reflect the multicultural model that Maniam envisioned in his article "The New Diaspora". Manicka's *Touching Earth* and Mano's *Prodigal Child,* who are the younger generation of writers, are having good reviews without any Malaysian characters at all, not even an Indian character. The diaspora is present in these novels but they are non-Indian. These writers are addressing diasporic issues but among other minority communities that are diaporic. The "internationalization" of community literatures is also affected by various other factors. One of it is institutional support as was discussed by K.S. Maniam. Institutional investment has the potential of promoting community literatures produced by Malaysian writers.

Novels by the younger generation of Malaysian writers of Indian origin support a unique feature which appeals to the world at large. Malaysia epitomizes Jawarhalal Nehru's motto 'Unity in diversity' to promote national and world peace. The multiracial and multicultural experience of the Malaysian Indian enables him to relate to the world at large with greater ease as compared to one from a homogenous society.

Rani Manicka is enjoying international recognition through various intellectual discussions held on her earlier novel *The Rice Mother* at several book clubs in England and also on both the East and West coasts of America. The *Rice Mother* has been translated into several European languages. Manicka's books are found in various other places such as "at Borders Singapore, at Heathrow in England, Melbourne, Australia, in Zanzibar, at the Slipway (Malaysia's version of Bintang Walk) with large posters pasted everywhere and in Tanzania".

## Defining and Delimiting the Literary Works

Literary works are always evolving with the changes in the society in which they are produced. The term diaspora itself is an unstable term and its status is at all times evolving. To be able to capture the state of being diasporic in an individual or community is just one moment in time. The moment it is captured, this volatile and unstable state is already evolving and changing.

If there arises a need to categorize literary works globally, current writings by Malaysian Indians should qualify as trans-cultural or trans-national literature based on the content of the work. As is the current trend among literary critics, the term Post-colonial literature and Commonwealth literature is a misnomer today. Globalization and its effects have created a new breed of writers in the space 'in-between' through 'hybridity'. The whole world revolves around fuzzy areas of hybrid cultures, races, ethnicities and traditions. World politics today supports the existence of 'mixed-breed' citizens from around the world.

## The Other Side of the Coin

However, while being able to relate to foreignness with comfort, diasporic writers are also intimidated by this exposure because they are constantly under pressure to integrate with the local culture. As such, to transmit and retain his/her heritage becomes a constant struggle, almost a battle. In the process, some assimilate and disappear. For example, the opening lines in Phillip Langran's "V.S. Naipaul: A Question of Detachment" states that

> Naipaul's mature work speaks eloquently of the conviction that the individual must constantly reassess his or her position in the world. (132)

Langran contends that Naipaul explores the confusion of racial, cultural and political loyalties that is the universal legacy of colonialism; his insistence on individual responsibility and intellectual striving becomes absolute.

Apart from racial discriminations, diasporic communities around the world face other forms of economical and political suppressions of various degrees as well. Thus, diasporic communities have resorted to creative literary works to reveal their position in the society and the world. They have made literature their voice platform. This is evident in the writings of Africans, Indians,

Australian aborigines, Chinese, Mauritians, Malaysians and writers who are in exile.

Pankaj Mishra, a literary critic who observes the above trend among diasporic communities in England states that there is an "ever-growing literature" that describes the varied lives of the colonial subjects in England. The attempt is to "remake" themselves for the new life in the old imperial centre. Diasporas around the world project their lives and channel their thoughts, fears, aspirations and expectations through the literature they produce. Hence, the findings of this study apart from exploring the diaspora in Malaysian literature, it could also reveal the expectations and aspirations of the Malaysian Indian community.

Mishra further states that there is "much publicity and excitement" about the above kind of literature which is academically categorized as Commonwealth, Multicultural, Diasporic, Indo-Anglican, Caribbean, African, etc. (Naipaul, V.S., viii). Exploiting the publicity and excitement created about this kind of literature gives room for Malaysian writers to venture into the international arena of publication with much ease and thus supporting the call to promote community literatures internationally by K.S. Maniam.

As a result, there exist Trans-Cultural works which:

> [a]cknowledges the impossibility of confining migrant writing within the straitjacket of national or regional labels. (Thieme 3)

Thieme further states that due to hybridization and metropolitan discourses there is a possibility of dismantling previously maintained, hierarchized notions of centrality, thus resulting in literary works that are known as post-colonial writings.

The trans-cultural exposure of the Malaysian writers has enriched the nation and more exotic writings will definitely emerge soon. This sentiment is also voiced in *Malaysian Literature in English: A Critical Reader* where the editors Muhammad A. Quayum and Peter C. Wicks state "Those newer, younger authors who nowadays choose to express themselves in English convey a view of the world that blends both national and cosmopolitan influences" (xiv). The reality of this influence is inevitable.

## The Inevitable Reality

The idea of 'real' and 'imagined' communities is inevitable in diaspora discourse. The Indian diaspora as it is today is dispersed to different parts of the world. They are minority communities in most parts of the world but a minority community, which is impacting the world in a big way, especially in the United States and the United Kingdom. As 'real' communities they form closely bonded minorities but as an 'imagined' community they are closely bonded as a huge global diaspora that is picking up momentum to impact the world through ethnic-based networking. The support given by the Indian Government is further strengthening their stand as a powerful global diaspora in the near future. There is a need to address the issue of loyalty and to accept the existence of multiple loyalties among the Indian diaspora just as multiple identities have become an accepted norm in the study of diaspora.

I believe it is a polygamous situation for the diaspora is loyal to two or three nations at the same time. I also believe that this is possible for it is not unusual in our lives that we take on different roles, loyalties and responsibilities to different people concurrently. As an analogy, it is possible for a man to often play the role of a son while at the same time he is a brother, lover, husband, father, uncle, and grandfather to another. Thus, it is possible to maintain multiple identities and multiple loyalties without affecting one another.

## Conclusion

The transformation that is experienced by the Indian diaspora in Malaysia seem to further promote a sense of tolerance which enables its members not only to sympathize but also to empathize with other communities in Malaysia and minority communities around the globe and this familiarity with alien terrains has strengthened the peace and harmony in the Malaysian multicultural and multiethnic setting.

## Notes

1. This article was a keynote address at the International Communities Conference, University of Southern Queensland, Australia 27–30 November 1996. Later it was published in Donald H. McMillen (ed.) *Globalization and Regional Communities: Geoeconomic, Sociocultural and Security Implications for Australia,* University of Southern Queensland Press, 1997, 18–23.

## References

Langran, Phillip. 1990. "V.S. Naipaul: A Question of Detachment". *Journal of Commonwealth Literature*, XXV.1.

Manaf, Nor Faridah Abdul, and Quayum, Mohammad A. 2001. *Colonial To Global: Malaysian Women's Writing in English 1940s–1990*. Kuala Lumpur: International Islamic University Malaysia.

Maniam, K.S. 1993. *The Return*. London: Skoob Books Publishing Ltd.

—. 2003. *Between Lives*. Selangor, Malaysia: Maya Press Sdn. Bhd.

—. 2004. "The New Diaspora". (28 December). <www.ucalgary.ca/UofC/eduweb/engl392/492/maniam-dias.html>.

Manicka, Rani. 2002. *The Rice Mother*. Great Britain: Hodder & Stoughton.

—. 2004. *Touching Earth*. Great Britain: Hodder & Stoughton.

Mano, Shoba. 2003. *Love's Treacherous Terrain*. Secunderabad: Om Paperbacks.

—. 2005. *Prodigal Child*. Sierra Vista, USA: Treble Hearts Books.

Naipaul, V.S. 2002. *The Writer and the World: Essays*. Introduced and edited by Pankaj Mishra. London: Picador; New York: Knopf.

Quayum, Mohammad A. and Wicks, Peter C., 2001. 'Introduction'. In Mohammad A., Quayum, and Peter C. Wicks (eds.), *Malaysian Literature in English: A Critical Reader*. Kuala Lumpur: Longman.

Rushdie, Salman, 1997. 'Introduction'. In Salman Rushdie and Elizabeth West (eds.), *The Vintage Book of Indian Writing (1947–1997)*. Britain: Vintage.

Sandten, Celile. 2000. "In Her Own Voice: Sujata Bhatt and the Aesthetic Articulation of the Diasporic Condition". *Journal of Commonwealth Literature*, 35(1): 99–119.

*The Arnold Anthology of Post-Colonial Literatures in English*. 1996. John Thieme (ed.). London: Arnold, 3–4.

# II

# New Indian Diaspora

# 7

# Migration of Highly Skilled Indians

## Case Studies of IT and Health Professionals*

BINOD KHADRIA**

The relation between brain drain and the exodus of health professionals, such as doctors and nurses, dates back to the early 1960s when large-scale immigration of doctors from the United Kingdom to the United States came into focus. The vacuum in the supply of health personnel created in the UK health sector was partly filled by immigration of Asian doctors in general and Indians in particular. Variations in the supply and demand of human resources in various other professions over the last 40 years across the developed and the developing countries have led to waves of migration and return migration with subsequent changes in the supply of human resources in science and technology (HRST), and changes in the policies regarding their mobility across countries. Indeed, the skilled

---

* First published as *STI Working Paper* 2004/6 (Copyright © 2004, Directorate for Science, Technology and Industry, Organization for Economic Co-operation and Development (OECD), France). Reprinted by Permission of the Author.

** The author would like to acknowledge the research assistance provided by his graduate students Narender Thakur, Perveen Kumar, Geeta Verma, Basant Potnuru, Sridhar Bhagavatula, Durgesh Rai and Kripabar Baruah in carrying out two painstaking primary field surveys in the cities of Bangalore and New Delhi that form the basis of this study. The study could not have been carried out without the co-operation of the many IT professionals and IT agencies in Bangalore, and the doctors, nurses and hospital administrators in New Delhi who were approached for interviews. The incisive comments and detailed queries made by Martin Schaaper of the OECD in course of the preparation of this Working Paper helped improve the focus and presentation of the study considerably. The responsibility for all the remaining shortcomings, however, lies with the author.

health workers, particularly the doctors and nurses, have continued to be on the centre-stage of this international migration of HRST in one continent or the other, although changes in technology and lowering of barriers between countries have brought about large-scale movement of professionals in new areas like information technology as well. India has received the utmost attention in the last years so far as the out-migration of IT professionals is concerned.

STI Working Paper 2004/7 (Khadria, 2004) reports on the results of a comprehensive study to estimate data on stocks and flows of human resources in science and technology (HRST) in India, and their migration overseas and/or return to India. Part of this study were two case studies that focus on two particular kinds of migration of highly skilled people, namely the return migration of information technology (IT) professionals to India, and the changing response of Indian doctors and nurses to the world demand for health workers. These two case studies form the subject of this Working Paper, which would best be read in conjunction with STI Working Paper 2004/7.

The case studies were carried out by means of two specific primary surveys—one of IT professionals in the city of Bangalore and their role in making the city a "corridor" for international mobility of Indian IT professionals (Section 2), and the other of health professionals (doctors and nurses) in the city of New Delhi (Section, 3).

## A Case Study of the Role of Return Migrants in the Development of Bangalore as a Corridor for International Mobility of its Professionals

### *The Case Study of Bangalore: Rationale for Selection and Methodology*

Focusing on return migration to India, this section presents the results of a field study that was conducted in the city of Bangalore in the month of November 2002. The field survey in Bangalore was intended to tap the experiences of return migrants in the host countries, particularly in terms of the gains derived as well as the difficulties faced by them during their stay abroad vis-à-vis their motivational expectations, and plans after return to India. The focal point of this entire exercise, however, was on identifying the role and importance of return migrants in the development of the city of

Bangalore as a "corridor" for movement of IT professionals internationally.

The selection of Bangalore for the study of return migrants is primarily based on the popular perception that the city is in the process of developing as 'a gateway to new global frontiers' and harbinger of a new global labour force that works in cyberspace (Stremlau, 1996: 154–58). Further, a survey conducted by the National Association of Software and Service Companies (NASSCOM, 1995) covering the headquarters of the top 200 software companies in India revealed that "68 companies were located in Bombay, 56 in Bangalore and 30 in New Delhi. The remaining one-quarter of the companies were distributed among Hyderabad, Madras, Calcutta and Pune". Besides, Bangalore has another major distinction of being located in a state, namely Karnataka, which has a long history of support for science and higher learning, and a flourishing tradition of engineering and technology through the establishment of several apex institutions, e.g., Bharat Electronics Limited (BEL, 1956), Hindustan Aeronautics Limited (HAL, 1960) and the Indian Institute of Science (IISc). Encouraged by this popular support for engineering and technology, and enriched by the development of professionalism, Bangalore has emerged as the key location for software development in India. Considering this, the so-called 'Silicon Valley of India' became an obvious choice for conducting this field survey.

For conducting the field survey, a very specific kind of population, comprising *all* skilled return migrants, had to be identified. Since no statistics are available about return migrants in India, this task could not have been accomplished even in Bangalore. To make the survey feasible though, a two-step process was adopted. As a first step, using informal contacts, some professionals were approached by e-mail and telephone. At the second stage, the willing respondents were interviewed. While approaching or contacting the respondent return migrants in Bangalore, care was taken to cover diverse types of software companies so as to make the sample as representative as possible.

Primary information was sought on a comprehensive questionnaire, designed by the author and his team (see Annex 1). The questionnaire contained 48 major items, each with some sub-items, distributed under five different headings, namely:

- Personal information;
- Information on out-migration;

- Information on return migration;
- Impact of return migration;
- Relationship with and involvement in diaspora associations.

The questionnaire was used to interview 45 respondents, mostly belonging to the field of information technology. Besides having written accounts of the responses noted down by the interviewers, several interviews were also tape-recorded for in-depth analysis later on. Nevertheless, as is clear from the sample design and the sample size, no statistical significance should be sought in this survey, the evidence presented here is purely anecdotic.

### *Results from the Survey*

The sample for the field survey consisted of 39 males and 6 females. The composition of the sample is skewed in favour of married professionals, as 35 out of 45 respondents are married, constituting just over three-fourths of the sample, and the remaining 10 are unmarried. Out of the 45 respondents, 21 were born in Karnataka, of which Bangalore is the capital, and 21 in other states. One respondent was born abroad, while two respondents did not report the place of birth in the written questionnaire, possibly due to oversight.

The age profile of the sample shows that almost two-thirds of the respondents (i.e., 30 out of 45) are between 25 and 35 years. As we move further on the age ladder, the number of respondents goes down substantially, and the lower (20–25 years) and upper (45–50) extreme class intervals have only one respondent each. The conclusion is that returning IT professionals to Bangalore are mostly young, with a mean age of 33 years.

The breakdown by educational qualification reveals that out of 45 respondents, 20 are graduates, followed by an equal number of postgraduates. Four respondents have research degrees at the Ph.D. level. One of the returned migrants reported that he had gone abroad after completing a three-year diploma course from the National Institute of Information Technology (NIIT)—a well-reputed institution at the diploma granting level in the field of computer education.

All the respondents have graduated from within India and almost half of them received their degrees from Karnataka state itself, except the sole foreign-born candidate who was educated abroad. Thirteen respondents have done their post graduation in

India and five have done this abroad. But unlike graduation and postgraduation, out of four research degree holders only one respondent has done his Ph.D. in India and the remaining three abroad. The notable point here is that all the respondents who did their postgraduation or Ph.D. degrees abroad had also received foreign fellowships.

The respondents' answers substantiated the fact that students in professional courses like engineering and IT are lured into foreign institutions more by the assurance of financial assistance than either the quality of education or its 'brand' name. In contrast to the common misnomer in India that most of the brain drain from India is taking place from the apex institutions of national/international reputation such as the Indian Institute of Technology (IITs), Indian Institute of Management (IIMs), Indian Institute of Science (IISc) or Regional Engineering Colleges (RECs), our sample shows that out of 45 respondents only two are from the category of IITs/IIMs/IISc and the majority of them (24) have completed their graduation from other state—and central-government universities and colleges, both private and public. But this is not true for postgraduation and research, wherein out of thirteen respondents, six have done their postgraduation at IITs/IIMs/IISc and one at REC. The lone research-degree holder respondent has been awarded his doctorate from one of the apex institutions of management in India, the IIM. The scenario emerging may be partly explained in terms of the fact that in a profession like IT, higher education (postgraduation and research) is a very costly affair, particularly in terms of the opportunity cost to the students, and most students are unwilling to pursue further higher studies unless compensatory financial packages are offered.

Table 1 shows that the United States is the most favoured destination for Indian highly skilled IT workers, as out of 56 total destinations for the 45 emigrants from India, 36 were in the United States. Several pull factors account for this choice, including better infrastructure in the professional establishments and favourable immigration policies for granting visas to IT professionals. The United Kingdom is found to be the second most sought after destination, particularly because of the traditional bond between the two countries and a close resemblance in their education systems and because of the conducive immigration policy of the British government in admitting S&T personnel. Due to the anticipated shortfall of skilled professionals in general and of IT professionals in

**Table 1**

*Countries of Sojourn of Return Migrants*

| | *No. of Respondents* |
|---|---|
| United States | 36 |
| United Kingdom | 7 |
| Germany | 4 |
| France | 3 |
| Belgium, Canada, Ghana, Hong Kong, Malaysia, Switzerland | 1 |
| Total | 56 |

particular in the twenty-first century, not only the traditional receiving countries like the United Kingdom, but also Germany, France, Japan, Belgium, Denmark, Ireland, Korea and Singapore have started opening their markets to Indian professionals (Khadria, 2001). Despite having been a traditional destination country for Indian migrants of all types (i.e., skilled, semi-skilled and unskilled), Canada is not represented adequately in the sample from Bangalore, as there is only one returned migrant who could be approached. Most of the returnees in the Bangalore sample have been to the United States and to the European countries and only a very small proportion has been to Asian and African countries.

The distribution of return migrants in terms of years of stay in the host countries reveals that more than one-third (38%) of the return migrants had gone overseas for a very short period, i.e., less than two years (see Figure 1). This temporary, short duration migration may be explained by the fact that the majority of the

**Figure 1**

*Length of Stay Abroad of Return Migrants (in years)*

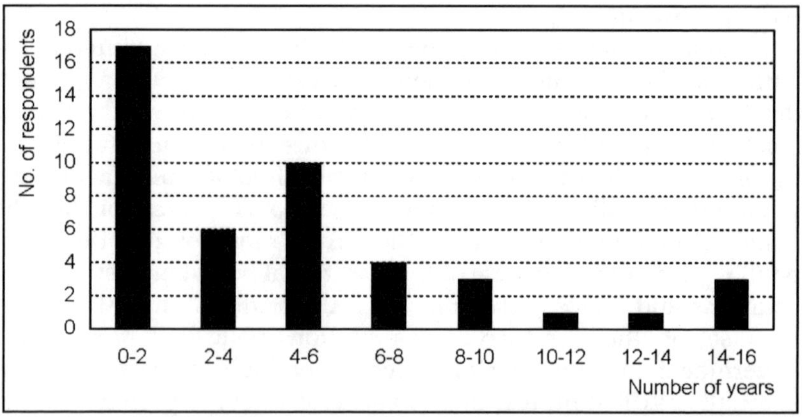

returned migrants had gone abroad on an assignment or project entrusted to them by their employers in Bangalore. Three out of every four respondents had stayed in the host countries for less than six years. Only three respondents had stayed overseas for 14–16 years, reflecting a low representation of long-term migrants in the sample. The average span of residence abroad for the entire sample comes out to be 4.6 years.

Concerning the return migration, almost half of the respondents have started working in Bangalore only a few years back (see Table 2). Three out of every four in the total sample have worked in Bangalore for less than 6 years, while only 12 respondents have stayed and worked in Bangalore for more than 6 years.

**Table 2**

*Employment Length of Return Migrants in Bangalore (in years)*

| | *0–2* | *2–4* | *4–6* | *6–8* | *8–10* | *10–12* |
|---|---|---|---|---|---|---|
| No. of Respondents | 19 | 6 | 8 | 6 | 4 | 2 |

It is clear from Figure 2 that employers have been the most important motivators for out-migration of professionals from Bangalore. They have allowed their skilled employees to avail the offers/opportunities of lucrative professional assignments (called "projects") abroad, particularly in the United States. Another important source of emigration for professionals from India is the

**Figure 2**

*Sources of Motivation for Emigration*

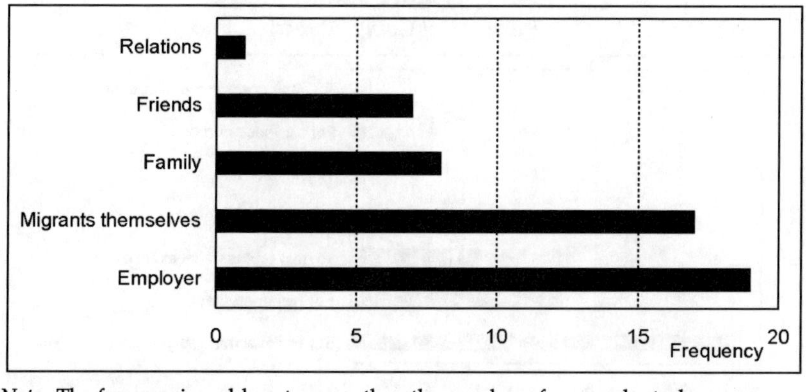


*Note:* The frequencies add up to more than the number of respondents, because some respondents chose more than one variable of motivation.

willingness of the respondents themselves, for they are found to be highly desirous of getting on to the greener pastures. The role of closely related people, including family, friends and relatives, does not seem to be very significant in precipitating the emigration of highly skilled workers.

Figure 3 provides the distribution of motivational factors behind out-migration, though from a different perspective. This figure shows that almost half of the respondents (23 out 45) went abroad mainly to grab the opportunity to work on project assignments, which were available to them through their employers in India. Eight respondents stated that one of their latent purposes behind going abroad was to gain professional experience, because, to them, work-experience abroad was of comparatively high value in India. Thirteen returnees stated that their purpose for going abroad was to get additional higher education in the host country, although only nine of them were successful in doing so. A very striking point that emerges from this figure is that not a single respondent had gone abroad to settle down permanently. Assuming that this follows from a true expression of returnees' intent in going abroad, it may lead the reader to conclude that the emigration of IT professionals from India was more of a temporary phenomenon aimed at fulfilling the short term gains and were preoccupied to come back. Of course, this result is biased by the fact that many of those willing to settle abroad may actually have done so, and therefore fall outside the scope of the target population.

**Figure 3**

*Purposes of Going Abroad*

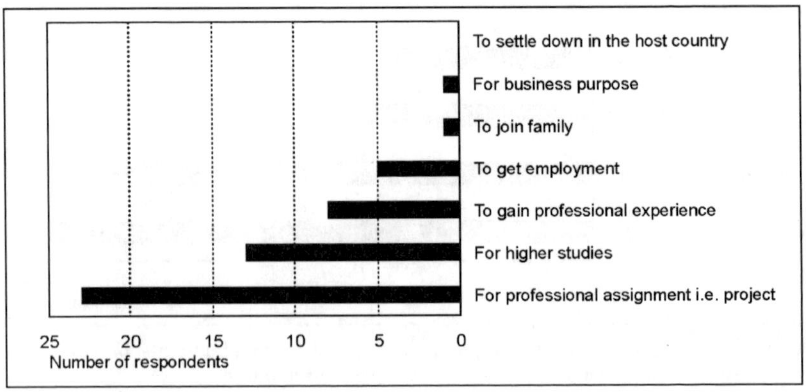

For identifying the push and pull factors behind the out-migration of returned professionals, the respondents were asked to select and explain the role of various factors, some of which have been included in the questionnaire. The responses have been recorded on a five-point scale, provided to the respondents, to weight the relative importance of each factor. Weights were given to each factor according to the following pattern: weight 1 for the factor(s) that played an extremely important role in the out-migration of the respondent; weight 2 for the factor(s) playing a moderately important role; and weight 3 for factor(s) considered important but not having enough intensity/capacity to make substantial alteration in the decision to go abroad. Weights 4 and 5 have been given to the respondents in order not to eliminate the unimportant factors from the list.

Figure 4 provides a list of nine factors along with their preference ranking in terms of weights given to each factor. The first three weights, as discussed above, are indicative of the "selection" response while the last two (weights 4 and 5) indicate the "rejection" response. "Votes" for answer '1', '2' or '3' were added up, without weighting them first.[1]

**Figure 4**

*Motivating Factors for Out-Migration of Return Migrants*

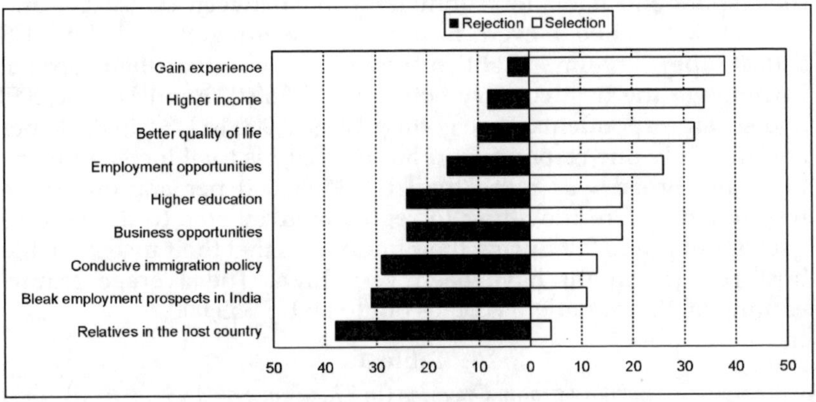


The figure shows that the largest number of respondents (38) expressed that the most important factor in their decision-making about going abroad was 'to gain experience that would later be highly valued in India'. Most of the respondents stated that since developed countries had an edge in technological advancement and were professionally more accomplished, they decided to cross the border and expose themselves to qualitatively better experiences there. Thirty-four respondents stated to have been lured by 'better income prospects in the host country'. The third important pull factor for out-migration has been 'better quality of life in the host country', as 32 of the respondents found it quite important in their decision for emigration. 'Better employment opportunities in the host country' has been stated as the fourth important factor in the decision-making for out migration. The other two pull factors, namely 'higher education' and 'expectations of better business opportunities in the host country' attracted 18 votes from the respondents and played a less significant role.

Table 3 presents the earnings of the respondent returnees when they were abroad. One of the major drawbacks of this earning profile is that it is based on the lumpsum estimates of incomes as verbally revealed by the respondents themselves. Besides, this earning profile reflects the past emoluments, which the respondents were getting when they were working abroad. Therefore, to get a standard estimate of earnings abroad in the current period, these amounts need to be adjusted by various rates of inflation. Despite these drawbacks, the earning profile shown in the table provides valuable information, which may be useful in analyzing the sample from a comparative perspective. The table shows that one-third of the respondents had a total annual income between US $40,000 and US $60,000, while eleven respondents were getting below US $40,000 per annum. Eight respondents reported their annual earnings in the host country between US $60,000 and US $80,000, and seven respondents were getting US $80,000 to US $1,00,000 per annum. Only one respondent reported that his total income during his stay abroad was more than US $1,00,000 per annum. Three respondents were unwilling to report their income to the investigators, but it was felt during their interviews that their income in the host country might have been very high. The average annual earning of 42 respondents comes out to be US $55,000.

**Table 3**

*Earning profile Overseas (in Thousands of US $)*

| | *0–20* | *20–40* | *40–60* | *60–80* | *80–100* | *100–120* | *No response* |
|---|---|---|---|---|---|---|---|
| No. of respondents | 4 | 7 | 15 | 8 | 7 | 1 | 3 |

Figure 5 depicts the role of catalytic agents that played a vital role in bringing the Indian expatriate professionals back home. It is apparent from the figure that the respondents themselves have been the most important motivating agents of return migration, as 29 of them emphasized that they have come back at their own initiative. The specific causes of their decision to come back will be discussed later. Family has been found as the second major motivational factor behind return migration of professionals. Nine respondents highlighted that it was their employers who called them back. The roles of another two agents, 'friends' and 'relatives', were only secondary and not decisive.

**Figure 5**

*Return Migration of Professionals: The Catalytic Agents*

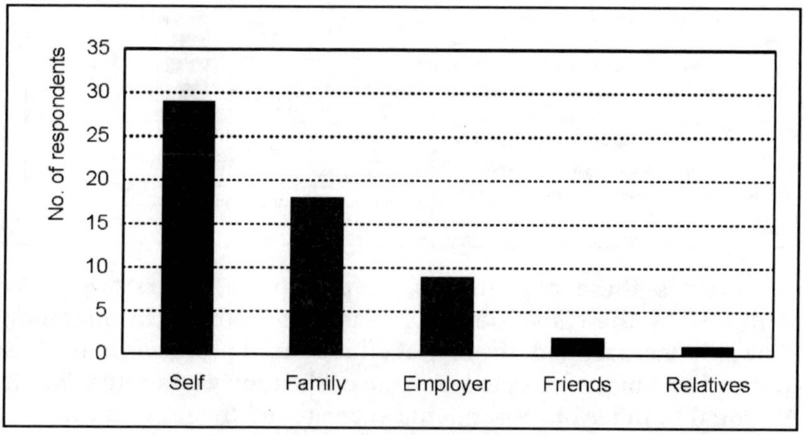


Figure 6 contains a list of twelve factors that motivated the respondents to come back to India. As before, weights 1 to 3 indicate that a factor was important, while weights 4 and 5 suggest that a factor was not an important motivation to return. The figure shows that 'family' has been the most important motivating factor in coming back, as 27 respondents have given it the first rank. One of the respondents, for example, explained that his parents were getting older and nobody was there to look after them in India, and so he did not have any other option but to come back. Just over half of the respondents identified the 'recognition of India as a major emerging IT power in the world' and the consequent increase in 'employment opportunities' in India, particularly in the IT sector, as the major motivators to come back. Eighteen respondents had decided to come back due to 'higher real earnings' in India. They were of the opinion that despite getting higher nominal wages abroad their real earnings were not so high, particularly because of the high cost of living abroad as compared to India. 'Expectations of better business and entrepreneurial opportunities in India' attracted one-third of the respondent returnees to India.

**Figure 6**

*Motivating Factors in Return Migration to India*

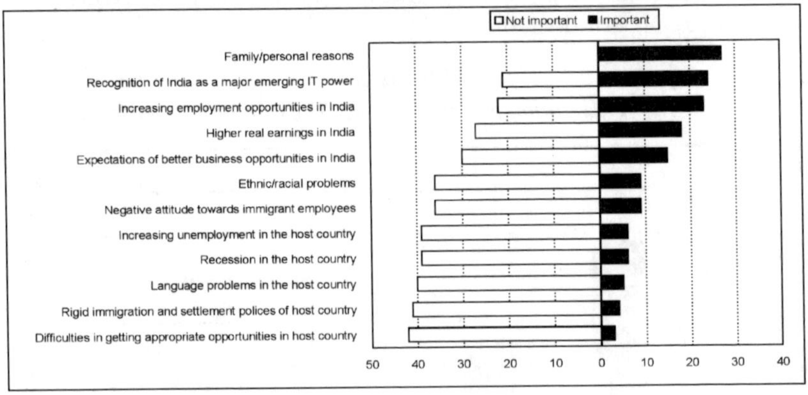


Besides these pull factors, several push factors were also identified by the respondents as causes of their return migration. Nine responses named 'the fear of ethnic/racial problems in the host country' as a major push to leave the host country and return home. An equal number of respondents experienced 'negative attitude of the employer towards immigrant employees' though some of them did not directly confront such problems during their stay abroad. For most of them, it was the fear psychosis of discrimination that pushed them back towards their home country. Six respondents returned due to the 'recession in the host country', and the consequent 'increase in unemployment in the host country' also discouraged six respondents from staying abroad.

Figure 7 is an extension of Figure 6, focusing on identifying the enticing factors in return of migrants back to India, specifically to the city of Bangalore. It contains a list of 12 factors which have played a crucial role in alluring return migrants towards Bangalore and make the city a 'corridor' for migration of IT and other professionals, both inward and outward. During the field survey, the respondents were asked to identify, select and explain the significance of ten clearly stated options covering a wide range of important factors including political, economic, social, educational and health factors in their decision to select Bangalore. Besides the specified options, two other factors, namely 'family in Bangalore', and 'climate of Bangalore' were also identified during the interviews as important factors that attracted them to the 'Silicon Valley of India'.

**Figure 7**

*Bangalore as a "Corridor" for Return Migration: the Enticing Factors*

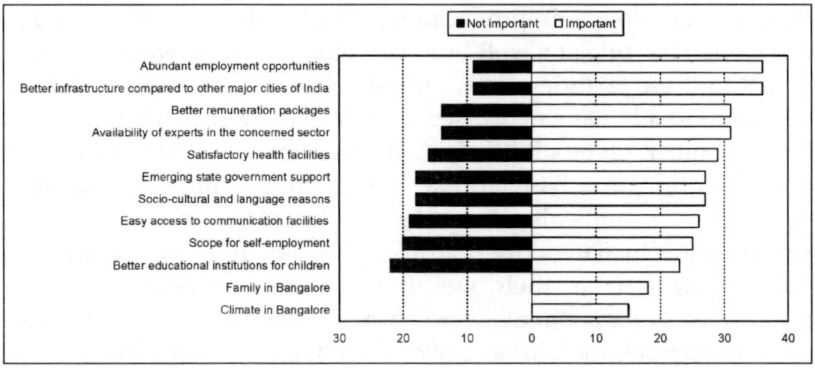


It is evident from the figure that 'abundant employment opportunities' in Bangalore, particularly in the IT sector, have allured a large proportion of the respondents to this 'cyber city' of India, for as many as 36 respondents have accepted the significance of this factor in their choice of Bangalore as the 'corridor' for their return from abroad. An equal number of respondents stated that availability of 'better infrastructure in comparison to other major cities of India' like New Delhi, Bombay, Hyderabad, Pune, etc. have lured them to Bangalore. 'Availability of experts in the concerned sector', i.e., the IT sector, has been attributed importance by 31 respondents, as an allurement in Bangalore. Thirty-one respondents have asserted that comparatively 'better remuneration packages' are available in Bangalore, particularly in the IT sector, which is a very important incentive to work. Twenty-nine respondents have identified the role of 'health facilities' as an important determinant for selecting Bangalore as a destination for their return from abroad. Affinity to the local society, language and culture have also played an extremely important role in attracting return migrants to Bangalore, as 27 respondents have agreed that they had decided to stay in Bangalore because of its 'peace-loving' and 'multilingual' society, and of course a 'truly cosmopolitan culture'. Twenty-seven respondents have recognized the 'emerging state government support' for newly emerging professions, like IT, as one of the important reasons to come back to Bangalore. 'Increasing scope for self-employment' in Bangalore has been also cited by 25 of the respondents as an important motivation for return to Bangalore and start their own establishments.

However, only a few of the respondents have actually started their self-employment programme. Twenty-six respondents have mentioned the role of a well-built communication network and easy access to these facilities as an important factor. A little over half of the respondents have expressed that availability of and access to a large number of qualitatively 'better educational institutions for their children', and Bangalore as a 'safe abode' for them and their coming generations also encouraged them to pursue their professional career in Bangalore. Eighteen respondents have decided to select Bangalore as their working residence because of family reasons, as 21 respondents were born and brought up in Karnataka state. Bangalore, the capital city of the state, was therefore a natural choice for these returning migrants. One-third of the respondents have cited the 'climate of Bangalore' as an important deciding factor for the selection of Bangalore in returning back from abroad.

Table 4 provides the annual earnings profile of the respondent return migrants in Bangalore. It is evident from the figures in each cell that as we move up the earnings ladder, the frequency of respondents goes down substantially. Out of 45 respondents, only four have reported to be earning more than US $21,000 per year. This may not seem much, but taking purchasing power into account raises this number to 1,08,000 PPP dollars. Five respondents have told that their annual earnings did not exceed US $4,000, or 22,000 when expressed in dollar PPPs. Twelve respondents reported their annual earnings between US $4,000 and US $8,000 per annum (22,000–43,000 in PPPs), followed by an equal number of respondents whose annual earnings were reported between US $8,000 and US $12,000 per annum (43,000–65,000 PPP). Eight respondents were found to earn between US $12,000 and US $21,000 per year (65,000–108,000 PPP). The average annual income of 41 respondents came out to be US $11,000 per annum, 59,000 in PPPs. The remaining four respondents in the sample refused to provide the estimates of their annual earnings.

When comparing return migrants' *current income* in Bangalore with their *earlier income* abroad, nineteen respondents stated that their current annual income was 'much lower than before', followed by ten other respondents who said that it was 'lower than before'. Eight respondents did not perceive any significant difference between the two earning profiles. Contrary to this, seven respondents expressed that in Bangalore they were in a comparatively better financial position. One respondent did not give a reply to this question.

**Table 4**

*Earnings Profile of Return Migrants in Bangalore*

| *Thousand rupees per annum* | *Thousand US $ per annum* | *Thousand PPP per annum* | *Number of Respondents* |
|---|---|---|---|
| 0–200 | 0–4 | 0–22 | 5 |
| 200–400 | 4–8 | 22–43 | 12 |
| 400–600 | 8–12 | 43–65 | 12 |
| 600–800 | 12–16 | 65–87 | 3 |
| 800–1000 | 16–21 | 87–108 | 5 |
| 1000–2000 | 21–25 | 108–130 | 1 |
| 1200–1400 | 25–29 | 130–151 | 1 |
| 1400–1600 | 29–33 | 151–173 | 1 |
| 1600–1800 | 33–37 | 173–195 | 0 |
| 1800–2000 | 37–41 | 195–216 | 1 |

It was noted that a large number of respondents, while abroad, had not sent any significant amounts of money back home to their families residing in India. Out of the 45 returnees, 24 said that they had sent remittances to their families while they were working abroad, but not 'on a regular basis'. Most had sent intermittently and a few of them had sent money only once or twice during their entire period of stay abroad. A large chunk of these remittances was spent by their family members on meeting the day-to-day expenses at home, except a few "who spent the money on buildings, buying a house, purchase of land, etc." The amount of remittances was also not quite large, mainly because a large number of return migrants had gone abroad for a short span of time and could not accumulate large amounts of money.

Table 5 provides an estimate of the foreign-earned money invested by returnees in Bangalore. The table shows that twelve returnees (one-fourth of the respondents) each invested below US $10,000,[2] and another ten invested between US $10,000 and US $20,000 each. The amounts of investment in Bangalore by another eight respondents were between US $20,000 and US $30,000 each. Only three respondents invested more than US $30,000 each.

**Table 5**

*Investment of foreign-earned Money in Bangalore by Returnees*

| *In 1000s of rupees* | *In 1000 US $* | *In 1000 PPP* | *Number of Respondents* |
|---|---|---|---|
| 0–500 | 0–10 | 0–54 | 12 |
| 500–1,000 | 10–20 | 54–108 | 10 |
| 1,000–1,500 | 20–30 | 108–162 | 8 |
| 1,500 and above | 30 and above | 162 and above | 3 |
| No response | | | 12 |

Further analysis of investment/expenditure by return migrants in Bangalore reveals that 'housing' got the highest priority, as 25 respondents reported to have spent a major portion of their foreign earnings/savings in purchasing/construction of shelter. 'Durable consumption goods' including electronic appliances and furniture got the next major part of their investment/expenditure, as 20 respondents mentioned it. Fourteen respondents revealed that a major share of their earnings abroad was invested in the education of their own children or those of their direct family. For example, one of the respondents has been bearing all the expenses of his younger brother currently studying in the Indian Institute of Technology in Mumbai (IITM). Five respondents have invested a huge proportion of their foreign earnings in business and three others in the stock market. It is to be noted here that almost all the respondents have invested/spent their money in more than one category of items.

While enquiring about the awareness of respondents regarding any incentive programme(s) or policies of central or state government(s) aimed at getting back to the country the Indian expatriate professionals abroad, i.e., NRIs (non-resident Indians) and PIOs (persons of Indian origin), only 11 respondents have responded positively. The remaining 34 respondents denied having any information, whether before returning to India or afterwards, about any state-sponsored incentive programme or policy to promote the return migration of IT professionals to India in general and to Bangalore in particular. Even of the 11 respondents, who were aware of the incentive programmes and policies, very few could actually get any help from these in and after their return to Bangalore. The incentives, as told by the respondents, were offered mostly in terms of tax rebates, housing facilities and financial assistance in establishing business in Bangalore. It leads us to conclude that official efforts to get the nation's talent back (if it is assumed to turn brain drain into brain gain) are not sufficient.

On the state of job-satisfaction in their present employment/business in Bangalore, 41 return migrants responded positively, and almost all of them displayed the same impression. Greater professional autonomy, world class institutional infrastructure, conducive working environment, a truly cosmopolitan culture of the city, and a large number of opportunities for career advancement have been enumerated as some of the most important factors in keeping their morale high in the present professional set-up in Bangalore. The remaining four respondents, who reacted negatively on the job-satisfaction in their present employment, cited bureaucratic hassles in getting the work done as the most prevalent problem in Bangalore. Besides, quite a few have expressed that 'dignity of labour' is not upheld in India, unlike in most developed countries. There is a lack of healthy professional ethics and practice amongst people.

When asked about the difficulties and problems in adjusting to the present working conditions in Bangalore, as many as 32 respondents explicitly expressed that they did not face any major hurdle in adjusting to their present working organizational climate. The background of respondents and their earlier exposure to India and its culture helped them a lot in adjusting back in Bangalore after their return from abroad. This finding, however, may seem a bit out of place to some who believe that after having accustomed to a more advanced socio-cultural set-up, it becomes a little difficult to re-adjust in a comparatively closed and traditional society. As if to satisfy such apprehensions, 13 respondents mentioned some problems in their re-adjustment in Bangalore. The major adjustment problems faced by them were caused due to the lethargic administrative procedures, inefficient handling of the day-to-day professional concerns, relatively unhealthy business ethics, poor research facilities (especially in academics) and poor work culture.

Twenty-five respondents revealed that they had tried to motivate their friends and colleagues and some relatives as well to return to India. However, not all of them were successful in this endeavour. Generation of a fairly large number of good employment opportunities, and many more lucrative opportunities for self-employment, especially in India's IT sector, a sense of feeling at home consequent to a socially comfortable and easy life—were the inducements that were cited by these respondents to their friends and colleagues abroad.

For analyzing the impact of return migration in Bangalore, the respondents were asked to react on the role of returnees in certain areas of development, e.g., in the economic domain, particularly in terms of remittances and prospective economic avenues in Bangalore, knowledge and skills gained overseas and their implications back home, development of physical infrastructure in India including Bangalore, development of education and other social services, etc.

When reacting to the question, 'which of the following do you consider the most important to your current work/business in Bangalore', thirty-seven respondents accepted that the 'knowledge and skills gained overseas through higher education and on-the-job training' is highly useful for their current jobs in Bangalore (see Figure 8). Two-thirds of the respondents expressed that the opportunity to work abroad helped equip themselves with the recent and most appropriate technologies. Only nine respondents recognized the 'role of professional networks established overseas' in their current jobs in Bangalore. They asserted that these networks helped them in providing information on several professional issues like technology, management, outsourcing, etc. Only three respondents recognized the importance of '(financial) capital accumulated overseas' in their current occupation in Bangalore. Interestingly, these three respondents had not stayed abroad for a very long time. Rather, it was the nature of their job and the remuneration packages overseas that helped them in earning a huge sum of money in a comparatively short span of time.

All the respondents except one acknowledged the 'contribution of skills, experience, knowledge, and ideas' which they have gained

**Figure 8**

*Gains from Return Migration*

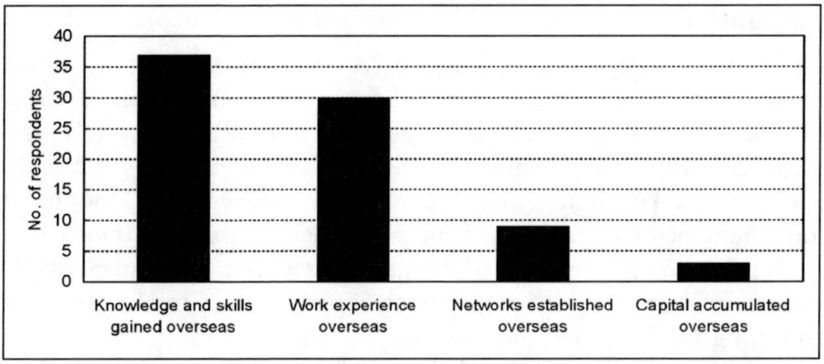


*Note:* The frequencies add up to more than the number of respondents because some respondents chose more than one variable of motivation.

while working abroad, in their present employment/business in Bangalore. A majority of them have elaborated that their experience helps them a lot while interacting with the clients, for most of the clients are from the United States and European countries. It helps them in acquiring technological innovations and coping with the rapid technological changes, improving management practices, and, above all, confidence building. Respondents from the academic world considered that it is the exposure to different work cultures and a sound academic base, which is of paramount importance and very useful in their current positions. As an exception to this, one respondent, a returned civil engineer from Malaysia, uttered in despair that "in no way the knowledge, skills and experience gained there helped me in my present position, because all that I do here is completely different from the nature of the job and work culture over there". He revealed that due to the economic downturn he lost his job in the host country and as a consequence came back to India, where he could not utilize his experience because of his failure in getting a good job in the concerned field. In his present occupation in Bangalore, he however expressed satisfaction, particularly because of increasing income prospects in the future. This apart, it has been expressed by almost all the respondents that their experiences abroad are well-recognized and valued by their employers and by colleagues as well. They receive more attention from their superiors and colleagues, who 'listen to them carefully on important matters'.

Additionally, employers and colleagues do not hesitate in assigning them important professional responsibilities.

### *Qualitative Observations by the Respondents*

When the respondents were asked to speak on the "positive and negative feelings" after coming back home to India, all of them expressed that positive feelings substantially outweigh the negatives. 'Physical proximity to the family as well as to the nation' and an independent environment were reported as the most important positive feelings. Several of them expressed their satisfaction on the development of Bangalore as a cosmopolitan city with an increasing number of employment opportunities in almost every emerging field.

Quite a few expressed that while working abroad they sometimes felt a sense of alienation from the surrounding society and its closed cultural facets, sometimes leading even to racial diatribes. Being back home, they ceased to feel alienated from the people around them. Rather, they started feeling as essential parts of a progressive Indian social system. Some of them felt that the climate of Bangalore was very pleasant and they liked it very much. So, for them, being in Bangalore was in itself a positive aspect of their return to India. Furthermore, the emergence of Bangalore as the 'Silicon Valley of India' made them feel proud about it and they wanted to become a part of it.

On the negative aspects of their life in Bangalore, the respondents were unhappy about the government's apathy and delay in reacting to the issues, concerns and developments taking place in the global economic scenario and its failure in controlling corruption, particularly in public offices. A heavy load of growing vehicular traffic, the disastrous state of pollution, especially in the metropolitan cities, Bangalore being no exception, nearly uncontrolled population growth and a poor state of infrastructure were stated as the major causes of their pessimism. Nearly 22 per cent of the respondents, however, still believed that since these types of problems were in any case not going to be removed altogether in the near future, they saw no reason to feel entirely pessimistic about returning to the home country on such grounds.

Thirty-five returnees expressed their desire to re-emigrate, but only if they got a very lucrative job offer from overseas. Since a major part of the sample was formed by professionals who went overseas on their employers' initiative, they expressed that they would certainly take a foreign trip if the employing authority, i.e., the companies, made the arrangements again. One such respondent was to catch a flight to the United Kingdom on his company's assignment on the day he was interviewed in Bangalore for this study. Amongst the choices of preferred destinations for foreign working trips, the United States came out as the most preferred choice, followed by the United Kingdom and Australia. Other European countries, namely France and Germany, were also mentioned among the list of preferred destination countries. Canada and Singapore were also listed high in the preference list, though by only a few respondents.

Thirty-nine respondents stated confidently that they would not settle down abroad permanently. It was expressed by most of these respondents that since they were getting world-class facilities at their work place in Bangalore, enjoying the healthy environment of the city and were very optimistic about India's place in the future world, they saw no point in leaving the home ground for permanent settlement elsewhere. To them it is an added advantage to be in close proximity to their families. Two respondents expressed the view that if they got a favourable opportunity, they might think about emigrating permanently. Four respondents expressed their inability to say anything with confidence at the moment on their decision to go abroad for permanent settlement and left everything to the circumstances both at home and overseas.

When the respondents were asked about their 'active involvement in the development process' of India, more than half (25 out of 45 returnees) responded positively. A majority of them felt that 'relevant education' is absolutely necessary for the development of society. Furthermore, to make education accessible to the masses, educational infrastructure needs to be built by providing adequate funds. It was also expressed that besides governmental efforts, private hands also had an important role to play in this nation-building endeavour. They urged that people should contribute generously for the uplifting of the masses. These respondents reported that they were contributing to the societal cause through several organizations and NGOs working on environmental issues, education of poor children and other social services.

## A Case Study of Migration Abroad of Indian Doctors and Nurses

### *The Case Study of Health Workers: Rationale for Selection and Methodology*

This section focuses on the out-migration of health workers (interchangeably called medical professionals), especially of doctors and nurses, from India to developed economies. It also highlights the issue of some foreign educated (mainly in Russia) returning doctors, which has given rise to the controversy regarding the official recognition of their educational credentials for practicing medicine in India. A case study was conducted in New Delhi because of its unique position in medical education, extensive institutional infrastructure, large-scale emigration of medical professionals—particularly from the All India Institute of Medical Sciences—and an easy access to the target population. The sample for the present study was selected from premier institution-cum-hospitals of medical education in New Delhi, namely All India Institute of Medical Sciences (AIIMS), Maulana Azad Medical College, Jayprakash Narayan Hospital, Safdarjung Hospital, Kalawati Saran Children's Hospital and Lady Hardinge Medical College. These institutions/hospitals were selected considering their high quality of medical facilities, diversity of students and diverse courses and areas of specialization. From these institutions, a total number of 82 professionals including 34 doctors and 40 nurses were approached and interviewed. In addition, 8 recently returned fresh medical graduates from CIS countries (mainly Russia) were also interviewed.

The questionnaire contained several items that sought information on the following dimensions (see Annexure 2):

1. Personal information including information on education;
2. Information about the decision to go abroad and the major motivational forces for their out-migration;
3. Perception of the prospective migrants about the quality of education abroad, on-the-job training and prospects for employment/professional growth.

### *The Case Study of Doctors: Data Presentation and Analysis*

This section focuses on the prospective migration of doctors and tries to find out the causes of their emigration and their perception about their professional status in the host country. It provides a detailed analysis of the information sought from the sample of 34 qualified doctors during the field survey. Out of the 34 respondent doctors, 29 were male and 5 were female. The distribution in terms of marital status shows that a large majority (30) of them were unmarried. All the respondent doctors were between 20 and 30 years of age, showing that the prospective migrants are quite young. It has been observed during the field survey that the 'inclination to go abroad' was stronger amongst the doctors belonging to the age group 25–30 years.

The respondent doctors came from different states of India, thus making our sample more or less representative of India as a whole. The highest number (6) were from New Delhi, followed by five from Punjab (the state from which migration takes place in a large-scale, mostly to Canada, the United States and the United Kingdom), four doctors belonged to Madhya Pradesh and three doctors each came from Assam, Bihar, Karnataka and Utter Pradesh. It was also observed that most of the doctors completed their last educational degree in New Delhi, which proves that New Delhi is amongst the favourite places of choice for medical education in the country.

Twenty-two responding doctors had completed their graduation degrees and were pursuing their postgraduation, while twelve respondents had already completed their postgraduation and were working on an internship at the time of the interview.

The All India Institute of Medical Sciences (AIIMS) stands at the first rank in terms of prospective emigration of doctors, with fifteen doctors in the sample. An earlier study conducted in 1992 to analyzes the extent of brain drain during the period 1956–80 from this apex institution of medical sciences reported a very high rate of out-migration of 56 per cent of graduating doctors. The second major chunk of the sample is drawn from Maulana Azad Medical College, New Delhi with eleven doctors interviewed from this institute. The remaining eight respondent doctors completed their degrees from seven different institutions. A further 27 respondents have got their degrees from institutions established in New Delhi, while the remaining seven respondents got them from outside of New Delhi. Most of the respondent doctors viewed that the "medical profession is a well respected profession and is full of innumerable opportunities for serving the society".

When asked about the sources of inspiration for emigration, the total of the first three weights,[3] as given in Figure 9, shows that 24 respondents wanted to go abroad mainly because of self-motivation. Twenty-three respondents said that they were given inspiration from their overseas friends. An equal number of respondents mentioned that their teachers/mentors/senior doctors inspired them to go abroad, at times by those who had already left the home country.[4] Fifteen respondents admitted that their friends in India have been motivating them. Family and relatives have also been cited by ten and seven respondents respectively, as important motivators for their decision to go abroad.

**Figure 9**

*Source of Inspiration for Emigration for Doctors*

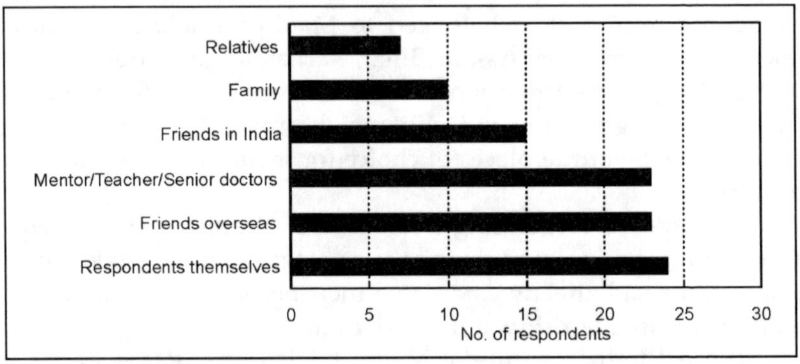


Figure 10 highlights the purpose of out-migration as stated by the respondent doctors. It shows that 29 doctors are planning to go abroad "to get jobs with better training opportunities." Moreover, 18 respondents stressed that it was the most important factor in their decision-making for out-migration. The next important factor is the desire "to ensure rapid progress in the medical profession", of which 28 respondents spoke in favour. Seventeen respondents expressed that their purpose was "to obtain a specific kind of training not easily available in India". Sixteen respondents wanted "to move abroad for getting good employment opportunities" in the host countries, while fifteen respondents mentioned that their purpose for going abroad was to get "medical experience not easily available in India". "Permanent settlement in the host country" was selected by eleven respondents as one of the important purposes for their out-migration. A small number of respondents stated that they would leave for abroad even if they could only get some project or research assignments. The forgoing discussion shows that "to get a job with better training opportunities overseas" and "to progress at a comparably faster pace in the professional career" were the most important considerations behind the intentions of out-migration of most of the doctors. These two broadly stated purposes lead us to conclude that after having had the education and on-the-job training in well-reputed institutions of medical education in India, doctors are still sceptical about their future professional growth within India, and they strongly feel that experience in foreign hospitals is highly valued in the Indian labour market for health workers.

**Figure 10**

*Purpose of Intended Out-Migration of Doctors*

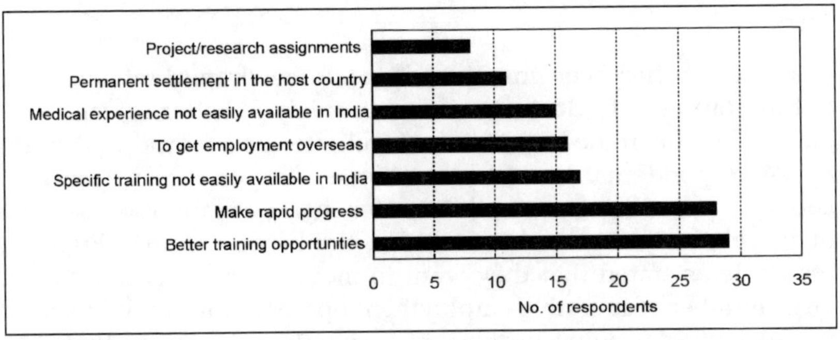


Figure 11 enlists 16 factors, which have helped the respondent doctors in choosing their favourite destination abroad. "Higher education" in the host country stands at the top of the list, since—except for one—all the respondents consider this an important factor ('extremely important' for 19, 'moderately important' for 8, and 'less important' for 6 respondents). The responding doctors feel that if they have to make rapid advancements in their professional career, they would certainly need better academic exposure and better professional infrastructure, which they feel is "not easily available in India". The total of 'selection response' category (i.e., weight 1, 2 and 3) shows that "better income prospects overseas" is an important pull factor for 24 respondent doctors, of which for 13 it is an "extremely important" one. "Availability of experts in the concerned field", i.e., in the medical profession in the

**Figure 11**

*Motivating Factors for Out-Migration of Doctors*

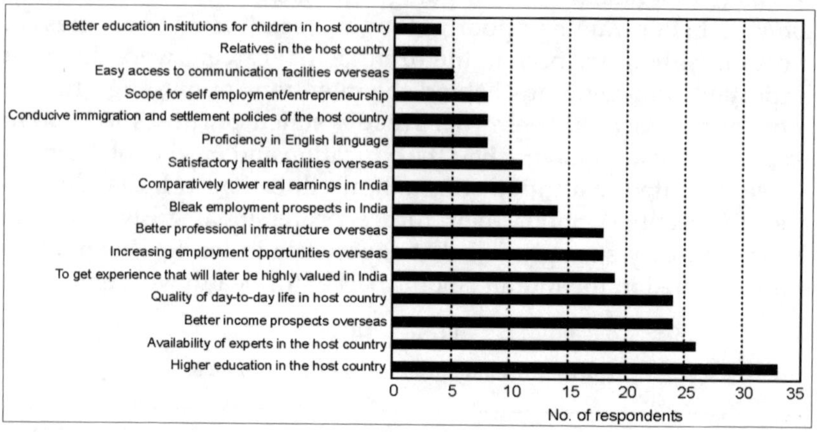


host country has been mentioned as another important cause for out-migration of doctors. Comparatively "better quality of day-to-day life in the host country" weighted as an important factor by 24 respondents. For 19 respondents, "experience in the host country" is an important pull factor for their out-migration because of its relatively high value in India, the home country. Eighteen respondents stated that they want to move overseas because of "a large number of lucrative employment opportunities in the medical profession". An equal number of respondents consider that they "would be having exposure to better infrastructure abroad" required for the profession. Around one-third of the respondents thought that in India real earnings were quite low when compared with several other countries, even despite having the same educational and professional qualification. Fourteen respondents have cited "bleak employment prospects" in India as a major push factor for the emigration of doctors to developed nations. "Satisfactory health facilities overseas" (11 respondents), "conducive immigration and settlement policies of the prospective destination countries" (8), "scope for self employment" (8), "access to qualitatively better school education for their children" (4) and "proficiency in the English language" (4) have been reported as some other important considerations for out-migration.

Figure 12 shows that the United States is the favourite destination for medical professionals, as 23 respondents have given it

**Figure 12**

*Preferred Destination Countries for Out-Migration of Doctors*

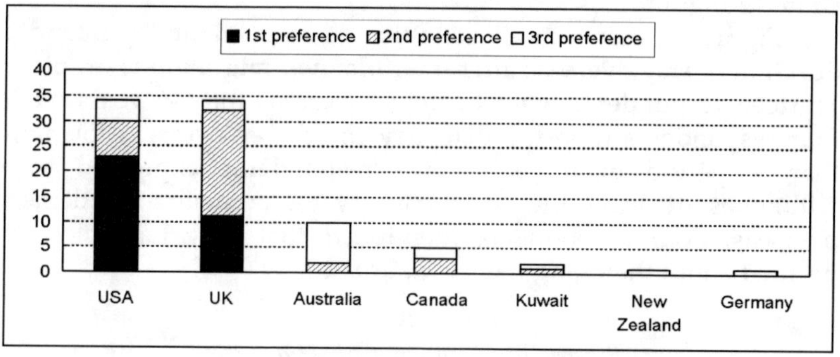


first preference. For seven doctors, the United States is the second choice, while for the remaining four it is third choice. The United Kingdom has come out as the second preferred destination, with 11 doctors giving it the first preference, 21 second preference, and the remaining two-third preference. Australia has emerged as the third preferred destination, followed by Canada, Kuwait, New Zealand and Germany.

It may be observed that the medical professionals in the sample had sufficient information about their destination country and the pre-requisites for making their entry possible. Twenty-one of them have even passed certain necessary eligibility tests. The remaining thirteen candidates have not appeared for any such test but are planning to sit for one in the coming year. Professionals who are going to the United States and Canada were very specific in their choices of institutions/hospitals to which they had applied. In contrast, doctors who were planning to go to the United Kingdom were not specific about the hospitals they wished to join; they pointed out that that it was only after clearing the second stage test of the two-tier process that they would be allowed to apply for specific institutions in the United Kingdom.

Cardiology and internal medicine are the most preferred specializations for the prospective migrant doctors to be pursued in the host country. It was observed during the fieldwork that, as an area of specialization, internal medicine was the most preferred specialization for those with the United States as destination, while surgery was the preferred specialization for those intending to go to the United Kingdom. However, due to the recently amended favourable immigration policy of the British government and consequently easy access, a large number of doctors prefer to go to the United Kingdom.

Figure 13 shows the distribution of respondents by intended duration of stay overseas after their planned migration takes place. Thirteen respondents want to move overseas for 4–6 years while four respondents reported that they could stay overseas for more than a period of 6 years. Five respondents expressed their willingness to leave the home country for permanent settlement overseas. Four respondents mentioned that they have not yet decided about their length of stay abroad.

**Figure 13**

*Prospective Duration of Stay Overseas*

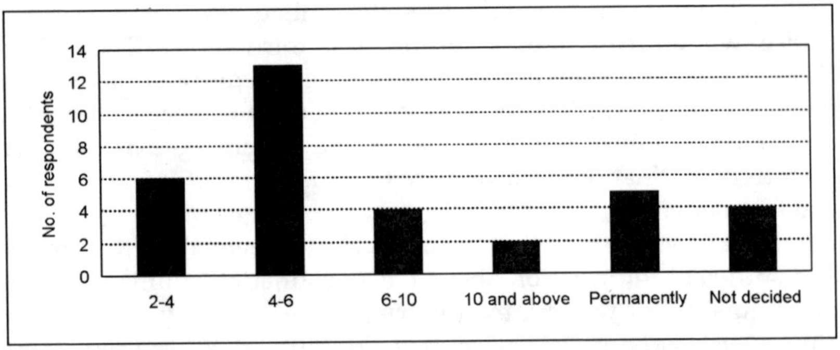


A large majority of doctors (28 out of 34) are hopeful that their career growth would be "faster than in India" in the host country, while five respondents mentioned that it would be "almost the same as in India". Contrarily, one respondent did not expect the professional growth to be faster overseas than in India.

On the intended career choices, the majority of the doctors (15 respondents) expressed their desire to pursue a career in the field of medical research. Ten responding doctors desired to be in public health services, followed by six respondents willing to start their professional career as private practitioners. A career in 'administration' of medical services and other international organizations like WHO, figured as the career choice of three doctors.

When the respondent doctors were asked to rate the quality of medical education and training in India, slightly more than three-fourth of the total sample reflected a sense of satisfaction.

Figure 14 shows five respondents to be "very satisfied" while another twenty-one respondents were "moderately satisfied" with the kind of education and training being provided in the Indian health sector. The remaining eight respondents expressed their dissatisfaction on the state of education and training in the medical field.

**Figure 14**

*Doctors' Perceptions about the Quality of Medical Education and Training in India*

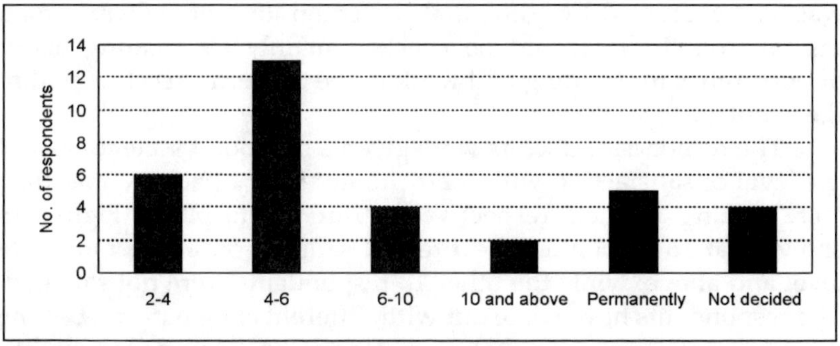


A majority of the respondent doctors (20) feel that if one is educated in United States or the United Kingdom, one's professional career growth would be faster in India in comparison to the India-educated doctors. On the contrary, six respondents were of the view that the future of foreign-educated doctors is not bright in India, while another seven have expressed their inability to say anything in concrete terms on the future of foreign educated doctors in India.

When asked about their prospective contribution in the development of the nation after their return from abroad, the respondents have mentioned many diverse ways of contributing. All the respondents have noble intentions about their prospective contributions in the nation's development. Some of them mentioned that they would contribute by sending remittances back home, getting involved in charity work by improving medical facilities, or by providing information, training and consultancy to those medical organizations which are working in rural areas. They can also provide their services through tele-medicine. A few respondents mentioned that capacity building of 'fellow doctors' to provide the latest medical treatment to the masses in India could be one way of contributing to national development. Nine respondents said that they would come back to India and provide their service for the cause of India's betterment. Speaking on the impact of large-scale emigration of highly skilled professionals from India on India's national development, eight respondents expressed it would have a negative impact because of the loss of human capital. Eight respondents however, were of the view that it would not have any adverse impact because of India's large pool of skilled professionals and educational capacity to fill the gaps caused by emigration. A view was also expressed by some that the emigration of skilled human capital from India would be checked mainly by creating better opportunities for training and work in the concerned sectors within the country.

The respondent doctors were given a five-point scale to weight the level of satisfaction with their present salary package that they were getting in their respective institutions/hospitals. Figure 15 shows that 16 respondents expressed satisfaction at the moderate level and above, while the other 18 respondents were not satisfied. The respondents have come out with different explanations, but the most notable point was that considering the educational qualification and the rigorous training they had, their remunerations were quite low. Moreover, in India, the private sector offers much more lucrative jobs in the medical profession than the public sector. Therefore, the public sector should also provide compatible salaries to the medical professionals.

**Figure 15**

*Level of Satisfaction with Present Salary in India*

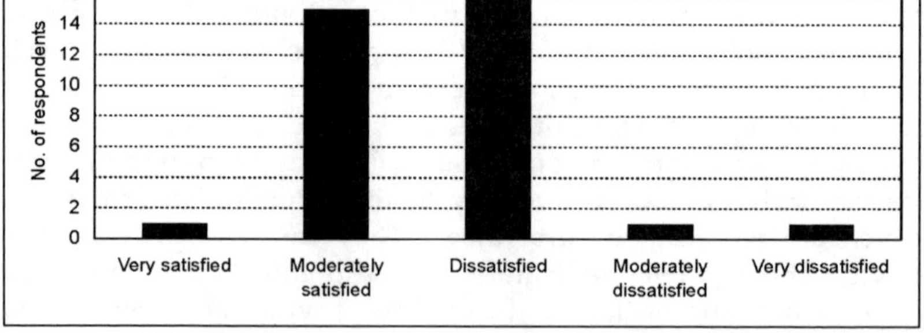

When the respondents were asked to react on a hypothetical possibility that if a handsome remuneration package was offered, would you move beyond your most favoured destination countries, 12 doctors answered positively, while the remaining 22 doctors showed no intention of changing their preferences only on a monetary account. Ten of them said that "quality of education and training (experience) are more important than money". Besides, quality of life, environment, professional freedom, and above all, the scope for pursuing a career in the chosen area of specialization were more important considerations in such a decision. When asked about the expected monetary returns in the host country, all of the respondents, except one, were hopeful of getting what they expected. Their argument was that there were plenty of employment opportunities overseas in the field of health services, and so they saw no reason to be sceptical about the size of the remuneration packet they would be offered in the destination country.

Furthermore, the respondents were asked about the difficulties faced by the medical professionals (especially doctors) while pursuing their career in India. A large number of respondent doctors made the point that to get into medical education was very difficult in India mainly due to limited number of seats and the consequently tough competition. The policy that a number places are reserved based on one's caste[5] (henceforth referred to as reservation policy) in the institutions of higher education, including medical education, was cited as one of the major drawbacks of the admission system, which resulted in the lowering down of the standard of education and the quality of professionals as well. Lack of proper training facilities, low quality of medical infrastructure, lack of proper guidance, bleak employment opportunities and lack of qualitative research endeavours were highlighted as some of the crucial hurdles in the advancement of the medical profession in India. When respondents were asked to anticipate the difficulties while pursuing their medical career overseas, most of the respondents felt that socio-cultural problem and racial bias could be the most severe problems overseas which they might have to face abroad. They also voiced the fear of becoming 'second-class citizens' in the host country.

## The Case Study of Nurses: Data Presentation and Analysis

This section presents the information related to nurses and their perception about out-migration overseas. The entire sample has been drawn from one medical institution of New Delhi, i.e., Kalawati Saran Children's Hospital. The analysis is based on the information provided by 40 nurses responding through a field survey.

Almost 60 per cent of the sample (24 nurses) is above 30 years of age. Three of them are in their late forties, and they all desire to move overseas because their immediate family members, including children, are staying abroad. Fifteen nurses aged between 25–30 years of age constitute 38 per cent of the sample. Only one respondent nurse is below 25 years. In comparison to the nurses, prospective emigrant doctors are quite young with an average age of 25 years while the average age of respondent nurses is 33 years. Furthermore, 35 nurses (88%) are married.

Around half of the nurses in the sample (18 nurses) are from Kerala, and one-fourth (10 nurses) are from New Delhi. The other twelve respondent nurses are from eight states—three each from Haryana and Uttar Pradesh, two each from Tamil Nadu and Maharashtra, and one each from Bihar and Himachal Pradesh.

Most of the nurses (32) have completed a diploma in nursing. Four nurses only have a graduation degree, while another four have done both a diploma and a graduation degree. It was understood during the survey that in the nursing profession, a diploma is considered an essential qualification, and if it is accompanied by a degree in nursing, upward mobility in the nursing career becomes easier.

Eleven nurses (more than one-fourth of the sample) belong to the pre-1990 vintage of education, and they now have more than thirteen years of work experience each. Twenty-six nurses completed their education during the 1990s, and only three respondents completed their education after the year 2000.

The highest number of nurses (10) in the sample are from Lady Hardinge Medical College, New Delhi. One reason for this is the fact that the Kalawati Saran Children's Hospital is itself affiliated to the college. This is followed by the Kerala University (4 nurses) and the Indira Gandhi National Open University at New Delhi (4 nurses). Some of the respondents mentioned that they preferred to have their diplomas as well as degrees in nursing from the Indira Gandhi National Open University, as it helped in their professional career growth to have completed their last educational degree from an institution based in New Delhi.

Twenty-seven nurses have been planning for one to two years to move overseas, and some of them have also qualified necessary tests like the TOEFL (Test of English as a Foreign Language). Five nurses were planning their out-migration for the last 6 years, but were waiting for the right opportunities of better training facilities abroad and better income prospects. Family location is one of the important factors, which is forcing them to stay back, as moving overseas involves movement of the entire family. Five nurses said they have been planning for out-migration only for the last 3–4 years, but have not been able to move for various reasons. A further seventeen nurses mentioned that they would migrate in 1–2 years, as certain eligibility tests needed to be met before going abroad. While fifteen nurses said they would take at least 3–4 years for migrating, eight nurses could not say anything on this issue.

Out of the 40 nurses, 11 respondents have passed the required tests (like TOEFL) to get into the hospitals overseas, while 29 nurses have not passed any tests yet.

Figure 16 reflects the motivating factors that have inspired the nurses' decisions for intended out-migration. "Friends overseas" is a strong factor that helped 20 nurses in taking this decision, apart from the self-motivation of 27 nurses. Family and friends in India are also decisive motivating factors for 16 nurses each, and 8 nurses said that they are going abroad to get employment on the advice of senior nurses, who have been abroad for sometime. Some nurses sought the help of consultants, who have come to play an important role in influencing the decision of out-migration.

**Figure 16**

*Source of Inspiration for Emigration for Nurses*

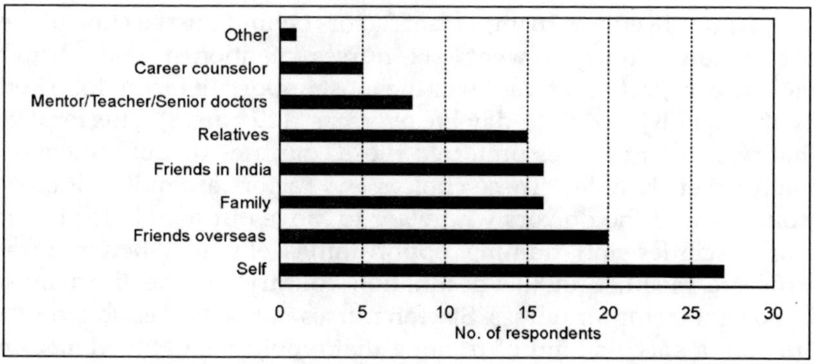

Figure 17 describes the purpose behind the intended out-migration of the respondent nurses. Out of 40 respondent nurses, 31 mentioned that "to get a job with better training opportunities" has been the main purpose to go abroad. They think they can always come back to India after a certain period of foreign training, which would be of value in Indian hospitals. Nineteen nurses want to move overseas because they want to progress faster in their medical career, which is not possible and feasible in India due to the reservation policies and caste-based politics in the job market (see Footnote 5). They also discussed the problems faced by them due to outdated medical facilities, which emerges as very important factor. They mentioned that careers in India are stagnant, education and training facilities are not good for nurses and pay packets are also not attractive. One respondent nurse said that she would be going abroad for her research assignment.

**Figure 17**

*Purpose of Intended Out-Migration of Nurses*

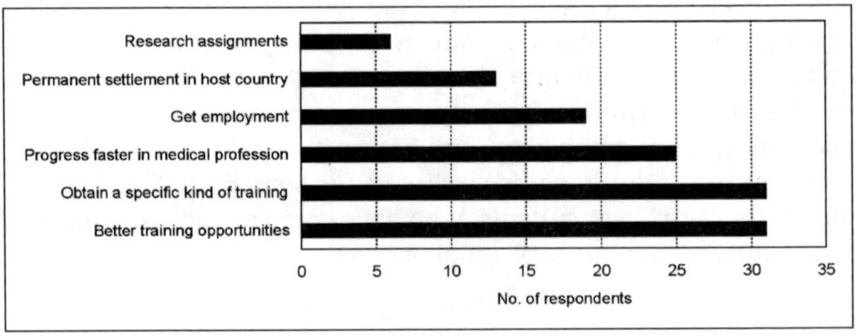


Figure 18 enlists 16 important factors behind the selection of the destination country. Twenty-six nurses mentioned that "better income prospects overseas" was the most important factor, followed by the "quality of day-to-day life overseas" (25 nurses). This implies that respondent nurses preferred those countries that offered good life for their families. These choices and factors are quite different from those of the doctors who want to move out mainly for better work facilities and training opportunities abroad. "Better infrastructure facilities in the destination country" is the third most important factor for nurses. Sixteen nurses out of 40 mentioned that "to gain a specific kind of training that would be highly valued in

India" they would move overseas. One of the other specific factors is that 17 respondent nurses are looking for "better school and education for their children" (first preference by nine nurses, second and third preferences by four nurses each). It is also to be noted here that only eight respondent nurses mention that they foresee "bleak or low employment opportunities in India." Therefore, one may draw a conclusion that respondent nurses want to move to those countries which have better opportunities and support for their families in terms of better infrastructure facilities, day-to-day lifestyle, schools for children, etc., apart from better income prospects overseas.

**Figure 18**

*Motivating Factors for Out-Migration of Nurses*

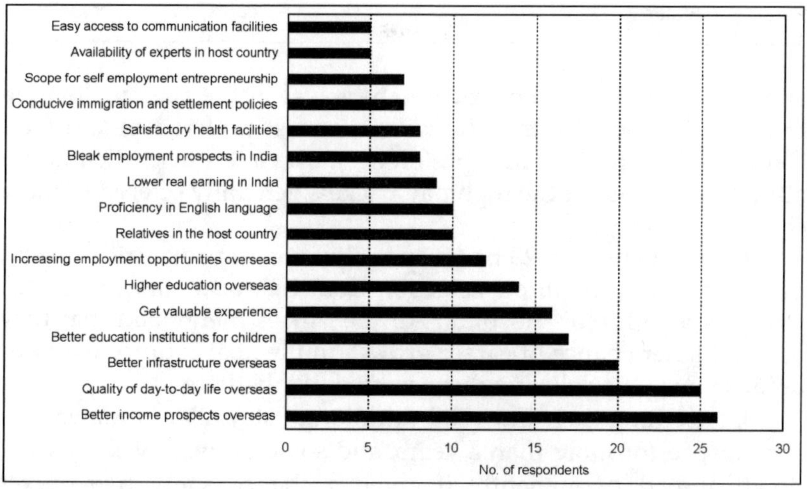


Figure 19 details the distribution of nurses by their favourite destination countries. Forty nurses were quite clear about their destination countries and had a specific choice for a particular country. The United States is their first choice (all 40 nurses choosing it in their first three preferences), followed by the United Kingdom (25, with 8 in first preference), both are chosen because of abundant employment opportunities. Third choice was Australia (25, with 3 in first preference) because of its climate and newly emerging employment opportunities, specifically after the IT boom. Nine nurses (with 2 in first preference) also considered Canada as a destination country. Some nurses have a liking for Switzerland, Germany

**Figure 19**

*Preferred Destination Countries for Out-Migration of Nurses*

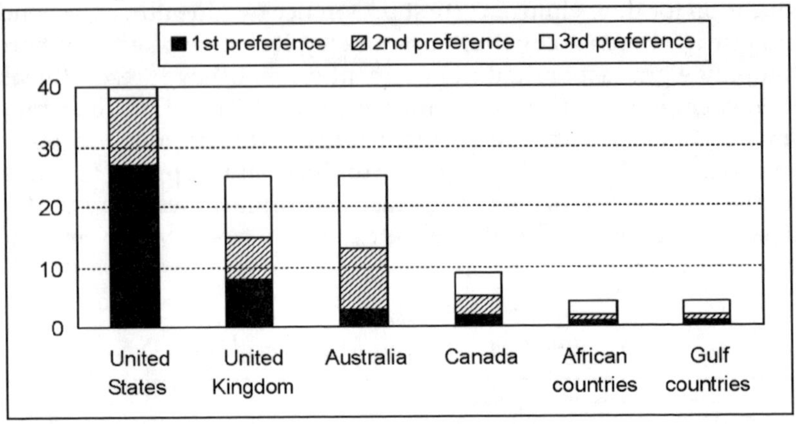


and Malaysia (not in the figure). There was also a clear inclination towards African countries (4, with 1 in first preference) and Gulf countries (4, with 1 in first preference). The latter in particular are attractive because of the high pay packets generally offered in these countries.

Out of 40 nurses, 23 had a specialization in paediatric nursery, mainly due to the sample selection from Kalawati Saran Hospital, which is a children's hospital. All the nurses mentioned that they have a higher chance of career growth in the host country overseas because their specialization was valued highly there.

Concerning their intended duration of stay, 25 nurses want to stay abroad for more than 4 years, and some of them wish to settle down abroad permanently if given a chance. Only five nurses mentioned that they would come back in 1–2 years, because they "want to serve the nation" with knowledge and training acquired abroad.

The breakdown of nurses by their perceptions about the relative career growth abroad as compared to in India shows that 39 nurses perceive that career growth is faster overseas. They also say that reservation policies and monotonous/pre-determined career paths are proving to be barriers in their career enhancement in India, whereas these factors are not there abroad where equal opportunity would allow them to be judged by their knowledge and competency.

Figure 20 reveals the perceptions of nurses about the education, training and experience provided by medical institutions in India. Twenty-three nurses mentioned that they are "moderately satisfied" with the facilities, while seven mentioned that they are "very satisfied". Nine nurses are "dissatisfied", the reason being absence of high quality training facilities for nurses and an absence of opportunities to attend any training programme to learn more about new research and technologies. One nurse is "very dissatisfied" because of the reservation policies. Overall, 30 nurses were satisfied with the training provided and 10 were dissatisfied.

**Figure 20**

*Level of Satisfaction with Education, Training and Experience in India*

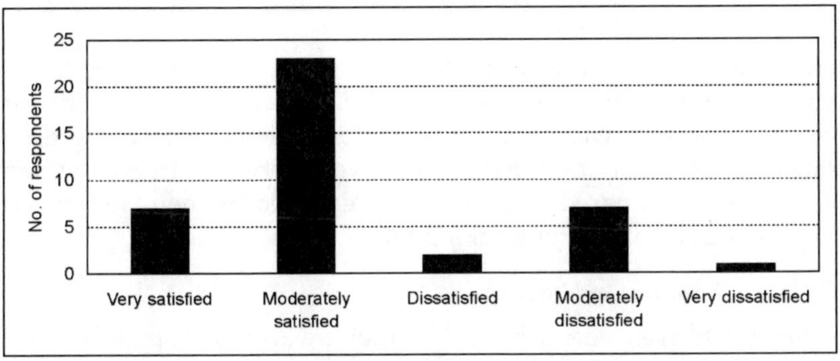


Reflecting on the perceptions of nurses about foreign credentials of nurses in India, according to seventeen respondents, foreign educated and trained nurses have a "very good" future in hospitals in general and private hospitals in particular. Ten nurses said that there were no differences between foreign and Indian credentials, because ultimately it was a matter of quality of hands-on training, whether it was overseas or in India. They also mentioned that Indian nurses are in high demand overseas, proving that Indian nurses are not behind foreign-educated nurses. Furthermore, they felt that the Indian health sector was progressing very fast, and therefore there would be more demand for nurses. However, eleven out of the forty nurses mentioned that it was very difficult to pursue a nursing career in India, as limited opportunities were available for career growth.

Figure 21 lists the level of monetary satisfaction derived by the nurses from their present salary in India. Thirty-four respondent

**Figure 21**

*Level of Satisfaction with Present Salary in India*

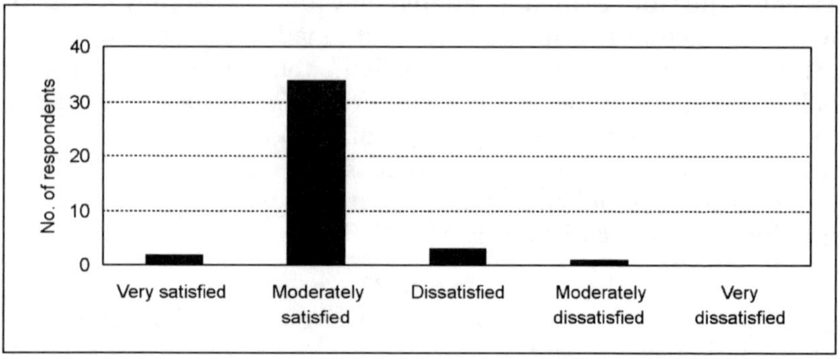


nurses were "moderately satisfied" with the present salary levels, but only two were "very satisfied." Three nurses were "dissatisfied," and one was "moderately dissatisfied" with the present salary. They mentioned that salaries were very low in government hospitals as compared to the services rendered by them, in terms of high workload and long working hours.

*Random Questions to Nurses*

When the nurses were asked about their awareness of possible difficulties that they might have to face overseas, 22 nurses confirmed this. The respondents mentioned that they might have to face a number of problems of adjustment to the new culture, such as accommodation, food, racial discrimination and language problems. Apart from these, disruption of family life, change of climate, new lifestyle and effective economic and penal disincentives linked to performance failure were also some other possible difficulties of which they were aware.

They also mentioned some of the facilities being provided by the foreign hospitals, for example accommodation, handsome pay packets, chances of further training for career enhancement and insurance (social security). However, the respondents considered that further training facility and income were the most favourable facilities offered abroad. They were mostly confident about receiving good future earnings in the host country with the only exception of one respondent, who was sceptical about the net benefits in case she was to take the services of foreign placement agencies which are charging high fees, sometimes exorbitantly.

When the nurses were asked about their contribution to the national development if they would not come back, they mentioned that they could do so in various ways. One of the important ways was through charity, i.e., donations in both cash and kind. The latter could include books, equipments, etc., particularly for the benefit of the children back in India. Some of the nurses mentioned that they would like to participate in knowledge sharing from abroad. However, twelve nurses could not answer this question. They mentioned that though it was difficult for them to tell what exactly they could do, they surely wanted to contribute to the nation's development. Most importantly, seven of the forty nurses mentioned that they would definitely come back to their home country, India.

Most respondents mentioned that after coming back they would serve the nation through better knowledge and service-experience gained abroad, and that they would also be involved in some charity work. They further emphasized that their enriched knowledge would be their main contribution in the national development of India.

When asked "what do you think about the situation when more and more skilled out-migration is taking place from India?", the respondents said that out-migration would take place in the future as well, because it would not depend on their migration decisions only, but also on the government policies related to education, employment, reservation, etc. They also argued that if one had to minimize migration, we ought to provide world-class training and other facilities with good income prospects to the next generation of highly-skilled Indians. If we fail to do this all, migration of future generations would also occur.

### *Foreign-educated Returning Indian Doctors*

Recently, the Medical Council of India (MCI) has made it mandatory for every overseas-qualified doctor to pass an examination before starting their career of medicine in India, particularly those returning from the Commonwealth of Independent States (CIS) countries—mainly Russia—a decision which, though contested, was later upheld by the Supreme Court of India after a few hearings. To understand the perception of the returnee doctors about this decision of the Indian government, as well as the quality of education they received abroad in these countries, eight returning doctors were interviewed informally. Out of these eight doctors, four were educated in Russia, two in Belarus, and two in the Ukraine. Of the eight doctors, three came from New Delhi and one each from Uttar Pradesh, Assam, Punjab, West Bengal and Haryana. All were unmarried, comprising seven males and one female.

*Motivating Factors to go Overseas for Medical Education*

Most of the doctors (6) responded that "family" was the main inspiring and motivating factor, as the best of medical education facilities were available abroad. "Friends in India", and "relatives" got the next highest scores. Thus, it is clear that family has been the main factor behind their going abroad. However, the interviewees observed that the most important factor was their failure to get admission into any good medical college/institution in India.

*Purpose of going Abroad for Getting a Medical Degree*

Almost all doctors (7) responded that higher education was the main factor. The second important reason for going abroad was to get a job with better training opportunities. For one doctor it was relatively easier to have access to high-standard medical education in the CIS countries than in India. One doctor also put forth the view that the average quality of medical education in Russia was much better than the average in India, which motivated him to go there.

*Important Factors in Choosing the Destination*

Almost all doctors (7) responded that quality of the medical education was the first important consideration in choosing the host country. Two of them said that 'the bleak employment prospect in India' was the first important factor for them. One (the lone female) doctor said that she had "relatives in the host country", and that the "quality of day-to-day life" too were very important factors. "Better infrastructure overseas", "availability of experts in the concerned medical field" in the host country were second most important factors for two doctors. Concerning the third important factor, it was 'bleak employment prospects in India' for two returning doctors, 'relatives in the host country' for another two and "quality of day-to-day life" for another three. They mentioned that conducive immigration policies also helped them in choosing these countries for their medical education.

*Favourite Destination Countries*

All respondent doctors (8) went abroad in 1995 and returned in 2001–2002. The first preferred destination for five doctors was Russia, while for one respondent it was the United Kingdom. Two respondents said that the United States and South Korea were their favourite destinations, respectively. As a second preferred destination, five doctors preferred Russia, while for one doctor it was the United Kingdom. For another two doctors, it was the United States and South Africa respectively. As a third preferred destination, some doctors opted for the United Kingdom, Australia and Fiji. For three doctors, their third preferred destinations were Russia, South Africa and Ireland respectively. Irrespective of these preferred destinations though, all the doctors had finally gone to the CIS countries. Out of the eight doctors, four had not qualified in any admission test of medical education in their preferred countries.

*Present Area of Specialization*

When asked about their specialization, three of them said they were general physicians, while others had diplomas in internal medicine, surgery, orthopaedic surgery, etc. As far as demand for their specialization in India was concerned, almost all the doctors sounded optimistic, except for one who was holding a negative view of the situation, mentioning that his degree could best be utilized in the position of medical officer in India.

*Difficulties in Pursuing Medical Education in India*

While four doctors said that there was no specific difficulty, the other four stressed difficulties arising from a limited number of seats, made worse by the reservation policies, tough competition, a lack of standardized quality higher education across the various institutions and rampant corruption—difficulties which forced them to go abroad for medical education.

*Jobs expected before Coming to India*

The expected jobs mentioned were those of medical officer and private practitioner. Two of the doctors were also hopeful of becoming consultants to various hospitals in India. As far as other career choices were concerned, public health services, community medicine and medical administration were the expected preferred jobs for four of the doctors. When asked about their professional growth in India compared to other countries, four doctors said it was slower in India, and two said it was more or less the same. Almost all doctors were "very much satisfied" with the kind of education/training they got overseas and only one was 'moderately satisfied'. Six doctors also added that there was no discrimination in job offers being made to them abroad.

*Perceptions About MCI's Decision to Introduce Compulsory Qualifying Test for Foreign-Educated Doctors*

Almost all returning doctors strongly opposed this decision with the argument that such a test was not adequate to judge the skill and quality of a doctor, as hands-on experience was also important in the making of a good doctor. Six doctors responded that there should not be any discriminatory policy against them, once MCI had recognized the foreign medical colleges from which they graduated. One of the doctors was of the view that this screening test should be conducted only after completion of an internship in India and should not pre-empt the permission to get registered for an internship. Two of them said that the entrance test should be conducted not only for those who got their medical education abroad, especially from Russia, but also for those who got medical degrees from any private institution in India.

The doctors educated in India and covered in this sample survey were also asked to give their reaction to the MCI's decision of making it mandatory for every overseas-qualified doctor to pass certain examination before starting his/her internship/career in medicine in India. Diverse opinions were expressed by these India-educated doctors. As high as 85 per cent of the respondents (29 doctors) supported the MCI's decision. They said that it was a good decision and every foreign-educated doctor should qualify the test before starting his/her professional career in India. Ten respondents suggested that MCI should publish a list of institutions abroad whose credentials are reputed and reliable. A few of them agreed with the policy, but felt that it should be implemented only after some qualitative modifications were incorporated.

*Credentials of Foreign-Educated Doctors in India*

As far as credentials of foreign-educated doctors were concerned, the eight returning doctors said that if MCI recognized their degree, they would have similar credentials as doctors educated in India, and so their future would be similar to those of Indian doctors.

*Expected Monetary Returns in India and Quid pro quo*

The doctors said they would get expected monetary returns in India if allowed to practice. However, three were not sure about the returns, particularly because of the uncertainty of being allowed to enter the profession in India due to MCI's decision. When asked about their potential contribution to India's development, four doctors responded by saying that they would undertake charity work and also provide scholarships to needy students; one doctor said he would contribute through activities of non-governmental organizations and another was of the opinion that he would serve the rural masses.

This survey reflects the awareness, perception and anxiety of foreign-educated doctors who want to serve in the home country, but are not allowed to pursue their medical career in India automatically. They are quite sure about their future, career growth and monetary prospects in the Indian medical profession if allowed to work. They seem to be very committed but their being barred from working in India raises many questions and contradictions between highly skilled migration being looked at as brain-drain on one hand and qualified returnees from abroad not considered as a brain-gain. One really needs to understand and resolve these contradictions and the dilemmas arising from them.

## Concluding Remarks

Bangalore has an important role in promoting the out and in-migration of professionals, including IT professionals and others from different fields like teaching, management, medicine and architecture, etc. During the IT-boom of the late 1990s and the beginning of 21st century, rapid economic growth in Bangalore led to the development of other economic activities. For example, during the Bangalore field survey, some architects said they had gained in terms of higher wage-rates triggered by the IT-boom in Bangalore. Similarly, in the case of medical professionals, a Commission on Graduates of Foreign Nursing Schools (CGFNS) Test Centre was opened in September 2001 in Bangalore. This initiative had been taken to better coordinate the out-migration of nurses (*Hindustan Times*, 2003). Already, four rounds of tests have been held for the selection of nurses for out-migration, the last one being scheduled on 12 March 2003. In each round as many as 1,500 nurses appeared for the examination. Estimates show that there is a shortage of 1,00,000 nursing personnel in US hospitals and this shortage has been projected to quadruple in the next few years.

The findings of both case studies show that young IT professionals as well as the medical professionals want to go abroad mainly to gain professional experience, which they think will be highly valued in India when they come back. In addition, they are encouraged by higher earnings, perks and high quality of life in the host country. However, unlike the IT professionals as well as most doctors, the majority of prospective nurses want to settle down abroad permanently, because they hardly perceive their career prospects to be bright in India. Amongst the doctors, only some are prepared to settle down abroad permanently if they get a chance. The fact that none of the respondent professionals in Bangalore gave priority to the idea of settling down abroad highlights a unique aspect behind Bangalore becoming a "corridor" for migration (outward and inward) of Indian HRST, which is not the case with health professionals from New Delhi. The IT professionals in Bangalore feel that they have growing opportunities for their career growth in India in general and Bangalore in particular. The other interviewed professionals (such as academics) in Bangalore also found themselves comfortable in the cosmopolitan city of Bangalore, though they believe New Delhi has better career prospects in academics.

The prospective returnee doctors from the CIS countries foresee a fast growing medical/health sector in India as the trigger behind their intentions to come back. However, eventually they perhaps would change their mind because they are directly dependent on the demand for medical services from people, who are largely poor in India and therefore unable to pay adequately for the services. In contrast, the IT professionals can feel confident about returning through the corridors like Bangalore because of their (a) dependence on a fast growing IT sector/companies, and (b) ease of re-migrating abroad through the corridor, and thus participate in circulatory migration.

After the wave of migration of doctors, IT personnel and nurses from India, the latest turn is of teachers. Newspapers show significant advertisements at regular intervals for the positions of teachers for countries like the United States, the United Kingdom, New Zealand, Australia, etc. An organization called "Recruiting New Teachers (RNT)" says that over the next 10 years the United States would need to hire two million teachers, because half of their teachers would retire during this period. These countries prefer Indian teachers because of the perception that Indians have good fluency in English and have received quality higher education.

## Notes

1. Weighting the answers was tried on some questions, but it did not significantly alter the results.
2. The conversion into US $ (with exchange rates) probably gives a good estimate of the value of the savings, because this money was earned abroad. The conversion into PPP, on the other hand, gives a better idea what the investment is worth in India.
3. See the section on IT professionals for an explanation of the ranking system.
4. Four respondent doctors had contacts with 'Maulana Azad Medical College Old Students Association (MAMCOSA)' and three had ties with 'AIIMSONIANS of America' through the Internet, while three others mentioned that they were influenced by their 'seniors' (doctors) through the AIIMS Students Union. However, all of them confirmed the role medical associations played in providing a platform to grapple with professional problems, supplying valuable information related to various jobs and educational openings in various countries, as well as the socio-cultural support.
5. In India, there is a Constitutional requirement of positive discrimination or affirmative action in education/employment whereby a quota of 22.5 per cent of all admissions in government institutions of education/of all government jobs is exclusively offered to (reserved for) applicants belonging to some designated minorities listed as Scheduled Castes and Scheduled Tribes.

## Bibliography

*Hindustan Times*. 2003. "Report on Prime Minister's Inaugural Speech at the Indian Science Congress in Bangalore". 16 February 2003 (and various other issues), New Delhi.

Khadria, B. 2001. "Offshore Universities and the Paradox of Factor-Endowment and Factor-Use in Trade-in-Services". Paper presented at the Sixth Biennial Oxford International Conference on Education and Development: Knowledge, Values and Policy, 19–21 September 2001, Oxford.

—. 2004. "Human Resources in Science and Technology in India and the International Mobility of Highly Skilled Indians". STI Working Paper, 2004/7, OECD, Paris.

Lateef, A. 1997. Linking up with the Global Economy: A Case Study of the Bangalore Software Industry. New Industrial Organization Programme, DP/96/1997, Geneva.

NASSCOM (National Association of Software and Service Companies). 1995. *Indian Software Directory, 1995–96*. New Delhi: NASSCOM.

Stremlau, J. 1996. "Dateline Bangalore: Third World Technopolis". *Journal of Foreign Policy*, March: 152–168, cited in A. Lateef (1997).

# 8

# Circulation of Indian IT Professionals to Hyderabad and Beyond

## Integrating India in a Global Workforce

ERIC LECLERC

India has become a major player in the production of software as it has benefited by the relocation of production facilities from the innovating countries. India's integration in the world's high technology market has not only radically changed its geo-economic position in the international arena, but it is also a powerful factor in the transformation of human mobility. New Information and Communication Technologies (ICTs) constitute a sector that highlights the openness of the Indian economy having an annual growth rate of around 28 per cent since 1999[1] and accounting for a total revenue of 29.5 billion (2006). Though this represents only 4.8 per cent of the GNP, it amounts to more than 25 per cent of India's exports ($23.4 billion). To analyze the impact of the Indian diaspora on the revolution of Information Technologies (IT) in India, we followed the actors in this revolution or the producers of software companies established in Hyderabad (Andhra Pradesh). Two sets of international actors can be studied in Hyderabad according to the scale (temporal and spatial) of their movements: those engaged in short-duration missions for their companies in India and non-resident Indians who have returned to their homeland on a more or less permanent basis. We have to move to Malaysia to study a third group, Indian IT workers abroad. In this paper, we will address the issues of the brain gain and the global workforce in the

IT sector. What can India expect from the brain gain in the IT sector? What challenges is India likely to face in a global IT labour market?

**The Brain Gain in the IT Sector in Hyderabad**

Why Hyderabad and not Bangalore? IT activities are generally associated with Bangalore (the "Silicon Plateau") rather than Hyderabad. The history of software began in both these cities in 1986 with the setting up of the Texas Instrument Research Center in Bangalore and the relocation of Intergraph in Hyderabad at the same time, but on a lower scale. However, Hyderabad holds fewer local winning cards than the capital of Karnataka (it has no IIT, no Indian Institute of Science[2]).

**Figure 1**
*HITEC City*

In Hyderabad, an external factor, namely the diaspora, produced a deeper impact on the IT revolution which occurred a decade later (1996) thanks to the solid political support from the new Chief Minister, Chandrababu Naïdu. With nearly 1,200 IT companies, including the giants (Microsoft, Wipro, TCS), now operating in the city and its exports reaching Rs 12.600 crores in 2005–2006,[3] Hyderabad's success is impressive. But what is the share of the Indian diaspora in this success? Indeed, the development of this new productive system attracts a large number of professionals from all over India, 80 per cent of the IT professionals in Hyderabad being migrants[4] whose main characteristics are:

- young (average age 27.5 years), male (75%) and mobile (50% come from regions more than 500 km away, well beyond the borders of Andhra Pradesh).

But there is also another flow, this one from the diaspora coming back to India: the Brain Gain. Among the software professionals questioned in 2003 in Hyderabad,[5] we located some examples of international reverse migration. This group is very different from the preceding sample. Its members are older (average age 35 years) due to their international experience. Their position in the company is higher with 80 per cent of the sample occupying managerial or administrative posts. Most have spent 3 to 4 years abroad but they can be divided into two distinct groups: long-term expatriates (5–6 years) and short-term expatriates (1–2 years).

- Members of the first group, who had lived abroad the longest, began their professional life abroad (United States) after higher studies, either in India or in the country of their first employment. After 5 to 6 years of professional life abroad, they returned to Hyderabad either as employees of a multinational corporations or to set up their own companies. As per the statements of the interviewees, emigration to the United States took place in the early nineties when it was almost compulsory to work in the software sector. They had to acquire the technical skills and work culture of a sector with international standards.
- On the contrary, the members of the second group, who had spent less time abroad, began their professional life in India. After going through the various hierarchical levels in their company and reaching managerial positions, they migrated to the West. So they already have a long career (8 to 9 years) in this sector in India. For those who went abroad through their company, this was a stage in their career.

We must consider these movements as circulation rather than migration. However, the "second generation effect", as Professor Khadria (1999) calls it, is very difficult to assess. Taking into account the three Ms, Money, Machine and Man, to measure the return of human capital, he concluded his study by dividing knowledge workers into two categories: first-generation NRIs (pre-1980 migrants), who are able to provide Money and Machine, and second-generation NRIs (post-1980 migrants), who return to India either to settle down permanently or for a temporary stay (the third

M, viz., Man). The persons we analyzed during our interviews were post-1993 migrants. They seem to be able to contribute to the return of human capital, the third out of there Ms, (though we have still not assessed in what proportion). In a recent study, Ann-lee Saxenian et al. (2002) pointed out that 24 per cent of Indians in Silicon Valley have invested money in India (as compared to only 10% of mainland Chinese) and that 45 per cent intend to return to their country of origin. Our hypothesis is that in the IT sector, economic and professional assimilation has taken place faster. So even fresh NRIs are able to return a part of their human capital. They have already raised the productivity of the Indian IT sector to international standards. In the IT sector, India can expect a faster return of human capital than in other sectors like health or academics.

What we observed in Hyderabad in 2003, was a simultaneous movement of people coming back and others going out of the country. It shows the complexity of the movements of IT professionals. It is less and less possible to assess the impact of the diaspora on a migratory approach (i.e., return of people), so we have conducted a study on mobility within the company and emigration of professionals abroad. Again, these movements are on a world scale because they involve the export of software companies. So the comparison between these professional movements and the movements of Indians returning to their country is meaningful.

## Circulation of IT Professionals from Hyderabad

We have been able to study the inflow of IT professionals settling in Hyderabad, and their exit abroad, but on a smaller scale because it was impossible to follow them everywhere. For young professionals today a first job in an Indian company may be a first step towards emigration to the United States or Europe. So we have decided to observe international movements within software companies and in one of their location abroad, in Malaysia. In the eighties and early nineties, the development of software in India was based on work on site (body shopping). This model is in regression with the decrease of H-1B visas for the United States. With the crisis in the new economy, the outsourcing process has gained momentum. More and more international companies are relying on outsourcing. Despite the disapproval of political leaders,[6] they intend to continue with it. According to a recent survey conducted by the Chicago consulting firm Diamond Cluster International,[7] 86 per cent of the companies polled expect to send more technology jobs overseas within the next 12 months. This figure was only 32 per cent two years ago. But this change doesn't put an end to the movement of people outside India. Despite the threat today to the L-1 visa being used for mobility inside a company, these movements have not disappeared. To understand how companies manage the distance factor, i.e., the distance between the place of production and the distribution of products, we asked questions about international professional movements on behalf of the company.[8]

These movements relate to two types of people: the higher level executives and employees at all training levels. We observed three situations depending on the category of the company type and it's size.

- In the case of large foreign companies (AVINEON, IIC SYSTEMS, DANLAW TECHNOLOGIES), which have opened software development or service centres in India, internal movements are very few. They are almost exclusively limited to managers who move to the firm's headquarters 5 to 6 times a year for about two weeks at a time.
- Multinationals (KEANE, INTERNATIONAL WILCO SYSTEMS, DELOITTE CONSULTING), which have opened a branch in India, are very similar in size and managerial habits; so managers move in the same way as in the previous type of companies. However, the employees' mobility is different. These companies send their employees for training to the parent company for durations close to six months. Moreover, half of these companies use a part of their employees to work on site for long periods (6 months). In spite of a rather similar company profile, mobility is much more significant for the latter and corresponds to a higher investment in India.
- Finally, the Indian companies which are smaller and fall into two categories: companies with a working strength of 50 to 60 (INNOSOFT, SYSTEL COMPUTERS) and small companies having around 10 employees. For the latter, only the managers move for long durations of 4 to 12 weeks to look for new clients. In medium-sized firms, in addition to the movements of managers there are also employee movements lasting for a few years. In fact, some of these Indian companies have set up

branches in the United States. They send some of their employees to do the work on the spot: this is a new form of body-shopping.

Changes in the economic and geographical situations between India and high technology countries generate movements on a world scale and in two directions, either of NRIs or expatriate employees to work in Indian or multinational branches of software companies. Thanks to the relocation in India of New Information Technology-related companies, circulation for purposes of marketing, management or training of employees has increased tremendously. The number of movements is not always proportional to the size of the companies since the smaller ones have to promote themselves on their own without any network for their distribution market. Movements within the company relate to activities demanding a face to face meeting. This finding confirmed F. Ascher's (1995) hypothesis that New Information and Communication Technologies lead to increased movements when it is impossible to communicate electronically. Its second assumption of an increased mobility proportionate to the new opportunities offered by New Information and Communication Technologies is also observed in Hyderabad.

## Andhra IT Professionals Abroad

During the two months' fieldwork in the Malaysian capital, we could study this population of Indian software professionals. We carried out around fifty interviews in Kuala Lumpur where they are exclusively located, in order to identify the characteristics of this new wave of Indian immigration in Malaysia. To fill the lack of computer skills, the legislation on the recruitment of the immigrant workers, however very strict in Malaysia, was adapted in the sector of the NICT. The companies recorded at the Multi-media Super Corridor can recruit as many foreign employees they want. The company submits its request to the authorities of the MSC which forwards it to the immigration department. After the criteria of education (diplomas) and professional experience of the potential immigrants (at least 3 years) have been checked, they deliver in one week a letter of approval which makes it possible to obtain the temporary visa of employment. In comparison with the official figures, the Indians account for 50 per cent of the foreign software professionals recruited by Malaysia. They are particularly required for the development of software.

The demographic structure of the sample shows (Graph 1) a composition in two groups: firstly, of young professionals (around 28 years) with the minimum of necessary professional experiment (3 years) to obtain their visa, and in addition an older group (around 35 years) at management level.

**Graph 1**

*Age Structure*

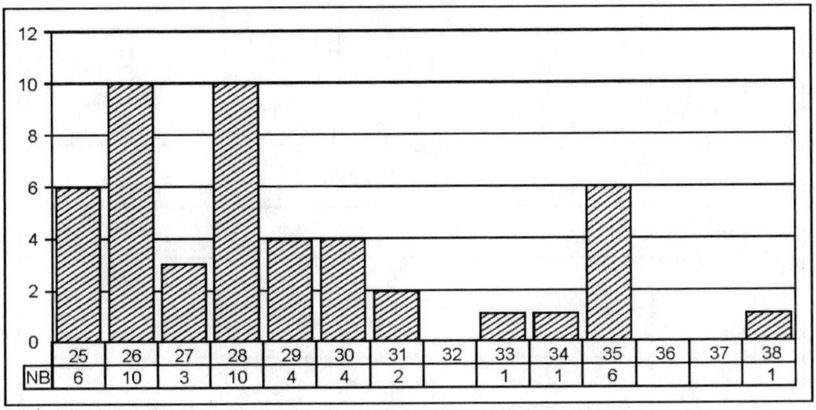


**Graph 2**

*Birth Place*

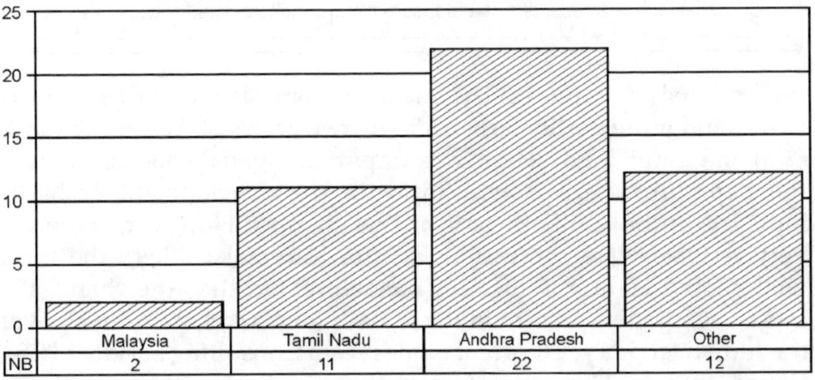


To locate this immigration compared to the preceding waves, we were also interested at the place of birth of the software

**Graph 3**

*First Choice*

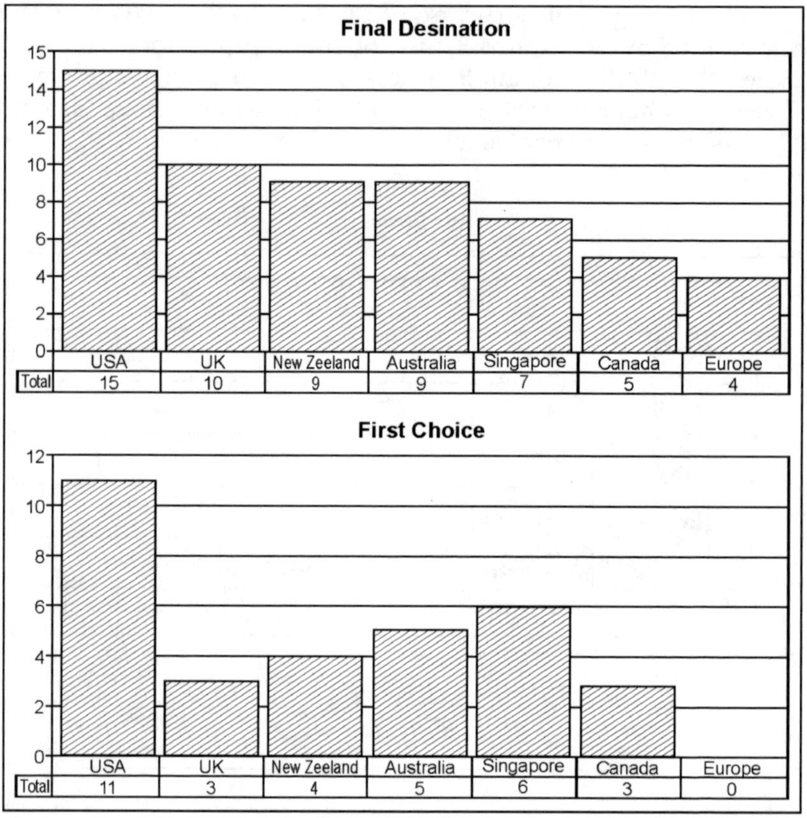


professionals (Graph 2). The majority come from southern India (70%), and more particularly from the two States of Andhra Pradesh (2/3) and Tamil Nadu (1/3). This important spatial concentration of the departure areas is relevant with the development of NTIC industry in the southern part of this country. However, there are very few software professionals from Karnataka where the most well-known IT hub is located, Bangalore. On the other hand, the Indian companies present in the Malaysian market are from all over the Indian territory. The great names, Tata Consulting Service (TCS), Wipro, Infosys, Hindustan Computers Limited are there. With the multinational firms of the sector, Hewlett Packard, Sun Microsystem, Oracle, Lucent, Microsoft, Siemens or Alcatel, they account for 14 per cent of the total number of companies installed in Malaysia.

To limit the recourse to a foreign labour, Malaysia tries to develop higher and technical training institutes like the multi-media university established in Cyberjaya. But these establishments which have its share of Indian professors, produces yet only young graduates without professional experience.

We sought to know at which stage of their career these Indian software professionals undertake this temporary migration. When we questioned them about their professional biography, we noted their short experiment for international migrants and especially for software professionals, a profession with a very fast turn-over. They are divided roughly into three-thirds, with two years of professional experiences for the first-third, then an additional year of experiment for each following third (30% the second employment, 30% the third employment, 30% the fourth employment, and 10% fifth).

The impression of a new career is corroborated by the fact that for 90 per cent of the Indian software professionals, it was their first expatriation. A more surprising fact, for two third of them, it is their first professional experience outside their state of birth, whereas the Indian software industry is characterized by a strong internal spatial mobility (Leclerc, 2003, 2004). To know if this temporary migration is part of a wider project, we also asked them what they would wish to do at the end of their Malaysian tenure. About 75 per cent wish to continue their migration towards other countries. The final destinations are the most developed Anglo-Saxon countries, the first country being the United States (Graph 3, Final Destination).

If their choice is detailed, according to the row of priority, one obtains results even more interesting. The first choice remains the United States, but in a more realistic way taking into account the difficulties of access to this country, it is Singapore, at the end of the Malaysian peninsula which takes the second place (Graphic 3, First choice). Australia and New Zealand are in good positions for the second choice. One sees a hierarchy of the destinations which corresponds at the various steps of a migratory movement which must be completed in the United States or, with equal share to the United Kingdom, in Australia and New Zealand. Studies on the software professionals highlighted these movements from Canada to the United States (Stackhouse, 2000), or from Australia to North America (Xiang, 2004). Since the attacks of September 11 and the reinforcement of the control of immigration, the immigrations in these two last destinations are in clear reduction. Malaysia is thus for many Indian software professionals, the door of entry into a global labour market, hierarchically organized.

**Conclusion**

The movements of IT professionals from India have to be correlated with similar movements of non-returned NRIs to India (80% of Silicon Valley Indians who have funded a company in India and travelled more than five times a year to this destination (Saxenian et al., 2002: 44). The circulation between the main poles of high technology in India and USA, has increased during the last decade. We need to analyze this phenomenon as a complex system of mobility where migration, circulation, temporary expatriation and also leisure movements are interlinked. What India can expect of its diaspora is less a matter of migration (return migration) than circulation. We have concluded from the first part of our study based on the survey of Returned NRIs, India can expect a faster return of human capital from IT professionals. The second part of the study suggests that this process of investment in India should be analyzed on a global scale. What the diaspora has already achieved is to connect some Indian metropolizes to the global economy. From the third part, we observe the creation of a global workforce of Indian IT professionals, so the export of brains is not over. Will this be enough to achieve a better return of human capital? The famous R.K. Narayana Murthy (2001) of Infosys believes in the growth of urban India and in a natural trickle-down effect to rural areas. But a widening gap between urban and rural areas may be very dangerous for India's social fabric in the near future. The connection of Indian metropolizes to a global urban network should not imply dissociation from the surrounding rural areas. The circulation of IT professionals is becoming more and more global. India and the Indian diaspora are playing an important role in this new global hi-tech workforce, but in this scenario, India may not be always at the centre-stage. The Indian diaspora has undoubtedly spread the positive values of mobility, widening opportunities for the young generation, but we must remember that they are not new values. The Sindworki merchants and Nattukottai Chettiar bankers whose history has been traced by C. Markovits (2000) or D.W. Rudner

(1995) already possessed these values, but perhaps they were not shared on the same scale as today.

## Notes

1. Source: National Association of Software and Service Companies (NASSCOM), see http://www.nasscom.in
2. For a complete analysis of the growth of Bangalore see Heitzman, J., 2004. *Network City*. OUP, Delhi.
3. These are only the software exports through the Software Technology Park of Hyderabad and we must add the export of services to this total, source http://www.stpp.soft.net/
4. Field work done by Stéphanie Morel during the first half of 2000. 121 employees in 17 software companies located mainly in Hitec-City were surveyed.
5. These data have been collected during field work in Hyderabad in January-February 2003 covering 13 interviews.
6. The outsourcing movement is an important issue in the developed countries. Regularly, it appears in the political debate both in North America and Europe.
7. Ref. Newspaper.
8. These data were collected during fieldwork in Hyderabad in January-February 2003 covering 25 interviews.

## References

Ascher, F. 1995. *Métapolis ou l'avenir des villes*. Paris: Odile Jacob.

Heitzman, J. 2004. *Network City*. Delhi: OUP.

Khadria, B. 1999. *The Migration of Knowledge Workers: Second Generation Effects of India's Brain Drain*. New Delhi: Sage Publications.

Leclerc, E. 2003. "Sur les marges de l'Archipel Mégapolitain Mondial, le pari des hautes technologies à Hyderabad (A.P., Inde)". In CME Interfaces (ed.). CEGUM, Université de Metz, Metz.

Markovits, C. 2000. *The Global World of Indian Merchants 1750–1947: Traders of Sind from Bukhara to Panama.* Cambridge Studies in Indian History and Society, Cambridge: Cambridge University Press.

Murthy, N.R.N. 2001. "Making India a Significant IT Player in This Millennium". In R. Thapar (ed.), *India, Another Millennium?*, pp. 212–240. New Delhi: Penguin Books.

Rudner, D.W. 1995. *Caste and Capitalism in Colonial India: The Nattukottai Chettiars*. New Delhi: Munshiram Manoharlal.

Saxenian, A., Motoyama, Y. and Quan, X. 2002. *Local and Global Networks of Immigrant Professionals in Silicon Valley*. San Francisco, CA: Public Policy Institute of California.

# 9

# Globalization, National Autonomy and Non-Resident Indians

MARGARET WALTON-ROBERTS

The convergence of territory and population with the boundaries of a distinctive civilization fortifies the ambition for autonomy as well as for a major role in world affairs.[1]

In this statement, B.R. Nayar argues that India's ability to maintain autonomy in the face of economic globalization is partly related to the size of territory and population. In this paper, I extend Nayar's analysis to consider how a divergence between population and territory also must be considered through an examination of the role played by India's non-resident Indians (NRIs) and persons of Indian origin (PIOs) population, both at the national and state level. The paper begins with a short review of globalization theories. I then offer a brief history of Indian out-migration, and highlight the magnitude of the economic contributions this NRI/PIO community has made to the Indian economy. I contextualize this overview with a discussion of some of the economic and cultural dimensions of NRI investment in the Doaba region of Punjab. In the conclusion, I support Nayar's argument that globalization processes (in this case, global migrant mobility and transnational connectivity), rather than undermining the power of the nation-state, can enhance its autonomy and self-assuredness. Tempering this conclusion, however, is my analysis of the finer scale of the Doaba region, which

First appeared in *Contemporary South Asia*, 13 (1), (March 2004) 53–69. 

suggests that, as with all complex processes, the consequences of NRI investment and capital flows are multifaceted.

## Globalization

Intense debate has revolved around the term 'globalization', but it has now been accepted as shorthand for the intensified and deepened cultural, economic, political and institutional interconnectedness and interdependency that has developed between corporations, communities and states, particularly since the 1970s.[2] Theorists, policy-makers, and even management consultancy gurus have debated the origins, nature and power of globalization.[3] Some have argued that the nation-state has lost control of its domestic economic and political functions to the International Monetary Fund (IMF) and other supra-national decision-making bodies.[4] Geographers resist accepting the prescriptive inevitability of such arguments, and contend that globalization must be seen as a set of interrelated tendencies that cumulate to produce heterogeneous and uneven processes that operate dialectically in the face of local difference.[5]

In the case of India, Nayar argues that the country's sovereignty has long faced the intrusion of foreign governments, even before the period when it formally began to globalize its economy. Yet, even when we examine processes of globalization as they are manifested in India, we do not observe a homogeneous effect. Rather, local diversity has permeated such change and produced outcomes qualitatively different across space. Globalization can be seen as having positive effects. For example, women's non-governmental organizations can bypass the state and access resources from international funding agencies in order to challenge the conditions (rooted in capitalist and patriarchal expansion) that undermine their rights.[6] Conversely, the influence of global corporations in India can result in environmental and social disaster.[7] The key is to be attuned to what changes result where in light of globalization processes, and how these might contribute to building contexts for positive social change. In the case of India, a significant cause and effect of globalization are the millions of emigrants, both temporary and permanent, that work beyond India's borders.

## Going Global: India's Human and Capital Mobility

India possesses a long history of border crossings, beginning in the pre-colonial period with the formation of important trading routes from Southern India.[8] In contrast, nineteenth-century and twentieth-century migration was channeled through colonial networks to Asia and new settler colonies such as Canada and Australia.[9] Since the 1960s, skilled Indian migrants have taken advantage of liberalized immigration policies in the West.[10] Migration source regions in India have been highly concentrated; for example, there are strong migratory networks connecting the states of Punjab, Kerala, Andhra Pradesh, Gujarat, Goa, Maharashtra and Tamil Nadu with Middle East countries. Similarly, migrants to the United Kingdom and Canada tend to come from Punjab and Gujarat. All these states have contributed to migration to the United States, Australia and West European countries.[11]

Recent estimates place the number of persons of Indian descent outside of India at around 20 million, spread across 48 countries. Eleven of these countries—including Canada, Malaysia, Mauritius, Myanmar, Saudi Arabia, South Africa, Trinidad and Tobago, the United Arab Emirates and the United States—are home to populations above half a million.[12] The information we can ascertain from these numbers is limited. For example, the link between population and political representation is clearly not evident in countries—such as the United States and the Gulf States—that do not accord political representation to temporary labour migrants. Also, many Indians who migrated overseas sometime ago are now part of communities with complex, distinctly hybridized national identifications (e.g., those in Fiji and the West Indies). Nonetheless, for a nation that has traditionally possessed limited capacity to collect reliable population statistics, the use of data collected through the cadastral apparatus of other states provides a useful measure of the Indian diaspora,[13] and provides a clear indication of an expansive Indian global presence.[14]

### *Relations between India and the NRI Diaspora*

Since independence, the Government of India (GoI) has missed several opportunities to develop comprehensive mechanisms to take advantage of its economically and increasingly politically powerful diaspora.[15] The GoI's traditional reluctance to become involved in political issues related to the diaspora under Prime Minister Jawaharlal Nehru transformed slowly into greater economic engagement in the 1970s and 1980s. More recently, the GoI has made efforts at enhancing NRI investment though economic liberalization. The efforts to encourage investment from Indians overseas in part reflect a change in the characteristics of the immigrant flow. Liberalized immigration regulations in most Western nations post-1960 attracted educated Indians to fill high-skilled labour shortages.[16] One major concern linked to this development was the effect of a 'brain drain' as emigrating skilled professionals were considered a loss to the national economy that produced them.[17] In an age of globalization, however, such international migration is no longer (if it ever was) a zero sum game.[18] The training and export of highly educated labour, particularly to the United States' information technology sector, offers India the potential to expand markets and forge global connections over the long term.[19]

Rather than regret the exodus of its highly educated people, the establishment of a High Level Committee (HLC) on the Indian diaspora in September 2000 suggests that India now officially recognizes the potential advantages this global community offers. In 2002, the committee released its detailed report:

> informing the Indian public of the achievements of the Indian diaspora, sensitizing it to their problems and their expectations from their mother country, proposing a new policy framework for creating a more conducive environment in India to leverage these invaluable human resources—and thus forging stronger ties between the Indian diaspora and India.[20]

The report presents an inventory of Indians overseas and a host of recommendations to facilitate greater economic and cultural interaction between India and its diaspora. Its main recommendation is the need to establish a dedicated 'singlewindow' organization, along the lines of a planning commission, to work with NRIs and Indian states to enhance investment and deal with the former's concerns.[21] This report marks a transition from years of neglect to officially and formally recognizing the role of NRIs and PIOs in India's development and global engagement. A review of that contribution suggests such recognition has been long overdue.

### *Migrant Remittances and Development*

Since the 1970s, social scientists have focused on the increasing international spread of various investment flows, interpreting them as indicators of the increasing globalization of capital markets.[22] Most of these interpretations lack any consideration of the movement of capital as an embodied action; that is, linked to people who also circulate around the globe. Worker remittances provide one of the few measurements of capital movement linked to migrants and, in countries such as India that are experiencing large labour out-migrations, they can contribute significantly to the economy. Despite the conventional view of remittances as 'squanderables', with little impact on economic improvement beyond construction and real estate,[23] the decline of other forms of income (such as donor aid) means that remittances are increasingly seen as a viable source of development revenue, as well as one of the few mechanisms of capital redistribution between developed and developing economies.[24] While uncertainty over the actual level of migrant-related remittances has contributed to their virtual erasure in discussions of economic transfers in the wider literature on globalization and development—some arguing that any official record 'grossly under-represents the true magnitude of these flows'[25]—some idea of their importance may be gleaned from work done by the IMF.[26]

Since the mid-1990s, India has been one of most significant recipients of worker remittances (see Figure 1).[27] The largest debtor nations in terms of worker remittances include major sites of Indian

**Figure 1**

*Top Worker Remittance: Receiving Countries, 1990–2001*

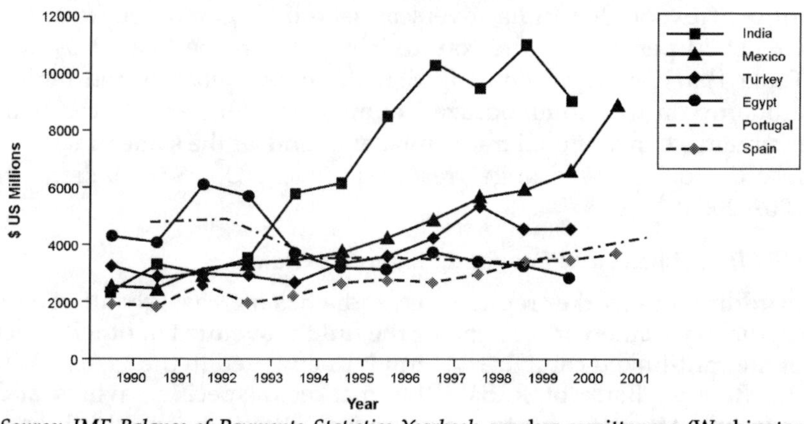


*Source: IMF Balance of Payments Statistics Yearbook*, worker remittances (Washington D.C.).

migrant settlement, indicating the intersection of global human and capital mobility (see Figure 2). The two major remittance debtor nations, Saudi Arabia and the United States, are key destinations for Indians (although, in both cases, the dominant form of migration is temporary in nature).[28] Remittances are especially evident if settlement is temporary or undocumented circular migration, because this increases the incentive to remit money home.[29] Therefore, the greater the uncertainty of settlement and tenure for Indian migrants overseas, the greater the potential economic returns to India.

Under the conditions of globalized labour markets, intense state regulation of international migration (including the reduction of rights accorded to temporary and undocumented workers) creates a scenario where the sending state can financially benefit from their own citizens' vulnerability. The two global movements of capital and migrants have to contend with very different regulatory regimes.[30] They also offer variable and contradictory results for participants at the scale of the individual and their nation. In light of India's commitment to engage with NRIs, it must be asked whether the state has effectively mobilized to protect the interests of the very people from whom it has derived the greatest financial returns.[31]

In addition to India's prominence among other remittance receiving nations, the contribution worker remittances have made to the country's official foreign income are very significant, exceeding foreign direct investment, external assistance, and NRI deposits combined (see Figure 3). In addition, if migration is considered a form of export for India, overseas labour migration represented almost 30 per cent of the country's exports in the late 1990s (see Table 1). There is no denying that the dependence of the Indian economy on this commoditized human transfer has allowed it to maintain a conventional trade imbalance and, at the same time, post record foreign exchange reserves (over US $71 billion in 2002–2003).[32]

### *NRI Investment and Economic Liberalization*

In addition to worker remittances, India has increasingly altered its regulatory frameworks to enable the fluid movement of other forms of migrant-linked capital. The term NRI emerged in the 1970s when the Reserve Bank of India (RBI) marketed specific savings and investment instruments to the successful Indian community abroad, especially those based in North America, Europe, South-East Asia

**Figure 2**
*Top Worker Remittance Debit Countries 1990–2001.*

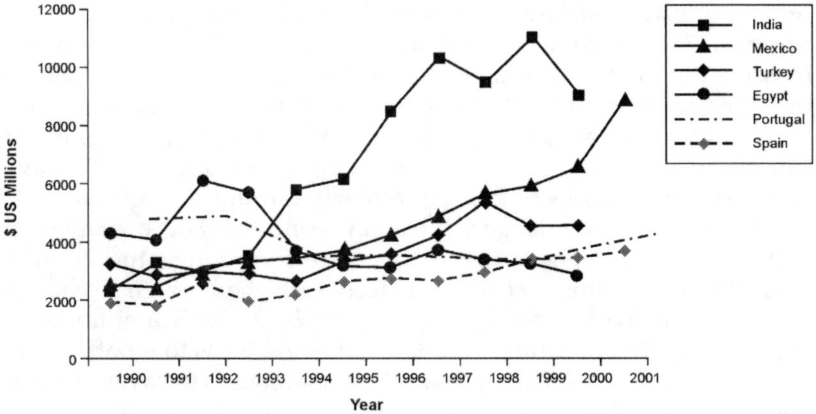


*Source:* *IMF Balance of Payments Statistics Yearbook,* worker remittances (Washington D.C.).

**Figure 3**
*Worker Remittance, NRI Deposits, External Assistance and Foreign Direct Investment Flows into India, 1990–1999.*

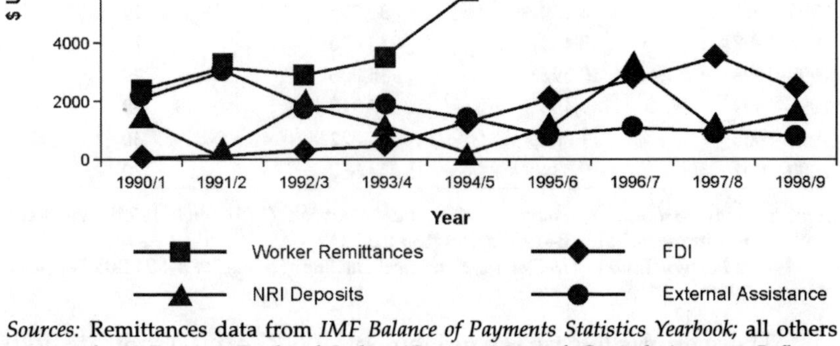


*Sources:* Remittances data from *IMF Balance of Payments Statistics Yearbook;* all others from Reserve Bank of India, 'Composition of Capital Account Inflows, 1990–1999', Appendix Table VI.6, in *Annual Report at <http://www.rbi.org.in/>.*

and the Middle East. Various NRI accounts were designed to encourage the investment of hard currency with Indian banks at globally competitive interest rates. Such investments, along with regular remittances, have been crucial in maintaining India's foreign reserves. This became obvious during the 1991 Gulf War when a massive evacuation of Indian workers from the Gulf states caused remittances to plummet, and panicked investors withdrew their money, causing foreign exchange reserves to shrink.[33] This event caused an acceleration of the liberalizing process, and NRIs have been key beneficiaries of this, particularly through the relaxation of investment regulations and currency controls. For example, in January 2000, currency controls were relaxed when the Foreign Exchange Regulation Act was replaced with the Foreign Exchange Management Act.[34] Additionally, in July 2002, the RBI announced the liberalization of capital accounts, allowing NRIs to repatriate up to US $2,30,000 from NRI Ordinary Rupee accounts to cover medical and educational expenses, including an annual amount of US $1,00,000 accrued from the sale of property held for no less than 10 years.[35]

**Table 1**

*Indian Worker's Remittances and Exports (all Figures in US$ million)*

| *Year* | *Worker Remittances** | *Exports*** | *Worker Remittances as % of Exports* |
|---|---|---|---|
| 1990–1991 | 2,352 | 18,145, | 13 |
| 1991–1992 | 3,275 | 17,865 | 18 |
| 1992–1993 | 2,891 | 18,537 | 16 |
| 1993–1994 | 3,495 | 22,238 | 16 |
| 1994–1995 | 5,782 | 26,330 | 22 |
| 1995–1996 | 6,139 | 31,795 | 19 |
| 1996–1997 | 8,453 | 33,470 | 25 |
| 1997–1998 | 10,297 | 35,006 | 29 |
| 1998–1999 | 9,453 | 33,218 | 28 |
| 1999–2000 | 11,001 | 36,822 | 30 |
| 2000–2001 | 9,034 | 44,560 | 20 |

*Sources:* **IMF Balance of Payments Statistics Yearbook (1997 and 1999),* Workers' remittances, Table B–19,Washington D.C..

*** *Foreign Trade in US Dollars, Statistical Outline of India, 1998–99* (Tata Services, 1998).

These efforts to ease the movement of NRI capital indicate both the growing mobility of Indians overseas, and the GoI's complicity with processes of economic globalization. As Saskia Sassen argues, 'global capital has made claims on national states, which have responded through the production of new forms of legality'.[36] In this case, however, the boundary between the national and the global is blurred, as India actively utilizes deeply cultural discourses of belonging to wrest investment from its diaspora. Such cultural discourses are widely employed by government and banking officials, and commonly stress ideas of national attachment to the feminized state:

> Remittances into India by NRIs are allowed to be repatriated back to the country where they remitted it from, so because India repatriates the funds, and welcomes the citizen, the sons of the soil wherever they live, they help their motherland .... So these NRI accounts, they offer certain facilities in India, in the process they help their motherland to grow.[37]

The image of the NRI investor therefore is shaped by complex cultural constructions of 'Indianness' that can act to both encourage and constrain involvement in India's development.[38] Add to this the emergence in the United States of a political 'Hindu' capitalist conservatism that meshes well with the Hindutva rhetoric of India's ruling Bharatiya Janata Party (BJP), and we see an interesting challenge to the orthodox argument of global investment as a rationalized, disembodied, denationalized 'race to the bottom'.[39] Instead, the case of India reveals how cultural rhetoric permeates the global investment mantra: 'The time has arrived to translate this reality in to his (Vajpayee's) vision of forging a constructive relationship between what he has described as the mother country and her children abroad.'[40] Indeed, India has incorporated the globalized NRI into its own discourse of territorially bounded Indian nationalism, illustrating Nina Glick Schiller's point that bounded territoriality 'still remains an important part of the imagery of the transnational nation-state'.[41] However, providing some material expression to this national embrace of the NRI has proved contentious.

While the allure of the NRI may be celebrated, cosmopolitan urban Indians often perceive them more variably, depending upon the wider economic context. As one young Delhi professional told me: 'You know middle class Indians have a different version of NRI. Rather than Non-Resident Indian, they say Non-Reliable Indian. They are the first to invest money if the interest rates are high, and the first to draw the money out if there is any trouble.'[42] Concern with the stability of NRI financial investments in India, including the possibility of panic withdrawals and the relative expense of such borrowing when linked with ongoing concerns over the issue of dual citizenship, reveals the complex relationship that exists between the 'motherland' and her estranged sons.[43] It presents a glimpse of the contradictions between a deeply territorial and nationalistic India and the growing power of Indians overseas.

### *NRIs and National Inclusion*

As the size of the diaspora increases, and India's economic health depends more and more on the remittances and investments channelled by NRIs, Indians overseas have created various organizations to represent their interests at both the state and international level. Groups such as the Global Organization of People of Indian Origin lobby various levels of the GoI to accord NRIs more official rights, from basic property protections to dual citizenship. The latter demand has caused much debate. Initially, NRI demands for formal citizenship association were appeased with a PIO card for foreign passport holders. The card presented a characteristic synthesis of the cultural and economic; a means of providing an emotional anchor for the NRI as well as material returns for India. For the GoI, the PIO card allowed for 'the sentiments of persons of Indian origin to be closer to their original country and to reinforce their emotional bonds, as well as respecting their desire to participate in the development of the country of their origin'.[44]

The HLC report indicated the general dissatisfaction NRIs felt with this arrangement, and recommended that dual citizenship be offered in certain cases. In 2003, the cabinet announced its intention to bring a bill before parliament to amend the 1955 Citizenship Act to permit Indians in certain countries to seek dual citizenship.[45] These events indicate that, despite the strong feelings of pride and chauvinism attached to Indian national identity, the Indian state's reluctance to grant 'flexible' citizenship has softened. This is indicative of the country's increasing receptiveness to forms of globalization that other countries have long embraced.[46] India's intention to pursue this matter supports the interpretation of dual citizenship as evidence of an individual migrant's success in securing economic and cultural capital across a global spectrum.[47]

One significant constituent within this equation is the geopolitical and economic importance of NRIs in the United States.

The HLC Report states that 'The Indian community in the United States constitutes an invaluable asset in strengthening India's relationship with the world's only superpower ... it is essential for India to create the necessary structures to facilitate this interaction.'[48] The United States-based NRI community has been constructed as an important component of a de-territorialized Hindu nation: 'Hindutva's practices in its US sites reflect the aspirations of Hindu nationalism in India and vice versa; together they form an entity that reinforces each of these parts but it cannot be reduced to either of them'.[49]

It is important to stress that, through such a construction, the heterogeneity of India and its diaspora is elided. The NRI becomes a displaced global actor endowed with immense economic wealth that can be drawn into India through the powerful cultural attachment that 'sons of the soil' retain for their motherland. Yet this grounded metaphorical attachment reveals an inconsistency between a global Indian national imaginary and the often more powerful local affinity that emigrants possess. Rather than see these as opposing scales, however, the point is to demonstrate how they operate in relation to each other, and how processes of globalization manifest themselves differentially across these spatial and social contexts. In order to examine this the following section considers Punjab, an important state in any consideration of India's diaspora, not only because of the global distribution of its emigrants and the active transnational linkages they maintain, but for its interesting contradictory position vis-à-vis the construction of a global Indian nationalism.

## Global Connections: Punjab and its Diaspora

The recent history of Sikh separatism in Punjab might make the GoI somewhat reticent to laud this particular diaspora as 'playing an important role in mobilizing political support for issues of vital concern to India in their new countries'.[50] However, in recent years, with the decline of the Congress Party and the rise of the BJP and its coalition of regional parties including the Akali Dal, Punjab has become more integrated into the political heart of India.[51] Indeed, the BJP government has constructed Sikhism as the 'militant "martial face" of Hinduism'.[52] Sikhs in Punjab have historically thrived within pluralistic social environments where power relations and structures are fluid, and individualism—expressed most obviously through competitive materialism and status—thrives.[53] In the villages of Punjab, especially in the Doaba region (which includes the Hoshiarpur, Kapurthala, Jalandhar and Nawanshahr districts), outmigration has long been a traditional coping mechanism for families facing dwindling land holdings and changing economic environments. Starting in the late nineteenth century, young males, particularly Jat Sikhs, travelled overseas to parts of Asia, Australia and North America.[54] In the post-1950 period, the rate and range of migration increased, and numerous villages in the Doaba area saw as many as 30 per cent of their residents move abroad.[55] Precise numbers of people of Punjabi origin living overseas are impossible to establish, but there may be as many as five million (documented and undocumented).[56]

The sheer number of overseas Punjabis—and their sustained connection with their homeland—is reflected in state-based responses to this group. In 1996, an NRI *Sabha* (assembly) was developed in Jalandhar, primarily to deal with NRI property concerns.[57] Subsequently, the NRI *Sabha* has fostered other cultural and investment initiatives, and the government of Punjab has responded to NRI concerns with property and tenancy-related policy changes. Punjab is also an interesting case to examine because, while the HLC Report examined three state-based NRI initiatives (in Kerala, Gujarat and Punjab), the authors commented relatively extensively on the Punjab case, describing its approach as 'innovative' and its organization as 'highly professional'.[58]

### Global Flows, Grounded Outcomes

Significant numbers of overseas Punjabis return to Punjab for extended visits and, with each visit, they become associated with financial success, and hence *taur* or *izzat* (honour). The effect of the money that circulates with this corporeal movement is variable, and offers grounded examples of the contingent and contradictory effect of globalization at various scales. Any effort to map the amount of money remitted on a regional level is hampered by both the invisibility of some transfers, and the lack of disaggregated financial data. However, estimates by rural bankers indicate that Doaba banks receive, on average, Rs 20–30 crore[59] (roughly US $5–7 million) in deposits per year from NRIs (this is in addition to long-term deposits from the 1960s).[60] Further evidence of the financial inflows to the region can be estimated from licensed moneychangers. The town of Phagwara is an important banking and currency exchange node for the Doaba region due to its central location on Punjab's main Grand Trunk road. Here, one moneychanger indicated that he changed Rs 5–6 lakh[61] (between US $11,000 and US $14,000) on a daily basis. Across the whole of Phagwara, he estimated that Rs 50 lakh were exchanged everyday (equivalent to over US $1,00,000 daily and over $36 million annually).[62]

While the material expression of these significant capital inflows is reflected across the landscape of Punjab through agricultural property, religious, health and educational investments, and other projects, the extent of these benefits are limited, both spatially and socially. This is because Jat Sikh families tend to receive the majority of such resources, and the benefit of related community projects and investments are specifically concentrated in the Doaba region of Punjab.[63] While that NRI capital contributes to the central economy of India, the local results of such inflows are more multifaceted. Financial exchange on the black market (of which Phagwara is seen as the centre), coupled with the common practice of financial bartering through transnational immigrant networks, deprives the state of hard currency to bolster its foreign reserves.[64] At the local level, unrecorded capital in the Punjab economy stemming from NRI inflows is thought to have encouraged corruption, thereby creating problems for the state administration.[65] Capital transfers from Sikh immigrants overseas also have posed a more direct threat to the central government.

In the early 1980s, the rising political pressure for a Sikh homeland under the Khalistan movement conflicted with Prime Minister Indira Gandhi's centralizing mission. Her government's choice to launch Operation Blue Star against the Khalistani militants holed up in Amritsar's Golden Temple complex led to her assassination, and the tragedy and carnage of the Delhi riots. These events marked a decade of terrorism and state oppression in Punjab, and the conflict pre-occupied the GoI until well into the 1990s.[66] Several scholars recognize that the Khalistan movement received support through transnational financial networks operating through the fairly liberalized capital exchange systems of the West.[67]

During the tumultuous period of the 1980s and 1990s in Punjab, the management of *gurdwaras* (Sikh temples) in sites of overseas Sikh settlement became the focus for intense conflict between various sections of this religious community. Charges of financial mismanagement and unexplained contributions to unknown charities raised concern that separatist groups were being funded though these channels.[68] The GoI retaliated by monitoring and blacklisting overseas associations it felt were connected to separatist actions, and pressured Western nations to be more vigilant of separatist groups that might utilize the institution of multiculturalism to raise funds.[69] This surveillance had a direct effect on Sikhs, both in Punjab and overseas. Opportunistic individuals involved in personal vendettas against others manipulated this situation, spreading false accusations to Indian security forces and foreign governments in order to constrain the rights and movement of others.[70]

This security crisis seriously truncated one aspect of globalization; that is, the movement of people between Punjab and overseas sites of settlement,[71] and had a particular relevance to the investments and connections maintained by NRIs in their 'home' state. Interviews with several district officials, legal practitioners and journalists to discuss NRI investment revealed some surprising consistency.[72] Most interviewees were conscious that Sikh Punjabi emigrants possessed a deep cultural desire to maintain links with their land and their culture. The main legal concerns they felt existed concerned the protection of property investments, and the need for a streamlined legal procedure to assist NRIs to deal with property and tenant disputes.[73] However, all the interviewees commented on how conflicts over property originated within the respective family networks of the NRIs themselves. A lawyer in Phagwara with experience of dealing with such disputes offered the following example of a typical case:

> NRIs think that their family will protect their interests, so they give them power of attorney over their affairs. Ten to fifteen years later, they discover that their brother has rented their land and paid them no money, or sold their land to their wife for a paltry sum, and the wife has legally sold the land again at the full market price. The NRI, once he discovers this has to resort to the courts to charge his brother with abuse of power of attorney, since the present owner legally owns the land. The case can take five to thirty years and, meanwhile, the brother in Punjab sells all his assets to his wife so that the brother cannot access anything. In order to process this litigation, the NRI has to either stay in India, or issue power of attorney to another person.[74]

Three factors are important in explaining this situation. First, it was argued that the 'bonds of the family' were being broken down by the materialism and consumerism that had been introduced into India as a result of globalization and economic liberalization.[75] Second, this process was exacerbated by the impact of the temporal, spatial and emotional separation between emigrants and their families. Third, it was argued that problems of estrangement were intensified during the 1980s and 1990s, as many Punjabis overseas were unable to visit because they either faced difficulties in securing a visa to return to India, or were concerned about the possibilities of being questioned by state and/or terrorist groups once in the country. Therefore, restrictions on travel built an ideal environment for some family members (often brothers) to appropriate property.

Some officials expressed the sentiment that the NRIs, in part, were responsible for the creation of intra-family property disputes. Local people were keen to emulate their overseas relations' building of status in the home village through profuse consumption and spending, especially on weddings and houses.[76] When remittances went down, or when family members had been left to tend to the land, rancour was created; especially in the absence of consistent visits from the NRI son abroad. The increasing value of land (to which NRI investment contributed) was also seen as a factor that encouraged some families to incorporate the emigrant sons' property.[77] As Sikhs faced a heady mix of increasing status and competition within a liberalized and consumer-driven economy, simultaneously marked by a restrictive internal political context, family disputes arose.[78] Thus, different forms of global incorporation—one the one hand, commodity consumption and, on the other, truncated human mobility—worked against each other at the scale of the transnational household.

## Conclusion

The bond many NRIs and PIOs maintain with the land of their ancestors contributes significantly to India's economic and social development, and shapes an increasingly global form of Indianness not ontologically rooted in the country's sovereign territory. While capital flows are evident at the national scale through remittances and NRI investments, the actual material effect of such transfers needs to be witnessed and measured qualitatively at the regional scale. The outcome of these inflows is mixed. Nationally, capital injections are important for economic stability (and provide evidence that India has been open to global flows of capital for some time, despite barriers to more orthodox forms of institutional investment).[79] At this national level, the rhetoric of the family, especially the notion of the greater Hindu family under the cultural nationalism of the BJP, is working to embrace the globally dispersed sons of the soil. However, at the regional, especially household scale, we find evidence of family bonds crumbling under the pressures linked to globalization.

Despite the complexity of these processes, one can conclude that globalization, in the guise of labour mobility, has encouraged greater global engagement and connectivity rather than undermined India's economic autonomy. The development of the HLC Report on the diaspora and the rapidity with which the BJP has moved to alter policy linked to dual citizenship suggest that we are moving into a new era. Now, processes of globalization—the movement of people, capital and ideas—are being exploited by India to the benefit of its national interest, despite the variable effects these processes create in localities such as Doaba in Punjab.

The BJP's interest in forging new relations with those flexible citizens beyond its borders may also reveal something about India's internal political relations. The interest espoused by the government-appointed HLC in building effective structures for engaging with NRIs has led it to examine the experiences of states—such as Kerala, Gujarat and Punjab—with large expatriate communities. The HLC Report authors stress 'that there is a very pressing need to link the state mechanism with the proposed, dedicated central mechanism',[80] and Punjab is one of the most active examples examined. This internal aspect of a report, ostensibly about global issues, raises interesting questions about space, politics and territoriality, and reveals how, in India's case, the nation-state can maintain, perhaps even strengthen, its autonomy in the face of globalization processes.

## Acknowledgements

Funding for the research presented in this paper was provided by the Indo-Canadian Shastri Institute, The Social Sciences and Humanities Research Council of Canada, and The Vancouver Centre of Excellence for Research on Immigration and Integration in the Metropolis (RIIM).

## Notes and References

1. B.R. Nayar, "Globalisation and India's National Autonomy", *Commonwealth and Comparative Politics*, Vol. 41, No. 2, 2003, pp. 1–34, p. 30.

2. A. Amin and N. Thrift, "Globalization, Socio-economics, Territoriality", In R. Lee and J. Wills (eds.), *Geographies of Economies* (London: Arnold, 1997), pp. 147–157.
3. See Nayar, op. cit., Ref. 1; P.F. Kelly, "The Geographies and Politics of Globalization", *Progress in Human Geography*, Vol. 23, No. 3, 1999, pp. 379–400; and P. Dicken, J. Peck and A. Tickell, "Unpacking the Global", In Lee and Wills (eds.), op. cit., Ref. 2, pp. 158–166.
4. See, For instance, Gilpin, R., *The Challenge of Global Capitalism: The World Economy in the 21st Century* (Princeton, NJ: Princeton University Press, 2000); B. Jessop, "Post-Fordism and the State", In A. Amin (ed.), *Post-Fordism: A Reader* (Oxford: Blackwell, 1994), pp. 251–279; and Harvie, C., *The Rise of Regional Europe* (London: Routledge, 1994).
5. See, For instance, Dicken et al., op. cit., Ref. 3, p. 160. See also Hirst P. and Thompson, G. *Globalisation in Question: The International Economy and the Possibilities of Governance* (Cambridge: Polity Press, 1996).
6. Ray, R., *Fields of Protest: Women's Movements in India* (Minneapolis, MN: University of Minnesota Press, 1999).
7. Cassels, J., *The Uncertain Promise of Law: Lessons from Bhopal* (Toronto: University of Toronto Press, 1993).
8. Blaut, J.M., *The Colonizer's Model of the World: Geographical Diffusionism and Eurocentric History* (London: Guildford Press, 1993).
9. See, For example, Tinker, Hugh, *A New System of Slavery: The Export of Indian Labour Overseas 1830–1920* (London: Oxford University Press, 1974); Mangat, J.S., *A History of Asians in East Africa* (Oxford, Clarendon Press, 1969); and Jensen, J.M., *Passage From India: Asian Indian Immigrants in North America* (New Haven, CT: Yale University Press, 1988).
10. For a more detailed discussion of the various Indian migrations over time, see M.C. Madhavan, 'Indian Emigrants: Numbers, Characteristics, and Economic Impact', *Population and Development Review*, Vol. 11, No. 3, 1985, pp. 457–481.
11. Ibid.
12. High Level Committee, *Report on the Indian Diaspora* at _http://indiandiaspora.nic.in/_, accessed 21 July 2003.
13. Following the practice of the High Level Committee Report, throughout this paper I use the term 'Diaspora' to refer to Indians overseas. However, note that Diaspora implies dispersal and an inability to return to one's homeland. I prefer the term 'transnational community' for Indian immigrants, because return to India is

possible and common (even for Sikhs now that the troubles of the 1980–1990s have receded).

14. K.S. Natarajan and V.S. Swarmy, "Data collection systems in India", paper delivered at the International Population Conference, New Delhi, 1989. Most articles highlighting the number of Indians overseas depend upon the figures provided by other governments. See, for example, T. Abraham, "NRI/PIO Community: A Perspective", at http://www.gopio.net/NRI_PIO_talk_mumbai.html; and D. Patel, 'South Asian Diasporas', *Himal,* December 1999, pp. 16–20.
15. Lall, M.C., *India's Missed Opportunity: India's Relationship with the Non Resident Indians* (Aldershot: Ashgate, 2001).
16. Helweg, A., "Indians of the Professions in Australia: Some Theoretical and Methodological Considerations", *Population Review,* Vol. 35, No. 1991, pp. 75–89.
17. Nayyar, Deepak, "International Labour Migration from India: A Macro-Economic Analysis", In Rashid Amjad (ed.), *To the Gulf and Back: Studies on the Economic Impact of Asian Labour Migration* (New Delhi: International Labour Organisation, 1989), pp. 95–141.
18. Saxenian, Anna Lee, *Silicon Valley's New Immigrant Entrepreneurs* (San Francisco, CA: Public Policy Institute of California, 1999).
19. Lindsay, Lowell B. and Christian, Bryan, *The Characteristics of Employers of H-1Bs* (Washington, D.C.: Institute for the Study of International Migration, 2000).
20. HLC Report, press release, 8 January 2002 at _http://indiandiaspora.nic.in/_, accessed 21 July 2003.
21. In 1999, the Government established an NRI/PIO office connected to the Ministry of External Affairs. Much of the current NRI Affairs office's attention is directed to the Gulf States, where three million Indians, mostly from Kerala and Punjab, are employed in semi-skilled occupations. The problems they deal with tend to be bureaucratic in nature, such as issues related to the repatriation of bodies of deceased Indians, contacting next of kin, and mediation in conflicts with employers. Interview with the deputy secretary of NRI Affairs, New Delhi, 22 February 2000.
22. S. Corbridge, N.J. Thrift and R.L. Martin (eds.), *Money, Power and Space* (Oxford: Blackwell, 1994).
23. See Choucri, N., "The Hidden Economy: A New View of Remittances in the Arab World", *World Development,* Vol. 14, No. 6, 1986, pp. 697–712; and Mehta, S., *Migration, A Spatial Perspective: A Case Study of Bist Doab-Punjab* (Jaipur: Rawat Publications, 1990).

24. See Connell, J., and Brown, R., "Migration and Remittances in the South Pacific: Towards New Perspectives", *Asian and Pacific Migration Journal,* Vol. 4, No. 1, 1995, pp. 1–34; R. Jones, "The Renewed Role of Remittances in The New World Order", *Economic Geography,* Vol. 74, No. 1, 1998, pp. 1–7; and S. Russell, "Remittances from International Migration: A Review in Prospective", *World Development,* Vol., 14, No. 6, 1986, pp. 677–696.
25. See Choucri, op. cit., Ref 23, p. 702.
26. Data are collected from individual countries and compiled by the IMF into tables identifying national credits and debits. The data is partial however, since some countries (such as Canada and the United Kingdom) do not register figures for worker remittances and are not represented in the tables. In addition, systems of calculation used by each state differ, making comparisons difficult. Nonetheless, the data provide one indication of the magnitude and geographical dimension of these transfers.
27. The Reserve Bank of India collects remittance data from banks and authorized currency exchangers, and quarterly surveys are conducted to ascertain unclassified receipts. See *IMF Balance of Payments Statistics Yearbook* (1999), p. 210, Washington D.C.
28. In the Middle East, migration is always contractual in nature. Workers' rights are limited since their status is always temporary, no matter how long they have actually been in the country. In Kuwait, migrant rights are determined by the Kafala system where the employer sponsors the migrant and takes full economic and legal responsibility for them during the contract period. This limits their freedom through various demands, such as surrendering their passport to their employer. See Longva, Anh Nga, "Keeping Migrant Workers in Check: The Kafala System in the Gulf", *Middle East Report 211,* Summer 1999, pp. 20–22. Indian immigrants to the United States are increasingly using the H-1B visa, which grants three years' work (renewable for another three years) authorization to highly skilled foreign persons. Although some individuals attempt to adjust their status to that of a permanent resident at the end of their stay, there is a per-country limit for such 'Green Card' applications. This option is certainly not available for all Indian workers. See Lowell B. Lindsay. *H-1B Temporary Workers: Estimating the Population* (Washington, D.C.: Institute for the Study of International Migration, 2000).
29. Kevin O'Neil, *Summary Report, Discussion on Migration and Development: Using Remittances and Circular Migration as Drivers for Development,* Migration Policy Institute at http://

www.migrationpolicy.org/pubs/sandiegoreport.doc_, accessed 1 August 2003.

30. Hirst and Thompson, op. cit., Ref 5.
31. The recent HLC Report makes a number of recommendations regarding the role of the Indian government in protecting the interests of its overseas temporary workers.
32. RBI data on foreign exchange reserves at _http://www.rbi.org.in_, accessed 30 July 2003.
33. See Lall, op. cit., Ref 15; and Nayar, op. cit., Ref. 1.
34. The Foreign Exchange Management Act employs civil rather than criminal charges against violators, and allows convertibility of capital in the current account (but not fixed assets or capital assets such as land). See RBI at _http://www.rbi.org.in_, accessed 21 March 2000.
35. RBI at _http://www.rbi.org.in_, accessed 9 July 2002.
36. Sassen, S., *Losing Control? Sovereignty in an Age of Globalization* (New York: Columbia University Press, 1996), p. 25.
37. Personal interview with the vice president/manager of the Vancouver branch of the State Bank of India, Vancouver, 2 December 1998.
38. Lessinger, Johanna, "Investing or Going Hme? A Transnational Strategy Among Indian Immigrants in the United States", in N. Glick-Schiller et al. (eds.), *Towards a Transnational Perspective on Migration: Race, Class, Ethnicity and Nationalism Reconsidered* (New York: Academy of Sciences, 1992) pp. 53–80.
39. See Chakravartty, P., "Liberalization and Non Resident Indians: Flexible Citizenship and India's Information Economy", In W.A. Cornelius and T.J. Espenshade (eds.), *The International Migration of the Highly Skilled: Demand, Supply and Development Consequence* (La Jolla: University of California-San Diego Center for Comparative Immigration Studies, 2001); Mathew, Biju, and Prashad, Vijay, "The Protean Forms of Yankee Hindutva", *Ethnic and Racial Studies*, Vol. 23, No. 3, 2000, pp. 516–534; and Rajagopal, A., "Hindu Nationalism in the US: Changing Configurations of Political Practice", *Ethnic and Racial Studies*, Vol. 23, No. 3, 2000, pp. 467–496.
40. HLC Report, op. cit., Ref 12, p. 5.
41. Glick-Schiller, Nina, "Citizens in Transnational Nation-states", In P. Dicken, K. Olds, P. Kelly, L. Kong and H. Yeung (eds.), *Globalization and the Asia Pacific: Contested Territories* (London: Routledge, 1999), p. 211.

42. Personal interview, Delhi, 9 November 1999.
43. The gendering of NRI discourse is a powerful reminder of the inherent chauvinism that circulates through these debates. Indeed, the limited discussion about NRIs and gender issues is focused on cases of marital fraud and victimization, with little agency accorded to women. See Roberts, M. Walton, "Rescaling Citizenship: Gendering Canadian Immigration Policy", *Political Geography*, Vol. 23, No. 3, 2004, pp. 265–281.
44. This pseudo-citizenship was ascribed validity for 20 years and costs US $1,000. See Indian Government press note delivered in New Delhi, 30 March 1999, see http://iic.nic.piocard,htm#pn, accessed 30 March 2004.
45. There are certain proposed restrictions, but the countries considered are Canada, the United States, the United Kingdom, Australia, Finland, Ireland, The Netherlands and Italy. See "India grants dual citizenship to NRIs: Canada is among eight nations singled out by India for granting dual citizenship to its expatriates with a number of restrictions", *The Link* at _http://www.thelinkpaper.ca/index.htm_, accessed 21 July 2003.
46. Spiro, P.J., *Embracing Dual Nationality* (Washington, D.C.: Carnegie Endowment for International Peace International Migration Policy, 2000).
47. Ong, Aihwa, *Flexible Citizenship: The Cultural Logics of Transnationality* (Durham, NC: Duke University Press, 1999).
48. HLC Report, op. cit., Ref 12, p. 21.
49. Rajagopal, op. cit., Ref 39, p. 489.
50. HLC Report, op. cit., Ref 12, p. 7.
51. This seems incongruent considering the earlier role of the Akali Dal in searching for separation, but the alliance represents a pragmatic arrangement that allows both an opportunity to advance their political ambitions. See Singh, Gurharpal, "India's Akali-BJP alliance: the 1977 Legislative Assembly Elections", *Asian Survey*, Vol. 38, No. 4, 1998, pp. 398–409.
52. Ibid., p. 399.
53. Pettigrew, Joyce, "Betrayal and Nation-building among the Sikhs", *The Journal of Commonwealth and Comparative Politics*, Vol. 29, No. 1, 1991, pp. 25–43.
54. See Kessinger, T.G., *Vilyatpur, 1848–1968: Social and Economic Change in a North Indian Village* (Berkeley: University of California Press, 1974); Fox, R., *Lions of the Punjab: Culture in the Making* (Berkeley: University of California Press, 1985); and Johnston, H., *The East*

*Indians in Canada* (Ottawa: Ethnic Groups: Canadian Historical Association, 1984).

55. During fieldwork in 1999–2000 in Doaba, I was advised that these rates are common. See Walton-Roberts, M., "Returning, Remitting, Reshaping: Non-resident Indians and the Transformation of Society and Space in Punjab, India", *Working Paper Series #01–15* (Vancouver: Centre of Excellence Research on Immigration and Integration in the Metropolis, August 2001).
56. Personal e-mail communication with the NRI *Sabha* in Jalandhar, 19 April 2000.
57. Interviews with Deputy District Commissioner Vijoy Kumar Singh, Kapurthala, 24 November 2000; and Satnam Manak, editor of *Ajit Samachar*, Jalandhar, 29 November 1999.
58. HLC Report, op. cit., Ref 12, pp. 541–542.
59. A crore is an Indian numerical term for 1,00,00,000.
60. Personal interview with Dhesian Kahna, manager of the Canara Bank, District Jalandhar, 27 January 2000.
61. A lakh is an Indian numerical term for 1,00,000.
62. Interviews with the branch manager of the State Bank of India, NRI Branch, Phagwara, and the owner of Bhandari's authorized money changer, Phagwara, 28 November 1999.
63. See Mehta, op. cit., Ref 23; and Walton-Roberts 2001, op. cit., Ref 55.
64. Discussions with one middle-class immigrant family in Patiala in February 2000 indicate that bartering financial exchanges with other transnational families with interests in both Punjab and Canada was common.
65. Interview with Deputy District Commissioner, Karpurthala, 24 November 1999.
66. Axel, B.K., *The Nation's Tortured Body: Violence, Representation, and the Formation of the Sikh Diaspora* (Durham, NC: Duke University Press, 2001).
67. See Tatla, D.S., *The Sikh Diaspora: The Search for Statehood* (London: University College London Press, 1999); and Unna, W., *Sikhs Abroad* (Calcutta: Statesman Commercial Press, 1985).
68. Canadian Security Intelligence Service documents suggest that the country was used 'as a base to arrange and direct terrorist activities in other countries .... This is a particular problem with some members of Sikh terrorist groups whose leaders continue to endeavour to use Canada as their headquarters'. See Bolan, Kim,

'Probe Sikh temples' finances, leader says', *Vancouver Sun*, 4 July 2000, p B1.

69. Personal interview with the Under Secretary of the Ministry of External Affairs, Delhi, 21 February 2000. See also Tatla, op. cit., Ref 67.
70. Puri, H., Judge, P.S. and Sekhon, J.S., *Terrorism in Punjab: Understanding Grassroots Reality* (New Delhi: Har-Ananad Publications, 1999). Also, in conversations with NRIs and residents in Doaba during fieldwork in 1999–2000, several cases of conflict over property or matrimony between NRIs and others led to false information being provided to the Indian government and to the Canadian or British High Commissions. See Walton-Roberts, 'Transnational Geographies: Indian Immigration to Canada', *The Canadian Geographer*, Vol. 47, No. 3, pp. 235–250.
71. Bolan, K. "India to Review Visa Blacklist", *Vancouver Sun*, 8 January 2001, p. B5.
72. Interviews with the respective editors of *Voice of Today, Press Trust of India, Ajit Samachar* and *Ajeet*, Jalandhar, 27–29 November 1999.
73. The second largest area of concern linked to NRIs was the incidence of marital fraud.
74. Field notes from an interview with Professor Balram Vaid, Phagwara, 4 December 1999.
75. Similar observations have been made with regard to changes in dowry. See W. Menski (ed.), *South Asians and The Dowry Problem* (Stoke-on-Trent: Trentham Books, 1998).
76. Interview with Deputy District Commissioner, Kapurthala, 24 November 1999.
77. Interview with the District Commissioner of Hoshiarpur and Giani Resham Hayre (president of the NRI *Sabha* in 2000), 19 February 2000.
78. Pettigrew, J., "Betrayal and Nation-building Among the Sikhs", *The Journal of Commonwealth and Comparative Politics*, Vol. 29, No. 1, 1991, pp. 25–43.
79. Nayar, B.R., "Opening up and Openness of Indian Economy", *Economic and Political Weekly*, 15 September 2001, pp. 3527–3535.
80. HLC Report, op. cit., Ref. 12, p. 544.

# 10

# Is there a Second Diasporic Generation? The Case of India's Hyderabadis

KAREN ISAKSEN LEONARD

The issue of generational changes in citizenship, identities, and relationships with the homeland is a significant and understudied one. My findings, based on a fifteen-year study of emigrants from Hyderabad, India, to seven sites abroad (Pakistan, the UK, Australia, the US, Canada, and the Gulf states of Kuwait and the UAE: Leonard, 2007) emphasize the limitations of the theories about diaspora, transnationalism, cosmopolitanism, and globalization when applied to the descendants of first-generation immigrants. The study, begun in the 1990s, traced primarily those who still identified to some extent with the Nizam's former state of Hyderabad, those who called themselves *mulkis* (Urdu for countrymen) and knew the cosmopolitan Indo-Muslim or Mughlai culture that once reigned in Hyderabad. The study emphasizes the ruptures of 1948 and 1956 (the 1948 Police Action, incorporating Hyderabad state into India, and India's 1956 Linguistic States Reorganization, ending Hyderabad state's independence and dividing it among three new linguistic states). It calls attention not only to the formulation of new identities abroad but to the changing urban landscape in Hyderabad city as it became the capital of the new Telugu-speaking state of Andhra Pradesh. Here, I focus on the second-generation Hyderabadi emigrants abroad, asking whether or not they can be considered diasporic, whether or not they self-identify as Hyderabadis in significant ways in their new homes.

I found that even though some first-generation migrants could be truly transnational or cosmopolitan, their children rarely, perhaps never, could be so. The parents (and grandparents, increasingly being moved to the new homelands) might think of the children as South Asian and Hyderabadi, heirs to an identity that was an extension in space and time of what Akhil Gupta and James Ferguson (1997: 7) call 'a prior natural identity rooted in locality and community,' but the Hyderabadi children being raised abroad do not and cannot share that ancestral world. Not sharing the physical space or sociocultural landscape nostalgically recalled by their elders, members of the second generation locate themselves firmly in the Pakistani, American, Australian, and other new contexts.

Actually, I found that even the first generation, those we social scientists call first generation because they are the migrants, the movers, only partially fulfilled William Safran's no doubt over-demanding six criteria for a diasporic population. Looking carefully at the first-generation emigrants exploded the notion of a 'diasporic community' and highlighted their differential reworkings of identities in the new sites. The first-generation migrants fulfilled only two parts of Safran's (1991) six part definition of diasporic populations: retaining collective memories of the homeland and defining a collective consciousness through a continuing relationship to the homeland.

How did the first-generation migrants retain collective memories of Hyderabad and define a collective consciousness through a continuing relationship to that homeland? Were their children able to do these things as well? Looking at the first-generation migrants abroad, I found that many of those over the age of fifty did self-identify as Hyderabadis and claim certain collective memories of the old Hyderabad state and its urban Indo-Muslim culture. They continued to use the term *mulki* as a meaningful social category even for Hyderabadis settled abroad. They still voiced the traditional historical narrative so central to their own family histories, that Hyderabad was a successful plural society, perhaps even a cultural synthesis (Leonard, 1973; Butt, 1990; Sirajuddin, 1990). As Andrew Shryock (1996: 39) wrote about an aspiring historian of the Beduoin tribes in Jordan, 'Muhammad is a victim of the *real historical power* of the Adwan [his own tribe]. His identity is firmly grounded in the shaykhly era, and the memory of local might—now reduced to a kind of haughty nostalgia—makes new identities hard to imagine in any terms other than loss.' Like

Shryock, I collected oral materials often based on genealogical notions of transmission and authenticity, and I found that first-generation Hyderabadis' ways of thinking were akin to what Shryock (1995: 5) has called a 'genealogical imagination,' 'a tendency to parse society into discrete, vertical chains of inheritance and transmission, some of them biological, others intellectual, and others still a combination of the two' Especially those first-generation Hyderabadis from the former ruling class tended to privilege that version of the past based on hierarchies of both caste and class.

And how did Hyderabadis put these memories into play in the diaspora, how did they organize themselves and retain links to the homeland? First, their romantic notions of Hyderabadi culture (often conceptualized as surviving better in the diaspora than in the homeland) found expression in the founding of Hyderabad associations in many cities abroad.[1] A Hyderabad or Deccan Association was also founded in Hyderabad itself, linked to many of those overseas.[2] Second, Hyderabadi immigrants founded or participated in Urdu literary associations, competing associations variously represented in the new countries of settlement and often in Hyderabad as well. Reports of Hyderabad association meetings and Urdu association meetings were regularly published in Hyderabad city's leading Urdu newspaper, *Siyasat*, a newspaper taken by many Hyderabadis outside of India.

Third, the first-generation immigrants abroad drew on their old boy and old girl networks from their schooling in Hyderabad. The very strongest network that many first-generation emigrants tried to sustain was that of classmates or schoolmates. 'We went to school together,' 'His sister was in my class,' 'She and my wife were classmates,' and variations on these remarks were almost always the first response when I named people I had met elsewhere. Being classmates or schoolmates most frequently explained expensive and difficult journeys to attend school reunions and the weddings of each others' children. Madras-i-Aliya, Mahbubiyah, Nizam College, St. George's Grammar School, Public School or Jagirdar's College, Osmania University, and Residency Women's College—these and other schools that shaped Hyderabad's mid-20th century upwardly mobile youth had lasting impacts.[3] Schoolmates and classmates filled both instrumental and expressive roles for the first-generation emigrants, and the classmate cohorts affected sibling and friendship and marital networks as well.

Fourth, consider religion, which was not, I would argue, terribly important in Hyderabad before the 1930s and 40s. The schools, above, so important in shaping lasting friendship networks among Muslims, Hindus, Anglo Indians, and Parsis were dominated by the Indo-Muslim or Mughlai culture of the ruling class. Even the Australian principal of the elite St. George's Grammar School had to know Hyderabadi Urdu and Mughlai culture. But this "Muslim side" of the state, as some elite Hindus, Parsis, and Anglo Indians abroad termed it, was based on culture, not religion—Hyderabad state's court culture was cosmopolitan and secular, not Islamic. However, in the diaspora, the place of Islam and Muslims in the Hyderabad of the past posed the most troubling issue in the formulation of new identities, an issue that tended to divide people. Especially in Pakistan, old Hyderabad was reinterpreted as an Islamic state, either a failed one or a conquered one.[4] This 'Islamic twist,' the shadow of an Islamic state behind the Nizam's throne, seemed especially empowering to lower-class Hyderabadi Muslim emigrants, a shadow emerging into full view overseas and embodied in Muslim organizations and institutions being built by pan-ethnic Muslim populations in the western sites as well (Leonard, 2003).

The second generation of Hyderabadis abroad presented a very different picture from the first generation. Did they, or could they, share their parents' memories of the homeland? James Clifford (1090: 85) has characterized people migrating as 'changed by their travel but marked by places of origin, by peculiar allegiances and alienations.' For members of the second generation, there was no question that their parents' 'peculiar allegiances and alienations,' however remembered, rejected, or reinvented, were not theirs. They rarely called themselves Hyderabadis and they defined their identities and communities quite differently from those of their parents. Young Anglo Indians in Australia called themselves Indian or Australian, not British; youngsters in the US have become Indian or Pakistani or Asian American; youngsters in Britain have become British Asian or British Muslim. When visiting Hyderabad, many said they were 'just tourists'. As they mature, the friends, occupations, spouses and patterns of family life of the young people reflect their diverging personal, ethnic, and national identities.

The role of the state emerged as central in all the diasporic settings, and the new national contexts impacted the children far more powerfully than their parents. Pakistan's Punjabi-dominated and increasingly polarized society had no comfortable place for a Hyderabadi or other *muhajir* (refugee, exile) identity; even the first-generation immigrants there immediately claimed a Pakistani identity. The second-generation Hyderabadis in Pakistan assumed a Pakistani identity as their birthright and then claimed to be Lahoris, Punjabis, Karachiites, and so on, rejecting self-identities as Hyderabadis even more emphatically than their parents. In the western countries, British, Canadian, Australian, and United States versions of cultural pluralism encouraged the claim that old Hyderabad had been a successful plural society, a claim made by the many Hyderabad associations formed by first-generation immigrants. But the children of the immigrants related notions of cultural pluralism to their new nations and the future, not to the old nation and the past.

Do members of the second generation engage in the collective organizations and activities of their parents? While the formation of Hyderabad associations, Urdu literary associations, and others based on social networks brought from Hyderabad were important measures of the persistence of the Hyderabadi identity for members of the first generation, they were measures of the breakdown of that identity among the youngsters. In the UK and North American cities like Toronto, Chicago, Los Angeles, and Houston, the efforts made to establish associations and maintain a Hyderabadi identity continue to use Urdu—but that marginalizes the young people. Growing up in English-speaking societies and being educated in English, second-generation Hyderabadis have failed to master the language so dear to not only Hyderabadi Muslims but all older Hyderabadis. Spoken Hyderabadi Urdu continues to distinguish both first and second-generation Hyderabadis from other speakers of Urdu,[5] but reading and writing Urdu has declined markedly among members of the second generation. Thus, the Urdu literary societies maintaining truly international first-generation linkages throughout the diaspora have failed, like the Hyderabad associations, to engage members of the second generation.

Third, the old boy and old girl school networks so important to the first-generation Hyderabadis abroad are totally different for members of the second generation who are being schooled in the new homelands, forming friendships with co-learners of Pakistani, Australian, British, or North American history and culture and heading for careers in their new nations. Their friends and their classmates derive almost entirely from their new localities and differ greatly from place to place. Members of the second generation have no shared educational experiences that link them to Hyderabad.

Fourth, religion has emerged as more important to members of the second generation abroad, but religion as shaped by religious and identity politics in each new site. A more Islamic identity has been taken up by some members of the second generation, notably in Australia, Canada, and the US, but the Islam with which they identity has nothing (or very little) to do with the ways the religion was understood and practiced back in Hyderabad. Second-generation Hindu, Parsi, and Anglo-Indian Christian Hyderabadis abroad are also sometimes choosing to embrace or develop their religious identities more or differently than was done by their parents in the homeland.

Finally, when looking at the youngsters, one needs to look at the marriages they are making, a possible measure of continuing commitment to a Hyderabadi identity. The earliest students to the UK, the US, and Canada sometimes married outside their communities. 'What's happened to the Mughal princess?' one immigrant put it, trying to frame for me the subject of the marriages of young Hyderabadis abroad. Ram Mohan Roy, a Hyderabadi Hindu in California, told me that, brought up in old Hyderabad in the culture of the Nizam's days before 1948, his boyhood dreams were always of a Mughal princess, an image very familiar from Persian and Urdu poetry and Indo-Muslim miniature paintings.[6] But in the diaspora, the dreams of Hyderabadi young people and the actual brides and grooms they confront are less easily imagined. Who stands in the place of the Mughal princess or prince for young members of the Hyderabad diaspora communities?

While Roy, who came on his own as a student before 1965, married a Greek American, the numerous post-1960s Hyderabadi professional immigrants in the western countries have tried to maintain the practice of arranged marriages for their children, making matches through relatives, advertisements, and, sometimes, functions held to bring youth together.[7] Indeed, most members of the second generation have moved cautiously with respect to making their own choices of spouse. Choosing one's own marriage partner is a direct challenge to parental preferences and authority in most cases, and doing so risks losing parental love and support. I found that, at least for their first marriages, the young people were more apt to try to make changes in the wedding festivities: inviting more of their own friends and fewer Hyderabadis of their parents' generation, having family members sit together instead of being segregated by gender, and letting Pakistani or Punjabi friends dance the *bhangra*.

Since the Hyderabadi young people abroad most often were consenting to arranged or semi-arranged marriages with others of Hyderabadi background, one could argue that there is a transnational marriage market among members of the second generation abroad, one with patterns of spousal preference, by countries and by gender, and one that is evidence of a diasporic second generation of Hyderabadis. The directions of bridegiving indicate a new North American centre of the Hyderabadi global marriage networks. Few brides were sent to India or Pakistan from abroad, although some families continued marriages that drew on close relatives wherever they were. A few brides went to Australia but it did not appear to be a magnet for brides from Hyderabad and Karachi. Hyderabadis went to Australia as couples, or Hyderabadi men tended to marry local Australians or New Zealanders, or grooms were brought from Hyderabad, pointing to the good prospects for employment. The UK drew upon Hyderabad and Pakistan for brides and also sent brides to the US, although the dominant pattern was to arrange marriages between young people of Hyderabadi background in the UK. The US and Canada attracted both brides and grooms from all other sites, although young men brought up in India or Pakistan were thought far more difficult to 'socialise' than young women from anywhere. But young women of Hyderabadi or Karachi background were apprehensive about marrying men brought up in the west.

The real point about this transnational pattern, however, is that it is one determined by members of the first generation abroad, not the second, and unfortunately a fairly high proportion of these arranged marriages are ending in divorce. I do not have reliable quantitative data on divorce, but the anecdotes were many and the marriage-making patterns are changing. Instead of following former family or caste networks across national boundaries, parents are now looking for partners for their children brought up in the same country. Also, when divorces occur, parents are increasingly giving their children the freedom to choose another partner. To parental surprise, some love marriages have worked out well. I heard of one American wife 'from a good family, the Gustafsons of Minnesota,' whose relatives were cosmopolitan enough to satisfy an elite Shia Muslim family from Hyderabad. Another American wife was highly praised by her Punjabi Hindu mother-in-law, who waited eagerly for her visits to Hyderabad. In fact, while generalizations predicted negative outcomes, in most instances families have come to terms with the non-Hyderabadi spouses of their children and grandchildren.

Finally, what were the ways in which members of the second generation could or could not share their parents' memories of the homeland? Hyderabadi emigrants initially moved without supporting casts, without the servants or members of the older generation who had been crucial to the transmission and maintenance of Hyderabadi culture. Very few migrants managed to take servants from home along (some professionals in the Gulf being the exception),[8] and while there has been a growing tendency to bring aging parents to live abroad, especially in Australia, Canada, and the US, it is usually too late for grandparents to transmit Hyderabadi culture meaningfully. Their belated presence instead emphasizes disruption rather than cultural continuity for the grandchildren.

The Hyderabadi experiences abroad speak to the selective mobilization of first-generation memories to claim places in new sites and the formation of new second-generation national identities. Jonathan Boyarin (1994: 23 et passim) commented that Maurice Halbwachs (in his seminal 1950 work 'On Collective Memory') spoke not of fantasies or of people defining themselves as a collective in the present, but of the invocation of memories based on family, schoolmates, and village, of the shared reminiscences linking given sets of people in the past. (For Hyderabadis, it was a city and not a village that was relevant.) Jacob Climo (1995: 176) defines transmitted or 'vicarious' memory as 'strong, personal identifications with historical collective memories that belong to people other than those who experienced them directly.' Vicarious memories, Climo specified, are passed through strong emotional attachments from generation to generation in groups that share not only a common historical identity but also the process of its redefinition. Talking to members of the second generation, one was struck by the absence of cross-generational vicarious memories. For the descendants of the Hyderabadis abroad, there could not be an absorption and assimilation of a continuing identity, but rather responses to an interruption, a consciousness of difference. At best, the descendants tried to constitute and interrogate their parents' memories, which in any case invoked a range of interpretations and uses of Hyderabadi culture. The powerful new conceptions of citizenship in the new nation-states re-oriented memories and shaped the evolving personal and national identities of the young people of Hyderabadi ancestry and even of their parents.

The generational differences emerged clearly in all of the research sites. Some young people of Hyderabadi background in both Canada and the US claimed to be 'first generation' because they were the first generation born or raised abroad. They thought of themselves as very different from their parents, decisively formed by the new context and not by Hyderabad. Western social scientists should acknowledge the unsettled nature of these generational categories in the minds of immigrants.[9] Who was a native and who was a newcomer was a controversial and socially meaningful issue (as it had been in old Hyderabad with its *mulki* and non-*mulki* categories and in Pakistan with the *muhajir* category), involving claims to citizenship and national identity, signaling cultural claims to power in new settings.

Elements of Hyderabadi culture did continue if they appeared useful to the children's futures, for example, multicultural values in a plural society, respect and courtesy in everyday relations with others, or the winning tastes of certain foods (*bagara began* or tamarind-flavoured eggplant and Hyderabadi *biryani*) as they entered the 'multicuisines' of the destination countries. The nation-states in which the Hyderabadi emigrants reside and work set the parameters for their participation in their new sites, marking members of the first generation to varying extents but very strongly shaping the identities of members of the second and subsequent generations. I found that, at least in this case, the diaspora has disappeared with the second generation. For that generation, Hyderabadi identity has become, as with Mary Waters's chiefly European ethnics in the US (1990), symbolic at best, an ethnic option rather than a diasporic determination.

## Notes

1. Ideas about old Hyderabad varied significantly, depending partly on one's age and status in the old society but also on one's status in the new location and the national narratives of the new states. Hyderabadi culture was being drawn upon differently, redefined, and sometimes consciously discarded in the new locations. It had at least three uses abroad. First, people celebrated the Hyderabadi

culture of the past and talked about the virtues of the old state, its royalty, and its cultural synthesis. This stance was a primarily private and nostalgic one and inspired most of the initial invitational Hyderabad Associations abroad. Second, people affirmed an ongoing Hyderabadi cultural synthesis and saw it as not only still meaningful but useful in the public arena, analogous to notions of secular pluralism in some of the new countries. This activist stance also played a role in the rhetoric of many Hyderabad Associations and it was used, too, by Hyderabadis working to build multicultural alliances, like political coalitions with other South Asians, religious interfaith efforts, or professional coalitions. A third stance involved fairly drastic reinterpretations of Hyderabadi culture, the most powerful ones invoking Islam to challenge the dominant narrative of the former state. One version was that Hyderabad was really an Islamic state all along and the cultural synthesis was a myth, a view that could be voiced by Hindus and Muslims alike. Another version was that Hyderabad was a failed Islamic state, that the cultural synthesis, while real, evidenced the Nizam's failure to establish a truly Islamic state.

2. Where the earliest immigrants were not from the elite or where Hyderabadi identity served no useful purpose, as in Australia and many American settings, or where Hyderabadi identity was a disadvantage, as in Pakistan, Hyderabad associations were not established or were weak. Where multiclass and often multinational groups supported other kinds of associations, like Urdu, Muslim, Indian or Pakistani associations, these thrived with varying degrees of Hyderabadi participation.
3. Antoun (1998) suggested that academics underestimate the importance of their own occupation, of the impact of higher education and the institutions that deliver it, and I agree.
4. To remember Hyderabad as either a successful or failed Islamic state well-served those Hyderabadis who sought to recapture or replace Hyderabad by migrating to Pakistan. To remember it as a failed Islamic state paradoxically has inspired some Muslims, minorities in predominantly Christian countries, to say that religious freedom in the west permitted them to be better Muslims abroad, where their religion was not tainted by Hindu practices. These Hyderabadi Muslims stress Islamic ideals and build alliances with other Muslims in the new settings, distancing themselves from Hyderabadis organizing on the basis of culture or language.
5. C.M. Naim, Professor of Urdu at the University of Chicago, remarked that the Hyderabadi habit of speaking Urdu when together meant that their children knew only Hyderabadi Urdu; he

found their ignorance of 'standard' Urdu was a problem when they attended his classes. But language was the only marker of difference for the second generation Hyderabadis, he said; they were like other second-generation immigrants from India in all other respects.

6. Possibly many young men from Hyderabad hoped to see a Mughal princess when they came to the part of the Hyderabadi Muslim marriage ceremony where, after the *nikah* or official part of the ceremony, the bride and groom sit side by side holding an open Qur'an with a mirror on one page, and, after reading a verse, look in the mirror and see each other.
7. Families and communities preferred marriages of various sorts (cousins, regional or national origins), with Muslims either deliberately crossing or maintaining the Pakistan/India boundary depending on family preferences. But the notion that extended family membership overcomes differences of national socialization has been tested often and increasingly found wanting.
8. The role of servants came up again and again, their presence, absence, or degree of cultural knowledge, an indicator of the strength of Hyderabadi culture in any site (including Hyderabad, where servants who know the old culture are now few and hard to get).
9. Some grandparents (especially men with successful careers behind them) also claimed to be first generation simply because they were the elders, even though they were following their children. These deliberate attempts to appropriate the term for themselves (by children and their grandparents) could be the diasporic English language equivalent of contests over *mulki*/non-*mulki* or *muhajir*/non-*muhajir* (exile or refugee/son of the soil) status in India and Pakistan. Interestingly, I found the same situation among the children of the Punjabi Mexican couples whom I studied in the 1980s, the same proud assertion that they were the 'first generation' of Americans (Leonard, 1992).

## References

Antoun, R.T. 1998. "Transnational Migration for Higher Education: A Comparison Jordanians in Greece and Pakistan". Paper, American Anthropological Association, Philadelphia, December 3.

Boyarin, J. 1994. "Space, Time, and the Politics of Memory". In J. Boyarin, (ed.) *Remapping Memory: The Politics of TimeSpace*. Minneapolis: University of Minnesota.

Butt, H.B. (ed.). 1990. *The Composite Nature of Hyderabadi Culture*. Hyderabad: Intercultural Cooperation Hyderabad Chapter and Osmania University.

Clifford, J. 1989. "Notes on Theory and Travel". In J. Clifford and V. Dhareshwar (eds.), *Traveling Theory Traveling Theorists*. Santa Cruz: Center for Cultural Studies.

Climo, J. 1995. "Prisoners of Silence: A Vicarious Holocaust Memory". In M.C. Teski and J. Climo (eds.), *The Labyrinth of Memory: Ethnographic Journeys*. Westport, Conn: Bergin and Garvey.

Gupta, A. and J. Ferguson. 1997. "Culture, Power, Place: Ethnography at the End of an Era". In A. Gupta and J. Ferguson (eds.), *Culture, Power, Place: Explorations in Critical Anthropology*. Durham: Duke University Press.

Leonard, K. 1973. "The Deccani Synthesis in Old Hyderabad: A Historiographic Essay". *Journal of the Pakistan Historical Society*, 205–18.

—. 1992. *Making Ethnic Choices: California's Punjabi Mexican Americans*. Philadelphia: Temple University Press.

—. 2003. *Muslims in the United States: the State of Research*. New York: Russell Sage Foundation.

—. 2007. *Locating Home: India's Hyderabadis Abroad*. Palo Alto: Stanford University Press.

Safran, W. 1991. "Diasporas in Modern Societies: Myths of Homeland and Return", *Diaspora*, 1(1).

Shryock, Andrew. 1995. "Writing Oral History in Tribal Jordan: Developments on the Margins of Literate Culture", *Anthropology Today*.

—. 1996. "Tribes and the Print Trade: Notes from the Margins of Literate Culture in Jordan". *American Anthropologist* 98:1.

Sirajuddin, S. 1990. "Deccan-Hyderabadi Culture". Hyderabad: Private manuscript.

Waters, M.C. 1990. *Ethnic Options: Choosing Identities in America*. Berkeley: University of California Press.

# 11

# Indian Diaspora: Emerging Issues in the Context of Greater India

V. BASIL HANS

> One good thing about Indians. Though one can take an Indian out of India, one cannot take India out of an Indian.[1]
>
> —Chandrashekaran

Diaspora and transnational studies are now amongst the most rapidly growing fields of study, globally. While anthropologists and sociologists have been in the forefront of such studies, it is now becoming clear that an open-ness, the very characteristic of any social science has been infused to diasporic studies too. This was bound to happen because from the theoretical angle, the politico-economic character of the diasporas was always evident, and from the practical point of view, the growth and changes of diasporic communities owe largely to significant political and economic policies and reforms. This amalgamation of perspectives has been a positive step towards a holistic study of diasporas. The study of Indian diaspora also has benefited largely from multi-disciplinary approach.[2] India's recent strategic shift from indifference to a pro-active dialogue with its diaspora should be seen in this context (Thandi, 2006).

The theoretical base of this paper stems from an urge to examine new/alternative approaches to diasporic studies in the context of widening scope of diaspora as a subject and intricacies of policy issues. For example, how can diasporic studies be made more meaningful by continuing to have historical moorings but along with a sociological bearing? Similarly, whether we need to construct a new international order of diaspora with working relationship between and among diasporic communities? Such questions need thorough examination particularly for developing countries now under reforms.

We are in the times where an ardent student of diasporic movements *desi-pardesi* and developments can never be complacent by discerning mere historical facts (and figures) related to NRIs and PIOs. Fathoming the diaspora or feeling for the homeland or fetching home-made goods were all once considered amply nostalgic. The diasporic Indians were supposed to be in their own 'islands', known only to their near and dear ones.[3] Now knowingly or unknowingly there is a demystification of the diaspora and inter-connectedness alongside internationalization of the market.[4] This paper is an attempt to look at Indian diaspora in its demystified form—the surreal yet substantial—in terms of its contribution to the economic and social development of India as much as to lead to the emergence of a greater India.

## Diaspora as a Critical Resource

India's development priorities and patterns took a healthy turn in the 1990s with emphasis being laid on development of human resource. It dawned upon our policy-makers that the economy's growth rate depends to a large extent on the investment in human capital and the time had come to rethink on the developmental strategies based on experience. With World Trade Organization (WTO) coming to the global economic scene as a forum of multilateral trade in 1995, far-reaching reforms were introduced for bringing about faster and flexible international transfer of resources. Foreign capital, including NRI investment became an important component of such transfers (Hans, 2000). The two pillars of WTO, viz., Trade Related Intellectual Property Rights (TRIPS) and Trade Related Investment Measures (TRIMS) enhanced the commercial value of knowledge and investments giving them global rights protection even while putting them to a creative public domain for better international access. India stands to gain from these measures through expansive market, free flow of resources and a better managed (rather than 'controlled') international trade and foreign exchange (Hans, 2002). More than one facet of these developments has created forces for diasporic resurgence. Giving a red carpet welcome to NRI investment and joint collaborations obviously meant a call to millions of Indians living abroad—the Non Resident Indians (NRIs) and the Persons of Indian Origin (PIOs).

With the General Agreement on Trade in Services (GATS) making services more attractive for investment and employment, the service sector became the primary growth sector responsible for the economy's take-off. This is one of the main causes of the Silicon Valley revolution, in which Indians constitute the epicentre. This means that Indian economy has moved from being a job-seeking economy to one that is being driven by demand in developed countries for services and migrant workers from developing countries. There are some 20 million ethnic Indians overseas, a diaspora that has an estimated US $300 billion in purchasing power (Banik and Bhaumik, 2006). What is of more interest and economic significance is that the diasporic development has a 'spread effect' with increasing interconnectedness and transnational operations. The manpower and the money power of the Indian community speak for themselves (see Table 1 for numerical strength of Indian diaspora).

**Table 1**

*India's Global Community: A Numerical Glimpse, 2001–2002*

| *Territory* | *Indian Diaspora* |
|---|---|
| The Gulf | 3.5 million |
| Burma | 2.9 million |
| USA | 2.5 million |
| Malaysia | 1.6 million |
| South Africa | 1.2 million |
| Caribbean | 9,50,000 |
| United Kingdom | 9,42,000 |
| Canada | 8,51,000 |
| Mauritius | 8,00,000 |
| Trinidad and Tobago | 5,00,600 |
| Netherlands | 3,00,000 |
| Canada | 1,50,000 |
| Singapore | 90,000 |
| Tanzania | 90,000 |
| Afghanistan | 45,000 |

*Source:* Compiled from (1) A. Banik and P.K. Bhaumik (2006), op. cit., p. 147, (2). http://en.wikipedia.org

The total Overseas Indian Population at present is 2,92,30,309. NRIs and PIOs are at the high-end of educational and income spectrums. For instance in New York, the average number of workers abroad per Indian is 1.5 and the median Indian household income is $50,000. Almost 41 per cent of working Indian males are in professional and managerial positions. Among females, this proportion is 58 per cent. The Indian median family annual income is $60,000 as against the national average of $38,885. The estimated annual buying power of Indians working abroad stands at $20 billion. Over 3,00,000 Indians are working in technology firms in California's Silicon Valley and their average income is estimated at $1,25,000 a year. About one-third of engineers there are of Indian descent; over 7 per cent of high-tech firms are led by Indian CEOs. In USA, one in every nine Indians is a millionaire. Sixty per cent of Indians there have a bachelors degree, 40 per cent have Masters/Ph.D./Professional degree. In Mauritius, the entire country is populated by PIOs. The number of PIO in USA is about 1.7 million and in Malaysia about 10 per cent of its total population. Statistics on NRIs reveal that the number ranges from 40,00,000 in Nepal to 25,000 in Hong Kong (see Table 2). In Vancouver and Toronto cities of Canada, Indian communities largely consist of white collar and professional workers (Hans, 2006; Banik and Bahumik, op. cit.). The Indian diaspora is now large and diversified.

**Table 2**

*NRI Population in Various Countries*

| *Country* | *NRIs* |
|---|---|
| Nepal | 40,00,000 |
| United Kingdom | 15,00,000 |
| UAE | 12,00,000 |
| Zimbabwe | 12,00,000 |
| Fiji | 3,50,000 |
| Canada | 1,50,000 |
| Yemen | 1,00,000 |
| New Zealand | 70,000 |
| Hong Kong | 25,000 |
| Malaysia | 15,000 |
| Mauritius | 11,116 |
| Panama | 5,000 |
| USA | NA |

*Source:* Compiled from V. Basil Hans, "Socio-economic Dimensions of Indian Diaspora in the Globalisation Era". In Ajaya Kumar Sahoo (ed.), *Sociological Perspectives on Globalisation*, Delhi: Kalpaz, p. 232, (2) GoI, "The Indian Diaspora Catalyzes India's Ambition, March 24, 2006. Available at http://ibef.org

## From Seeking Fruits to Searching Roots

The ones who left the Indian shores hundreds of years ago were largely those went for educational pursuits and/or job prospects. The numbers of such immigrants in USA and other developed countries swelled so much that many politicians warned of brain drain. But for several reasons Indians—as a characteristic of most Asians—have begun feeling nostalgic and are being attracted by the smell and sound of their (first) home. Bikram Vohra feels that the Indian's unquenchable desire to identify with the home country has never diminished. Even tenth generation immigrants maintain the same values and traditions as does the home country, often with more fervour and commitment. He is reminded of the famous lines of poetry:

> Breathes there a man with soul so dead
> Who never to himself has said,
> This is my own, "my native land."

'In the poem he retraces his footsteps back to the land of his forefathers. We too, as Indians abroad, engage in a continual effort to hark back to our roots, to be one again with the mother country. India's triumphs bring joy to our hearts, India's pain echoes within us. This need to be one with our roots has been at the core of the Indian global movement'.[5]

What is quite interesting is that whether emigrant Indians live in tightly held urban clusters or spread out suburbia they have not been insulated from feeling for India (ns). Either due to isolation or due to we-feeling (kept alive by experiencing Indian-ness in food, films, festivals and fashions), the new generation of Indian diaspora has begun searching its roots in Indian soil. In USA, this trend is seen in attempts to update the old immigrant story and forging of a new Asian-American identity, not (necessarily) wholly recognizable in any of their parent's native lands but, in its hybrid nature, vibrantly American (Chu and Mustafa, 2006). The more recent Indian-American curve is: early isolation, rapid immersion and assimilation and then a reappreciation of ethnic roots. The 'east meets west' balances well and is in tune with India's 'unity in diversity'.

It is not surprising therefore, that several of the diasporic Indians do not want to be called 'forever foreigners'. Some have reached that conclusion due to some kind of social exclusion experienced by them at some stage, and a sort of social awakening leading to a cultural one. They are getting bonded over the peculiarity of being 'between two worlds'. There is thus, a cultural renaissance of the Indian diaspora. In more than one ways globalization has given a spur to this search of roots (anthropological dimension) and search of identity (socio-political dimension). It is so because 'globalization' meaning economic 'integration', came to replace terms like 'internationalisation' and 'transnationalization' as a more suitable concept for describing the ever intensifying networks of cross border human interaction (Jogdand and Michael, 2003).[6] Then there is the universal function of globalization, viz., establishing interconnectivity which also is responsible for the present grandeur of diaspora in general.

The notion of grandeur was no doubt present even in the early nationalist project in India and in the imaginations and convictions of the then elite. But even though it was coupled with the prevalent ideational and ideological currents, it was more a part of an anti-colonial project. In the post-colonial development this notion has absorbed the enlightenment of modern (welfare) state and international relations. Clearly, therefore, the mindset of the pervasive Indian diaspora is not one of separation from the new home nor a jarring break from the past but a step by step journey towards a 'Greater India'.[7] Apparently, this is part of normative globalism and Indian diaspora's engagement with an ancient civilization occupying a prominent geopolitical space[8] (Weiss, op. cit.). Moreover, the Indians Abroad are happy and appreciative of what the Government of India is doing for them—relaxation of investments rules, introduction of PIO Cards, Dual Citizenship and so forth. Whether, positive globalism or normative globalism, the idea of interconnectedness has liberally and verbally meant 'building bridges' (rather than fences!). Increasing importance to all facets of tourism, trade and foreign capital does lend support to this thesis. Borderless economy for the diaspora has meant opportunities galore. But we must see beyond the financial and technological spheres of globalization to make a Greater India.

## Constructing a Greater India[9]

The strength of Indian diaspora has never been so keenly assessed now than ever before. Their potential in constructing a Greater India by joining hands with resident Indians can now be measured at a higher scale. The process of construction is not to carve out any separate territory for the diaspora but to create a psychosocial space of action. The factors determining this process are economic as well as non-economic.

The process has been evolutionary with some spurts on occasions (like the *Pravasi Bharatiya Divas*). The process is on from both ends: India and its diaspora. And then we have a 'state-centred approach' and a 'community-centred approach'. The former approach focuses on public policies, political institutions and has limited community involvement. This is more a 'state-diaspora interaction'. The latter focuses on diasporic governance through social institutions. The state-diasporic interaction approach in many countries needs to be made more flexible, than what it is at present. The era of reforms and globalization has come as a beacon light in this direction. For example, financial activities of NRIs in India—both philanthropic and profit-motivated—need to be looked with a broader perspective that is more respectable for all concerned. A general toning up of administration may be required, which should not be delayed.

The second approach is a bottom-up approach with ethnicity as a social capital and people's participation as a tool. This is a 'community-community interaction' or a 'people to people' approach. For example, tourism, education, media, marketing and other services can be activated to strengthen diasporic ties beyond cultural exchange. Health tourism, sports tourism, marriage (and child adoption tourism?) etc., are some of the new and fast growing areas which have much to offer for diasporic development. Even the traditional exchange of offshore knowledge can be modified to the present needs of intellectual capital—exchange and investment—rather than mere study of foreign languages, history and culture. 'Cross-country Study and Research Team' with the essentiality of 'community-living and community developing' concept could be a workable model in this regard. Something that can make the visiting Indians feel as 'participative Indians' rather than mere 'passenger Indians' would be of great help. The reciprocity would then be seen when Indians visit abroad and visit Indians there: replacing aloofness with togetherness. We need to strive towards making India and Indian diaspora a common, standard 'currency' whose face value is equal to its intrinsic value.

The emerging issues in the process are of identity and consciousness; reciprocity between Indians and Indians Abroad; homeland and return; and so on. The construction in simple is coming together of India and its diaspora. This construction is an evolution of a different kind. It has successfully replaced the 'brain-drain' slogan of the bygone era with the idea of 'brain trust'.

Treating people as assets has helped. With the enforcement of IPRs, India is able to get credit where and when it is due (Hans, 2006b). Indians everywhere are engaged in building knowledge infrastructure as well as knowledge diffusion. The shyness of capital and static attitude of entrepreneurship have largely been overcome. The many success stories of Indian entrepreneurs provide ample evidence. There is an inter-play of several economic and non-economic factors in the process. For example, besides the exchange of financial and intellectual resources between India and its diaspora, cultural and emotional aspects are being emphasized that are mutually beneficial. India wants the NRIs to be real Indians but without forsaking their duty in the countries of their residence. That is how the country can claim legitimate pride in the process and its outcome.

India's advantage lies in its long history of people's migration and global adventurism added by the diverse wealth. Thanks to interconnectedness people have become real wealth creators. Indians and diasporic Indians are finding new avenues for mutual development. From the side of the diaspora this has been possible through the dynamics of collective action within their communities and links to local communities in homelands. From the side of the homeland there is a constant provision of healthy inputs to its diaspora in the form of incentives as well as moral support. Thus, from both sides the responses are positive and conducive. Regular exchange of information, the role of media and entertainment have in a large measure contributed to the generation of cooperative responses and initiatives both to diaspora formation and construction of Greater India.

No doubt the construction has to take place smoothly, abiding with the law of the land. Misrepresentation of ideas and identities needs to be avoided. Construction of Greater India with state-centred approach and people-centred approach should have one common goal: cohesion. The pace and pattern of construction may vary across communities but cooperation between India and its diaspora should be fostered in a fair way. The governments of the host countries also have a proactive role to play in this regard. This is where good governance enters. Good governance requires that rules be observed strictly.[10] The rules of construction define the roles of the stakeholders or participants, their positions and array of choices, access to information, limits to authority and so on. For a developing country like India with a framework of democracy and a sense of "unity in diversity", diasporic development needs cooperative governance more than corporate governance. For example, in the field of healthcare—where the Indian diaspora is most active within India—we could bring in some changes. Health care can be treated as an industry for developing social infrastructure in the country. This will also help us graduate from thinking diasporic development to doing diasporic development, specifically development that is not simple visible but viable. The same can be done in the filed of education too. In all such exercises, the role of institutions is never reduced but redirected; they are needed to give guidance for governance.

The rules of the game should be clear to both homeland and host countries and should be followed earnestly. All the players should understand what is required, permitted and prohibited. The construction of Greater India is thus, 'inclusive' and should continue to be so.

**Conclusion**

With a one billion plus total population (of which 58% comprises young people) and a total overseas population of 2,92,30,309 there is much good that can be achieved. The process of constructing a Greater India both with state-centred approach and a community-centred approach is on. The purpose of this paper is not to choose between the two, but to understand its dynamics and derivatives for the present and the future. There could be sub-processes linkages to this process. Z.K. Araoz and A. Araoz have suggested a national strategy for developing a culture of innovation with a collaboration of Indians and diasporic Indians, a special programme say 'Culture of Innovation' (CI) Programme (Araoz and Araoz, 2004).

There are several issues to be addressed in the process. New challenges and opportunities are likely to come on the way. The contours of connectivity are bound to change with the passage of time and with every advancement of India and its diaspora. Then we must redraw and/or stretch the lines of paradigm we work with. The youth of today has a dynamic role to play in fostering cohesion among and between communities. Rightly therefore, the Government of India has started the Youth Internship Programme, particularly for those diasporic Indians who have not visited India for the past ten years. With better governance of India and its diaspora in a larger context, we will be able to contribute much to international institutional governance and to garner more support and strength for the establishment of new international socio-economic order. For that we must read and reread Indian diaspora and work with the diaspora with a 'historical sociology approach' (Hans, 2005)—as that adopted by Prof. Chandrashekhar Bhat of the Centre for Studies of Indian Diaspora, Hyderabad and his followers. It is also then that the old and the new Indian diaspora converge.

## Notes

1. This is similar to the interrogative version of the dilemma of cultural syncretism posed in Wayne Wang's 1984 (Chinese?) film *Dim Sum*: "You can take the girl out of Chinatown, but can you take the Chinatown out of the girl". For this and other examples drawn from Asian-American cultural texts to observe shifting factors of culture such as demographics, languages, etc., in the context of intergenerationality and degrees of identification with and in relation to 'homeland' see Lisa Lowe, "Heterogeneity, Hybridity, Multiplicity: Making Asian-American Differences" in *Theorizing Diaspora*, ed. J.E. Braziel and A. Mannur (Oxford: Blackwell Publishing, 2003).
2. One of the clearest evidences for this is seen in the admission of the fact that economic integration via globalization has had much critical inputs supplied by the diaspora. In India, for instance, whether in Punjab or Kerala or Karnataka, the diasporan influence—in IT, Health, Tourism etc.,—is visible. Like many other relationships, the relationship between 'diaspora' and 'homeland' is also two-way. Unfortunately, however, there seems to be much talk on what a diaspora can do to its homeland than the other way round. The result: more ridges than bridges.
3. A few decades ago the contact of Indians with their diasporic kith and kin was confined to rarest visits beyond the shores, the airmail letters exchanged (often festival greetings) and the monolithic process of trunk calls. So it was a "trunk calls to hold all" relationship!
4. The difference between the two, however, is very thin. For instance, the NRI becoming the talk-of-the-town in India's Silicon Valley in the 90s—is it the result of pure resurgence? Is it a corollary of interna-

tionalization of the market (globalization, for short)? The simultaneous upsurge of interest in market management and diasporic development, is it coincidence? These are questions that have to be addressed in the economics of modern diaspora.

5. See Bikram Vohra, 'Great Indian Diaspora'. Available at http//yahind.com, YaHind-Serving India Globally, Copyright 2003–2006.
6. See also A. Hoogvelt, *Globalization and the Post-Colonial World*, London: Macmillan Press Limited, 1997.
7. The notion of grandeur in the two eras seems to have some common features or factors. One is the spread of religion. For instance, some nationalist writers point out to the early influence of India on kingdoms in Southeast Asia through the spread of Hinduism and Buddhism. There are also those who see in the emigration of Indian workers to Southeast Asia, the Caribbean, etc., an achievement of gaining a commanding position in the Indian Ocean and making a concrete presence worldwide. See Bimla Prasad, *The Origins of Indian Foreign Policy: Indian National Congress and World affairs 1885–1947*, Calcutta: Bookland.
8. However, it is too early to say if this approach of Indian diaspora towards India is just a compromise or a serious effort at constructing a greater India that could cast a broad net to muster adequate support for interconnectivity promoting policies. One thing however, is certain: there are stabilized initiatives on both sides of the shore and unified interests.
9. This part of the discussion draws heavily from Sawyer's approach to diasporic studies as found in Sawyer, 'Diaspora and Development', lecture 1. ppt.
10. We need to determine the elements of governance and utilize them effectively in a New Institutional Arrangement for Development (NIAD).

## References

Agencies. 2006. "Nipaul Believes India is Facing 'Cultural Fracture' ". *The Economic Times*, Saturday 11 November, 12.

Alamgir, Jalal. 2003. "Managing Openness in India: The Social Construction of a Globalist Narrative". In Linda Weiss (ed.), *States in the Global Economy*, pp. 225–44. Cambridge: Cambridge University Press.

Araoz, Karani and Alberto Araoz. 2004. *Building a Culture of Innovation: The Role of the Intellectual Diaspora*. Proposal sent to the Pravasi Bharatiya Divas, New Delhi, January.

Banik, Arindam and Bhaumik, Pradip K. 2006. "How Critical is Rural Employment: To Bridge Urban-Rural Divide". *The Hindu Business Line*, 28 February, reproduced in *Manpower Journal*, 41(1):145–48.

Bates, Crispin. 2003. "Introduction: Community and Identity among South Asians in Diaspora". In Crispin Bates (ed.), *Community, Empire and Migration: South Asians in Diaspora*, 1–45. Hyderabad: Orient Longman Private Limited.

Biwas, Shreya. 2006. "Diaspora Quota Fails to Sell in Colleges". *The Economic Times*, Saturday 11 November: 7.

Braziel, Jana Evans, and Anita Mannur (ed.). 2003. *Theorizing Diaspora*. Oxford: Blackwell Publishing Limited.

Chandrashekaran, S. 2004. "Indians Abroad", *Manorama Year Book*, pp. 560–70. Kottayam: Malayala Manorama Press.

Chu, Jeff and Nadia Mustafa. 2006. "Between Two Worlds: Generation of Immigrants' Kids forges a New Identity". *Time*, 167(17) 1 May, 40–45.

Hans, V.B. 2000. *A Handbook of Economics of Development*. Mangalore: Mangala Publications.

—. 2002. *Money, Banking and Finance*. Mangalore: Mangala Publications.

—. 2005. "Indian Diaspora in the Globalisation Era: Avenue for New Dialogues in Development". Paper presented at the International Conference on "Indian Diaspora: Trends, Issues and Challenges", February 24–25. Centre for Study of Indian Diaspora, University of Hyderabad, Hyderabad.

—. 2006. "Socio-economic Dimensions of Indian Diaspora in the Globalisation Era". In Ajaya Kumar Sahoo (ed.), *Sociological Perspectives on Globalisation*, pp. 229–253. Delhi: Kalpaz.

—. 2006b. "Intellectual Property Rights and India: Issues and Imperative". *The Journal of World Intellectual Rights*, 2 (1–2): 229–239.

Hansen, Thomas Blom. 2003. "Bridging the Gulf: Global Horizons, Mobility and Local Identity among Muslims in Mumbai". In Crispin Bates (ed.), *Community, Empire and Migration: South Asians in Diaspora*, pp. 261–285. Hyderabad: Orient Longman Private Limited.

Jogdand, P.G. and S.M. Michael (eds.) 2003. *Globalization and Social Movements: Struggle for a Humane Society*. Jaipur: Rawat Publications.

Kaur, Amarjit. 2003. "Sojourners and Settlers: South Indians and Communal Identity in Malaysia" in Crispin Bates (ed.), *Community, Empire and Migration: South Asians in Diaspora*, pp. 185–205. Orient Longman Private Limited, Hyderabad.

Sawyer. 2005. "Diaspora and Development". *Political Science Y673*, Spring, January 11.

Thandi, Shinder S. 2006. 'Preface'. In A.K. Sahoo (ed.), *Sociological Perspectives on Globalisation*, pp. 7–9. Delhi: Kalpaz.

Thiara, Ravi K. 2003. "Imagining? Ethnic Identity and Indians in South Africa". In Crispin Bates (ed.), *Community, Empire and Migration: South Asians in Diaspora*, pp. 123–152. Hyderabad: Orient Longman Private Limited.

## Websites:

http://en.wikipedia.org
http://ibef.org
http://indiandiaspora.nic
http://www.yahind.com

# 12

# Meena Alexander's *Nampally Road*

## Female Subjectivity and the Ethics of Care and Commitment at the Shock of Return

DOLORES HERRERO

Meena Alexander is a daughter and writer of the Indian diaspora. Her writings reflect her own lived diasporic experiences: on one hand those of uprooting, exile, trauma, separation and loneliness, but on the other those of hope and a privileged multiple vision that can alone transcend rigid national and cultural barriers. There is general agreement that Meena Alexander is yet another diasporic Indian writer of novels 'firmly situated in time and space', novels which 'are concerned with the concrete and immediate inequalities and injustices prevalent in India', since they 'question values prevalent in Indian society today, social and political structures, and the erosion of democratic institutions as they investigate Indian identity' (Mathai, 1996: 437). Alexander's works systematically question the so-called myths of the nation by negotiating the contradictory meanings that lie at the core of apparently coherent and whole discourses of nation and selfhood, mainly as regards the articulation, configuration and enforcement of traditional notions of the 'female identity'. To quote Rebecca Sultana's words:

> Alexander's writing disturbs and reconfigures the representations of the nation by situating her novels and personal narratives upon the politics of displacement. This displacement is figured in terms of a diasporic feminist vision that allows for a questioning of patriarchal narratives of nation and identity. In doing so, her texts also rewrite normative identity categories such as those of nation, race, gender, and postcoloniality. (1999: 62)

Although the diasporic condition can often mean displacement, isolation and confusion, a rather more positive view can also be upheld since, as Homi Bhabha extensively argued in his well-known work *The Location of Culture* (1994), the diaspora can also be seen as an empowered and liminal space whose ambivalent in-between condition allows for the generation of counter-hegemonic discourses that defy and question fixed geo-political boundaries. To put it differently, the diaspora can become a resistive site from which to interrogate, as Alexander does, not only class and gender conflicts, but also nationalism and its influence, both on a grand scale and on rather more local spheres. Born in Allahabad, India, Alexander moved to Sudan when she was five. Some years later she went to England for higher education and then returned to India to teach in Delhi and Hyderabad (the setting of her novel *Nampally Road*) before finally moving to New York in 1979. Her nomadic life has meant, among other things, her learning and mastery of many tongues, together with her persistent interest in 'fault lines' (significantly enough, this is the title of Alexander's autobiography), that is, the areas of fracture, but also of connection, however feeble this connection may be, between one cultural tradition and another.[1]

Alexander's sense of displacement has always been partially countered by the Gandhian ideology that she inherited from her nationalist grandfather, whose influence undoubtedly contributed to the awakening of her cultural identity. As she put it in an interview: 'My grandfather was a great idealist who really believed that there was a new India waiting, a new world based on issues like land reform and equality for all people' (in Grewal, 1988: 23). Unlike Mukherjee's exhilaration about the immigrant condition, Alexander's feelings are rather more ambivalent. When referring to her days in England, she affirms: 'I always felt that what I really was, was being left out as an Indian woman and also as someone [...] from the Third World [...] I had to go back to India' (in Grewal, 1988: 25). A similar sensation takes hold of Mira Kannadical, the protagonist of *Nampally Road*. Mira couldn't feel comfortable in England, the strain there was becoming too much to bear. In her anguish and solitude, she reached the conclusion that returning to India was the only remedy and solution to her anxiety.

> When I began my English sojourn I found myself at a great disadvantage as far as the loneliness of life was concerned. I suffered from dislocation. [...] I felt my nerves all jangled with the effort. I

> was trapped in the effort to remake myself and all the Husserlian epistemology I studied, flat sere stuff filled with post-Cartesian precision that respected no one's soul, did nothing to help. The job offered in Hyderabad could give me a way out. I returned to India determined to start afresh, make up a self that had some continuity with what I was. (*NR*: 29–30)

Mira tries to forge a sense of identity, an identity independent of her surroundings, amidst a world that strives to impose clear-cut and rigid definitions, classifications and labels upon people. She wants to establish links, connections between different places, and also between past, present and future. Like Alexander herself, Mira does not want to feel 'cracked by multiple migrations. Uprooted so many times she can connect nothing with nothing' (*FL*: 3). Mira strives to acknowledge the violent densities of place and to make a fusion of multiple worlds since, as she sees it, that is the only way in which ethnicities can be re-imagined and a truly multicultural world can be achieved. On the other hand, as Rosemary Marangoly George has observed (1996: 171), her diasporic condition makes her view the present in terms of its distance from the past and future, while never forgetting the experience of homelessness. Mira's cultural schizophrenia wavers on the varying ways in which different elements of identity (sex, gender, nationality, etc.) interact with one another in order to form new political discourses on identity and to create new selves. However, this process of self-creation implies several related struggles: not only that of creating an identity despite a patchwork past, but also those of fighting against established and deeply-rooted social assumptions, fighting against traditions and definitions enforced within particular communities and, most important of all, finding your own discourse, your own channels and means of expression. Hence the importance of literature, understood as the exploration of writing and language. Mira's obsession with writing against all odds equals Alexander's when the latter proclaimed: 'My writing comes out of my vision. [...] The whole point of being a writer for me is to be able to lay out what comes to me, with all the complexity of language that I delight in' (in Assisi, 2006: 3). Mira wants to organize/write her previous existence into a coherent whole:

> It was my fond hope that by writing a few poems, or a few prose pieces, I could start to stitch it all together: my birth in India a few years after national independence, my colonial education, my

> rebellion against the arranged marriage my mother had in mind for me, my years of research in England. (*NR*: 30)

But, however hard she tries, she finds this process rather more difficult than she had first imagined: 'Though I tried I could not really write my story. Each time I tried to write, everything splintered into little bits. I could not figure out a line or a theme for myself. [...] No one needed my writing. It could make no difference' (*NR*: 28). Mira finds herself entangled in the city's ongoing political unrest that took place during the time of Indian martial law in the 1970s. She tries to write and define her role and identity in relation to an India that is undergoing serious civil and social upheaval, an India that, much to her bewilderment, she can no longer comprehend: 'As for the Indian past, what was it to me? Sometimes I felt it was a motley collection of events that rose in my mind, rather like those bleached stones in the abandoned graveyard the boy picked his way through. I had no clear picture of what unified it all, what our history might mean' (*NR*: 28). To make matters worse, she realizes that her Romantic philosophy is wholly useless and futile at this time of unrest and confusion. Teaching western classics is quite at odds with her own history and the environment in which she is teaching these texts. Wordsworth can no longer be her model, no matter how well he might have understood the complex mechanisms of suffering and desire. Mira's incapacity to articulate her position arises from the tragic events around her. The novel is set in India, but Indian culture has been modified by western culture. Yet, Mira refuses to abandon her cultural heritage to exclusively cling to western education. Instead, she tries to relate her knowledge of western literature to the political situation in Hyderabad. In other words, the ideas she teaches and writes are deeply imbued with both Indian and English cultures and clearly affect her expression of identity, which is therefore marked by confusion and difference. Although so far unable to reconcile the past and the present in a language of her own making, Mira's attempt is nonetheless a beacon of hope for the future. As Shilpa Davé has put it:

> Mira's search for a universal language translates into a vision with multiple possibilities and opens up identity and culture to various influences, not just to a monolithic Western culture. Alexander depicts concepts of difference in her novel and supports pluralism as a means of reconciling an individual to a community. [...] Writing becomes a way of weaving her past and present into a

> presentable form that enacts her identity. [...] The influence of environment or culture is integrated into the vision of the individual with the intent of modifying the worldview into an all-encompassing cultural society. In essence, identity becomes multicultural instead of unicultural. (2001: 17)

And communal instead of individualistic, for that matter. Mira feels the need to get increasingly involved with those around her, if only to make her own life and existence meaningful. 'The life that made sense was all around me in Little Mother and Ramu and the young students, the orange sellers and the violent and wretched, ourselves included. It was already there. [...] We were in it, all together, that's all I knew. And there was no way out' (*NR*: 28). There is no way her idealistic concept of nationalism can escape this brutal socio-political reality. Corrupt politicians, represented in the figure of Limca Gowda and his Ever Ready Men, have distorted the message of the founders of the nation, who hardly considered the possibility of generally spread communal discord, and have misused power in order to exploit the poor and consolidate the influence and control of party politics. Gandhi, the 'Father of the Nation', as is written under his statue's high pedestal, 'stare[s] into a future that ha[s] disowned him' (*NR*: 47), and Jawaharlal Nehru, the founder of modern India, has become 'an aristocrat lacking a phone line with the future' (*NR*: 57).

The climax of the novel is the rape of Rameeza Bee, a poor Muslim woman, by a group of policemen, and the subsequent beating and killing of her husband. This brutal attack against members of a disenfranchised minority triggers off a series of violent events: the police station is burnt down by an angered crowd and the city is besieged by riots that bring together people from the lower castes and classes. The rape of Rameeza Bee will also be the turning-point in Mira's life, the catalyst that will let her go beyond the monochrome political activism of her lover, Ramu, who will gradually be replaced by Rameeza in Mira's heart. Not in vain is Rameeza described as 'the dark irruption' that 'break[s] into the circle of desire' (*NR*: 42). Mira will eventually transcend her ineffectual fractured vision of things in order to become part of a female continuum, a sisterhood that defies patriarchy and culturally imposed conventions, and heals the wounds of silence and oppression for so long inflicted upon women. The lenses on display at the Optical Palace, which were 'all kinds of colours, pink, purple, blue, green, gray' (*NR*: 52), had formerly pointed to the faint possibility of transforming external reality but, above all, of offering a multitude of fractured, and therefore partial and imperfect, images of the world. Diasporic people cannot possibly have a singular and unified vision, which in turn implies, to quote Mira's own words, that 'the self is always two. Always broken [...] given the world as it is, there's nowhere people like us can be whole. The best I can do is leapfrog over the cracks in the earth, over the black fissures' (*NR*: 92).

Yet, this lack of unity does not leave the narrator empty and helpless, since it is the infinitely layered identity that all diasporic people, and diasporic women in particular, have that allows Mira to have several visions through several pairs of eyes, and thus become part of a female communal project. Mira's leap is no longer a leap into the dark, but her fusion and transition 'from one woman's body into another. From this Mira that you know into Little Mother, into Rameeza, into Rosamma, into that woman in the truck on the way to the Public Gardens. A severed head, a heart, a nostril with a breathing hole, a breast, a bloodied womb' (*NR*: 92–93). The relationship that Mira establishes with, on one hand her mother substitute and mentor Durgabai (significantly called 'Little Mother'), who works at a women's health centre and resists government oppression by ministering to women who are victims of the culture and the system, and on the other hand with Rameeza, the innocent villager who is cruelly raped, tortured and beaten, plays a significant role in Mira's evolution and maturity process, both as a human being and as a writer. As Shilpa Davé has put it, 'by the end of the novel, Mira finds expression through a community of women; a dream language that is unique to Rameeza, Durgabai, and Mira' (1993: 110). The ultimate solution seems to consist of adopting a postcolonial/critical attitude and discarding the English written word, one of the main weapons at the service of the colonial enterprise. This corroborates the strength of the 'peculiarly fruitful alliance between feminism and postcolonialism' that Terry Eagleton attributes to 'the plight of women in such societies, forced as they are to assume many of its most wretched burdens' (1996: 205), and also Rahul Krishna Gairola's contention that 'it is no wonder that many prominent postcolonial theorists (and writers) are women, and most discussions of the subaltern subject inextricably involve a discussion of the (dis)placement of women in colonial/postcolonial/neo-colonial contexts' (2000: para. 2). Like Alexander herself, Mira eventually gets rid of the mask of the English language to reveal her 'differe/ant' face. To quote Alexander's words:

> Sometimes I think of the English language as a pale skin that has covered up my flesh, the broken parts of my world. In order to free my face, in order to appear, I have had to use my teeth and nails, I have had to tear that fine skin, to speak out my discrepant otherness. (in Gairola. 2000: 19)

In the end, Mira embraces a communal dream language that allows these women to express themselves and break free from the boundaries and restrictions of patriarchal definitions, which, contrary to what Shilpa Davé argues, are not only western, but western and eastern alike. To give but one example, at one point in the novel Mira's connection with Durgabai/Little Mother is so strong that she concludes: 'They have a power of feverish motion, these dreams of ours, they trap us, yet cut us free from the pots and pans and syringes of our daily lives' (*NR*: 62). After the rape, Rameeza finds it impossible to articulate her pain in verbal language, and draws a simple composition of triangles instead. Rameeza's inability to write (she clumsily picks up the pencil in her fist) clearly points to, and echoes, Mira's. Unlike Ramu, who soon minimizes the multiple meanings of Rameeza's drawing by interpreting it as a prison and thus making it serve his own political agenda, Mira immediately realizes the connection between Rameeza's drawing and her own nightmarish dream of the pyramid, made of bricks which were nothing but human flesh, and black water climbing higher and higher (*NR*: 65). Mira is therefore able to interpret the lack of articulated language as intense fragmentation and pain. By understanding Rameeza's ordeal, Mira begins to understand her own plight, her own problematic relationship with language. In the end, a community of women bound together by shared visions and dream imagery becomes a metaphor for the diasporic layered identity. The three women fuse so as to become one and the same, but also ultimately complex, thing. It is this collective identity that will enable Mira to write in the future. At the end of the novel, Mira identifies with Rameeza. Just as Rameeza's mouth is beginning to heal, Mira's ability to write herself into existence is now seen as being ultimately possible.

> As I moved forward the figure advanced. A woman. I knew her from real life and from my dreams. A young woman, almost my age, her head covered in an old sari. Her eyes were as dark as the soot that fell from the city of cardboard. I touched her hurt hand. [...] I looked at Rameeza. She edged closer to me. Her mouth was healing slowly. (*NR*: 106)

Just as is suggested in Deepa Mehta's polemical film *Fire*, the sari here can be said to function as an allegorical body wrap that confines the Indian woman to traditional cultural and gender roles. Significantly enough, it is her head, that is, her capacity to rethink and reinvent herself, that is being covered. Similarly, her dark eyes and hurt hand point to the oppression and violence that lie at the core of the other side of the patriarchal story. It is therefore clear that this collective woman helps Meena Alexander to 'question—insistently and painfully—inherited cultural orthodoxies of "Indianness" that have hitherto prescribed their place and identity as women' (Chanda, Ho and Mathai, 1997: 58). Mira, for instance, cannot put up with the orthodox notion of womanhood that the swamiji is trying to defend, and consequently exclaims with 'a ferocity in [her] voice that he could not mistake': 'what do you do with a woman [...] What happens to her knowledge? Is she just mere pollution?' (*NR*: 85–86). *Nampally Road* asks thorny questions about gender roles, woman's place, and notions of 'home' in a postcolonial India that strives, with much difficulty, to make the transition from tradition to modernity as swift and untraumatic as possible.

As Partha Chatterjee has argued (1993: 116–134), the origin of the modern or 'new Indian woman' can be traced back to the anti-colonial attempt to delimit an area of self-determination by clearly splitting the spiritual and material domains, the inner and the outer worlds. In the difficult transition from imperial colony to post-colonial state, from tradition to modernity, it is the woman who systematically becomes the recipient of traditional values, since she is made to integrate within herself the virtues of traditional Indian womanhood and the practical advantages of modernity while remaining immune to the attractions of westernization. This 'new Indian woman' enjoys a greater degree of autonomy and freedom, it is true, but this freedom is, more often than not, illusory, since it can only be exerted within a demarcated space and in certain circumstances, and it greatly depends on self-regulation. Moreover, such self-regulation relies, more often than not, on coercion and complicity when women are spoken for by a patriarchal society, the main aim of which is to keep them silent and under control. As Durgabai at one point in the novel exclaims when referring to the poor women she tries to help, 'It's terrible, the fate of some of our young girls' (*NR*: 16). The new Indian women like Mira have to find their own voices, their own language, their own discourse and representation, because the images of them that are in circulation keep on reiterating and enforcing the nationalist appropriation of women's identity. In short, what culture (advertising, the mass media, etc.) circulates are often illusions of happiness which, should they remain uncontested, will prevent women from being the masters of their own lives. However much she loves Ramu and respects his political project, Mira feels rather more closely linked and attached to the women who, like herself, *care* and are risking their peace and physical well-being in order to fight for their dignity and freedom. As Mira sees it, the latter enterprise is much more urgent and real.

> I felt the grandeur of his vision. But I could not see where it could lead. I saw the old woman again, Maitreyi, in her crumpled blue sari, hunched before the microphone, then her body shrinking into the great crowd. That crowd could erupt into sheer rage. I saw Rameeza's bruised cheeks. (*NR*: 97)

These women have managed to bind themselves together and support each other by cutting across social, educational and cultural boundaries, that is, by obliterating differences and advocating instead what many contemporary critics would label as an alternative feminist ethics of care, based on mutual understanding and compassion.[2] Judging from all the things so far said, it would be no exaggeration to conclude that *Nampally Road* is concerned, not only with the inequalities and injustices still prevalent in post-independence India, but also with the problematic nature of the diasporic condition and the ethics of care and commitment at the shock of return and, most important of all, with doing away with unfair and rigid patriarchal categories and classifications and celebrating a shared and liberating experience among women, especially women who have been suppressed by the combined oppression of religion, patriarchy and colonialism.

## Acknowledgements

The research carried out for the writing of this paper was financed by the MCYT (Ministerio de Cienciay Tecnología). DGI/FEDER, Proyecto HUM2004–00344/FILO.

## Notes

1. As Carolyn Walters explains (2006: 1), not in vain did Alexander decide to change her name from 'Mary Elizabeth' to 'Meena' when she was fifteen. This act of defiance—and of liberation—enabled her, the author herself explains in *Fault Lines* (74), to get rid of the colonial burden while proclaiming her multi-lingual nature, since 'Meena' means 'fish' in Sanskrit, 'jewelling' in Urdu, and 'port' in Arabic.
2. As is well known, to counter the lethal effects of patriarchal morality, based upon supposedly detached and aseptic analyses of right-wrong and the endorsement of rights and rules, many women writers, aware as they were of the dangers of relying on generalizing notions and labels, have developed an alternative ethics of care based on principles of sympathy, nurturing and compassion. Carol Gilligan's works, in particular her book *In a Different Voice* (1982), can be said to have pioneered the development of this movement. Gilligan states that 'the moral imperative' that emerges from a woman's perspective is "an injunction to care, a responsibility to discern and alleviate the real and recognizable trouble of this world" (1982: 19). While men's main concern is not to interfere with the rights of others, Gilligan goes on to argue, women are chiefly concerned with responsibility and relationships rather than rights and rules. In other words, women's moral judgements are, on the whole, not normative, but contextual and narrative. In her more recent work (1995: 121–26), Gilligan establishes a clear distinction between a feminine ethic and a feminist ethic of care. A feminine ethic is one that entails social obligations and self-sacrifice, and which is therefore concomitant with patriarchy. A feminist ethic of care begins with connection, that is, a thorough appreciation of how human lives and emotions are interconnected, to the point of becoming the voice of resistance. Moreover, the world-wide silencing of women, many postcolonial feminist critics have argued, could in turn be extrapolated to the whole colonial process and be thus indicative of patriarchal and colonial morality. Winnie Tomm (in Haney, 2002: 144), to give but one example, claims: "Patriarchal

morality is based on the desire for power over the other, beginning with sexual power over women and extending to political power over nations. The politics of sex has the same source as the politics of wars: ignorance, fear, and hostility toward the other". To claim the well-known feminist tenet that 'the personal is always political' inevitably implies a discussion of an ethics that calls for responsibility in our actions and solidarity and reciprocity in our interactions. The women's contributions so far mentioned were not an isolated phenomenon, however. Although clearly feminist, they should also be regarded as part of a much wider critical trend, namely, *ethical criticism*, a movement that emerged and developed in the 1980s and 1990s, mainly as a reaction against the cultural radicalism and relativism propounded by certain ideological conceptions of the postmodern era.

## References

Alexander, M. 1991. *Nampally Road*. San Francisco, California: Mercury House Incorporated.

——. 1993 *Fault Lines: A Memoir*. New York: Feminist Press.

Assisi, F.C. 2006. "Meena Alexander: Poet and Daughter of the Indian Diaspora". www.indolink.com/displayArticleS.php?id=120105041513 (retrieved 25/10/2006).

Bhabha, H. 1994. *The Location of Culture*. London and New York. Routledge.

Chanda, G.S., E.Y.L. Ho and K. Mathai. 1997. "Women in 'India': Four Recent Novels". *Wasafiri*, 26: 58–62.

Chatterjee, P. 1993. *The Nation and Its Fragments: Colonial and Postcolonial Histories*. Princeton: Princeton UP.

Davé, S. 1993. "The Doors to Home and History: Post-Colonial Identities in Meena Alexander and Bharati Mukherjee". *Amerasia Journal*, 19(3): 103–113.

——. 2001. '*Nampally Road* by Meena Alexander'. In C.S. Wong and S.H. Sumida, (eds.), *A Resource Guide to Asian American Literature*, pp. 13–20. New York: Modern Language Association of America.

Eagleton, T. 1996. *Literary Theory: An Introduction*. 2nd ed. Minneapolis: Minnesota U.P.

Gairola, R.K. 2000. "Western Experiences: Education and 'Third World Women' in the Fictions of Tsitsi Dangarembga and Meena

Alexander". http://social.chass.ncsu.edu/jouvert/v4i2/gairol.htm (retrieved 25/10/2006).

George, R.M. 1996. *The Politics of Home: Postcolonial Relocations and Twentieth-Century Fiction*. New York: Cambridge U.P.

Gilligan, C. 1982. *In a Different Voice: Psychological Theory and Women's Development*. Cambridge, Mass.: Harvard University Press.

—. 1995. "Hearing the Difference: Theorizing Connection". *Hypatia* 10(2): 121–26.

Grewal, I. 1988. "Interview with Meena Alexander". *Dispatch*: 379–80.

Haney, D.G. 2002. "Ethics and Identity: Postcolonial Feminist Perspectives". In W.S. Haney and N.O. Pagan, (eds.), *Ethics and Subjectivity in Literary and Cultural Studies*, pp. 143–158. Bern: Peter Lang.

Mathai, K. 1996. "National Identity in Recent Indian Novels in English". In W. Zach and K.L. Goodwin (eds.), *Nationalism vs. Internationalism: (Inter)National Dimensions of Literatures in English*, pp. 435–441. Tübingen, Germany: Stauffenburg.

Sultana, R. 1999. "Rewriting Nationalism: A Comparison of *The Tiger's Daughter* and *Nampally Road*". Conference of Collegue Teachers of English Studies 64 (September, 1999): 62–70.

Walters, C. 1998, 2006. "Meena Alexander". www.english.emory.edu/Bahri/Alexander.html (retrieved 25/10/2006).

# Contributors

**Ajaya Kumar Sahoo**, Lecturer, Centre for the Study of Indian Diaspora, School of Social Sciences, University of Hyderabad, Hyderabad.

**Binod Khadria**, Professor, Zakhir Hussain Centre for Educational Studies, Jawaharlal Nehru University, New Delhi.

**Brij Maharaj**, Professor, Department of Geography, University of KwaZulu-Natal, Pietermaritzburg, South Africa.

**Dolores Herrero**, Professor, Department of English Literature, University of Zaragoza, Spain.

**Eric Leclerc**, Associate Professor, Department of Geography, University of Rouen, Rouen, France.

**Gauri Bhattacharya**, Senior Lecturer, School of Social Work, Columbia University, New York, United States.

**Karen Isaksen Leonard**, Professor of Anthropology and Asian American Studies, University of California, Irvine, USA.

**Karthiyaini Devarajoo**, Faculty of Modern Languages and Communication, University Putra Malaysia, Malaysia.

**Kumar Mahabir**, Assistant Professor, School for Studies in Learning, Cognition and Education, University of Trinidad and Tobago, West Indies.

**Laxmi Narayan Kadekar**, Reader, Department of Sociology, University of Hyderabad, Hyderabad.

**Margaret Walton-Roberts**, Associate Professor, Department of Geography and Environmental Studies, Wilfrid Laurier University, Canada.

**Mohan K. Gautam**, Professor, Department of Anthropology, Leiden University, Van Ledenberchstraat 8, 2334 AT Leiden, The Netherlands.

**P. Pratap Kumar**, Professor, Department of History and Religion, University of KwaZulu-Natal, Durban, South Africa.

**Vinesh Y. Hookoomsing**, Professor and Head, Department of Linguistic, University of Mauritius, Reduit, Mauritius.

**V. Basil Hans**, Head of the Arts Department, St Aloysius Evening College, Mangalore, India.

# Index